International Technical Supp

Leveraging IBM Cognos 8 BI for Linux on IBM System z

February 2010

SG24-7812-00

Note: Before using this information and the product it supports, read the information in "Notices" on page xv.

First Edition (February 2010)

This edition applies to Version 8 of IBM Cognos 8 BI with the addition of Linux for System z support (product number 5724-W12) and Go! Mobile (product number 5724-W20).

Contents

Figures

Tables

Examples

Notices

This information was developed for products and services offered in the U.S.A.

IBM may not offer the products, services, or features discussed in this document in other countries. Consult your local IBM representative for information on the products and services currently available in your area. Any reference to an IBM product, program, or service is not intended to state or imply that only that IBM product, program, or service may be used. Any functionally equivalent product, program, or service that does not infringe any IBM intellectual property right may be used instead. However, it is the user's responsibility to evaluate and verify the operation of any non-IBM product, program, or service.

IBM may have patents or pending patent applications covering subject matter described in this document. The furnishing of this document does not give you any license to these patents. You can send license inquiries, in writing, to:
IBM Director of Licensing, IBM Corporation, North Castle Drive, Armonk, NY 10504-1785 U.S.A.

The following paragraph does not apply to the United Kingdom or any other country where such provisions are inconsistent with local law: INTERNATIONAL BUSINESS MACHINES CORPORATION PROVIDES THIS PUBLICATION "AS IS" WITHOUT WARRANTY OF ANY KIND, EITHER EXPRESS OR IMPLIED, INCLUDING, BUT NOT LIMITED TO, THE IMPLIED WARRANTIES OF NON-INFRINGEMENT, MERCHANTABILITY OR FITNESS FOR A PARTICULAR PURPOSE. Some states do not allow disclaimer of express or implied warranties in certain transactions, therefore, this statement may not apply to you.

This information could include technical inaccuracies or typographical errors. Changes are periodically made to the information herein; these changes will be incorporated in new editions of the publication. IBM may make improvements and/or changes in the product(s) and/or the program(s) described in this publication at any time without notice.

Any references in this information to non-IBM Web sites are provided for convenience only and do not in any manner serve as an endorsement of those Web sites. The materials at those Web sites are not part of the materials for this IBM product and use of those Web sites is at your own risk.

IBM may use or distribute any of the information you supply in any way it believes appropriate without incurring any obligation to you.

Information concerning non-IBM products was obtained from the suppliers of those products, their published announcements or other publicly available sources. IBM has not tested those products and cannot confirm the accuracy of performance, compatibility or any other claims related to non-IBM products. Questions on the capabilities of non-IBM products should be addressed to the suppliers of those products.

This information contains examples of data and reports used in daily business operations. To illustrate them as completely as possible, the examples include the names of individuals, companies, brands, and products. All of these names are fictitious and any similarity to the names and addresses used by an actual business enterprise is entirely coincidental.

COPYRIGHT LICENSE:

This information contains sample application programs in source language, which illustrate programming techniques on various operating platforms. You may copy, modify, and distribute these sample programs in any form without payment to IBM, for the purposes of developing, using, marketing or distributing application programs conforming to the application programming interface for the operating platform for which the sample programs are written. These examples have not been thoroughly tested under all conditions. IBM, therefore, cannot guarantee or imply reliability, serviceability, or function of these programs.

Trademarks

IBM, the IBM logo, and ibm.com are trademarks or registered trademarks of International Business Machines Corporation in the United States, other countries, or both. These and other IBM trademarked terms are marked on their first occurrence in this information with the appropriate symbol (® or ™), indicating US registered or common law trademarks owned by IBM at the time this information was published. Such trademarks may also be registered or common law trademarks in other countries. A current list of IBM trademarks is available on the Web at `http://www.ibm.com/legal/copytrade.shtml`

The following terms are trademarks of the International Business Machines Corporation in the United States, other countries, or both:

- AIX®
- Cognos®
- Cube Views®
- DataStage®
- DB2®
- DRDA®
- DS8000®
- FICON®
- FlashCopy®
- GDPS®
- HiperSockets™
- IBM®
- Impromptu®
- IMS™
- Informix®
- InfoSphere™
- Parallel Sysplex®
- PowerPlay®
- Rational Rose®
- Rational®
- Redbooks®
- Redbooks (logo) ®
- Sametime®
- System Storage™
- System z10™
- System z9®
- System z®
- Tivoli®
- WebSphere®
- z/OS®
- z/VM®
- z9®

The following terms are trademarks of other companies:

Adobe, the Adobe logo, and the PostScript logo are either registered trademarks or trademarks of Adobe Systems Incorporated in the United States, and/or other countries.

PowerPlay, the AMD Arrow logo, and combinations thereof, are trademarks of Advanced Micro Devices, Inc.

Cognos, PowerCube, and the Cognos logo are trademarks or registered trademarks of Cognos Incorporated, an IBM Company, in the United States and/or other countries.

Oracle, JD Edwards, PeopleSoft, Siebel, and TopLink are registered trademarks of Oracle Corporation and/or its affiliates.

Adobe Flash, Adobe, and Portable Document Format (PDF) are either registered trademarks or trademarks of Adobe Systems Incorporated in the United States, other countries, or both.

Java, and all Java-based trademarks are trademarks of Sun Microsystems, Inc. in the United States, other countries, or both.

Microsoft, Windows, and the Windows logo are trademarks of Microsoft Corporation in the United States, other countries, or both.

UNIX is a registered trademark of The Open Group in the United States and other countries.

Linux is a trademark of Linus Torvalds in the United States, other countries, or both.

Other company, product, or service names may be trademarks or service marks of others.

Preface

In this IBM® Redbooks® publication, we describe the role Cognos® plays in an Information On Demand (IOD) solution for IBM System z® and detail the functions of IBM Cognos 8 BI for Linux® on System z in current deployment scenarios. We show typical deployment architectures that show how to access disparate data sources both on and off the System z platform and show how the functions of the Cognos family of products provides a way to consolidate different BI solutions on System z.

We provide examples of Cognos functions for resolving business requirements using reporting and OLAP capabilities as well as general deployment considerations of IBM Cognos 8 BI for Linux on System z.

This publication is meant to help the Cognos Business Intelligence professional understand the strong points of System z architecture and the database specialist appreciate the Cognos family of products.

The team who wrote this book

This book was produced by a team of specialists from around the world working at IBM Silicon Valley Lab (SVL), San Jose.

Paolo Bruni is an Information Management software Project Leader at the International Technical Support Organization based in Silicon Valley Lab, San Jose. During Paolo's many years with IBM, in development, in the field, and at the ITSO, his work has been mostly related to database systems.

André Kres is an Information Management IT Architect at the Business Intelligence Centre of Competence in Germany. He has 10 years of experience in the area of Business Intelligence with IBM and in various other IT roles before IBM. He holds a Bachelor's degree in Business Computing (Dipl Inf.) from the University of Applied Science in Mittweida, Germany. His area of expertise is architecting BI solutions that require a broad knowledge of technologies, such as Web access, relational and multidimensional databases, Windows®, Linux, AIX®, and System z platforms, as well as Business Intelligence functions, such as OLAP and data modelling for BI.

Riccardo Paganelli is a Cognos IT Specialist in Italy. He has 12 years of experience in the Business Intelligence field and has a deep knowledge of the most commonly used platforms. He has worked at IBM and Cognos for more than 4 years. His areas of expertise include OLAP and Data Warehouse modeling and effective dashboards design.

James Wilson is an IBM Certified Consulting IT Specialist in the United States. He has 28 years of experience in the System z technical field. He holds a degree in Computer Information Systems from West Texas State University. His areas of expertise include Information Integration, Replication, and Business Intelligence on System z and Linux on System z.

Figure 1 From left to right: James, André, Paolo, and Riccardo

Thanks to the following people for their contributions to this project:

Jaime Anaya
Alvin Cho
Ann Jackson
Beth Hamel
Dave Jeffries
Sundari Voruganti
Don Weil
IBM SVL, San Jose

Jim Beacom
Amanda Bright
Dean Browne
Nigel Campbell
Doug Catton
Brecht Desmeijter
Jason Gartner
Anna Lynch
Marilyn O'Keefe
Corey Pickford
Daniel Wagemann
IBM Cognos, Ottawa

Gary Crupi
Tim Lighter
Andy Perkins
Jonathan Sloan
IBM USA

Andrew Keenan
IBM Australia

Frank Neumann
IBM Boeblingen, Germany

Cedrine Madera
IBM Montpelier, France

Emma Jacobs
International Technical Support Organization

Become a published author

Join us for a two- to six-week residency program! Help write a book dealing with specific products or solutions, while getting hands-on experience with leading-edge technologies. You will have the opportunity to team with IBM technical professionals, Business Partners, and Clients.

Your efforts will help increase product acceptance and customer satisfaction. As a bonus, you will develop a network of contacts in IBM development labs, and increase your productivity and marketability.

Find out more about the residency program, browse the residency index, and apply online at:

ibm.com/redbooks/residencies.html

Comments welcome

Your comments are important to us!

We want our books to be as helpful as possible. Send us your comments about this book or other IBM Redbooks publications in one of the following ways:

- Use the online **Contact us** review Redbooks form found at:

  ibm.com/redbooks

- Send your comments in an e-mail to:

  redbooks@us.ibm.com

- Mail your comments to:

  IBM Corporation, International Technical Support Organization
  Dept. HYTD Mail Station P099
  2455 South Road
  Poughkeepsie, NY 12601-5400

1

Introduction

Over the last several years, businesses have heavily invested in Business Intelligence (BI). Large enterprises may discover that they have multiple disjointed BI installations or silos of information. More and more of these companies are looking towards a consolidated BI deployment that can cut across departments and produce enterprise views, while at the same time reducing the overall cost of BI deployments. IBM Cognos 8 BI, the world's leading BI solution from IBM, has recently expanded its functionality to include the capability to run on Linux on IBM System z to better deliver mission critical enterprise BI. In this chapter, we discuss the merits of running Cognos 8 BI and why it is important for an enterprise that already has a significant investment in BI to consider consolidating their BI system onto System z.

This chapter contains the following topics:

- Consolidating your BI environment on System z
- Benefits of the System z environment
- Standardized reporting using Cognos 8 BI

1.1 Consolidating your BI environment on System z

Enterprises are increasing the value to their business by harnessing the power of BI to gain a competitive edge. Many of today's BI systems are comprised of multiple, departmental BI systems. These multiple BI systems may access different data warehouses, some of which could be quite large and may be consolidated with near real-time operational data stores (ODS). In order to maximize the effectiveness of the BI system, data may need to be pulled from multiple sources, such as financial, marketing, and inventory databases. By consolidating BI systems, the business can obtain the benefits of consistent information across the business lines, better performance and scalability, and better data currency. Finally, and most importantly, by consolidating your BI environment, the business will have access to trusted information incorporated from all business lines to support decision making at all levels from the department, through the lines of business, to the entire enterprise.

1.1.1 Business drivers for BI consolidation

BI consolidation can help the enterprise discover competitive advantages. An enterprise usually has multiple drivers for consolidation. Consider the following items:

- Locating and accessing comprehensive data to make business decisions is difficult.
- Obtaining accurate information across business lines or functions is difficult.
- There is a need for *trusted* information.
- Multiple data warehouses lead to more expenses because of duplication of data. In addition, when these warehouses are coupled with BI silos, incorrect information is much more likely to occur because the different departments are using different warehouses that are not synchronized, which leads to different business conclusions.
- Multiple BI silos leads to duplication of effort, inefficient use of resources, and the inability to share best practices. When coupled with duplication in people resources to support and service the different BI systems, the enterprise operates with a higher total cost of ownership (TCO) than if they had consolidation of BI silos.
- Multiple heterogeneous data stores exist.

1.1.2 Information On Demand

Information On Demand (IOD) is a comprehensive architecture for unlocking the business value of information for competitive advantage by enabling organizations to establish and leverage trusted information to optimize business performance. Consolidating the BI environment may be an important first step that will allow warehouse consolidation while shielding users from potential outages. The warehouses can perform BI without impacting the users. While Information On Demand includes BI and data warehousing, this initiative espouses a much more comprehensive vision where trusted information is available in context to any user, any application, and at any time, and not just in reports available to a select group of business analysts. In addition to enabling organizations to leverage information better, Information On Demand includes the ability to establish accurate, trusted information for a single version of the truth, managed over time, and built on an efficient and solid foundation for managing data and content over its life cycle. Cognos 8 BI is an integral part of the IBM Information on Demand architecture. For more information about how Cognos 8 BI fits into IOD, refer to 1.3.5, "Metadata and information integration" on page 20.

1.2 Benefits of the System z environment

The merits of System z have been well established. The System z platform is the platform to leverage service, performance, scalability, reliability, availability, bullet-proof security, green capabilities, and virtualization, which all play their part in providing the best TCO for many applications, including BI and warehousing deployments. All of the components in the IOD stack draw strength from the core merits of System z by extending the value to companies that deploy on System z through integration and exploitation. For example, by simply deploying Cognos on Linux on System z, you can take advantage of most of the merits of System z mentioned here.

The mainframe market also has taken advantage of advancements in technology, which has become a key factor in server consolidation trends. IBM statistics show that mainframe data represents 60% of business structured data assets, with a growth of 20% per year.

These powerful capabilities have led to a resurgence of the mainframe because, among other advantages, it allows the enterprises to:

- Run the business with respect to the environment.
- Increase competitiveness by applying new cost reduction strategies.
- Improve IT efficiency in terms of performance, reliability, and quality of service.

Hardware consolidation is not only a matter of saving money; it is also a way to help a company achieve certain goals. For example, using less power and air conditioning results in energy savings that in turn help reduce a company's carbon footprint.

Costs matter, and freeing resources, in terms of time, people, and money, for more strategic activities, also impacts the efficiency of the entire IT infrastructure. The indisputable qualities of mainframes in terms of efficiency, reliability, performance, scalability and security, reaches the state of the art on System z. Reducing the costs of ownership and the number of requests for maintenance, combined with the power of a high performance platform, bring benefits to any aspect of business processes.

Furthermore, a more efficient infrastructure allows IT to be proactive, which saves time and resources to test and apply new, forward-looking, and more valuable solutions, which leads to a perceivable appreciation of the entire service.

In addition to the proven capabilities of System z to manage OLTP data, IBM completes the scenario by offering IBM InfoSphere™ products, such as DataStage®, which can orchestrate ETL data streams and deliver high performing data marts and data warehouses on DB2®. The secure Web tier leverages IBM WebSphere® Application Server to respond to the enterprise's needs in regard to publishing and distributing access to information.

This is a natural environment to consolidate BI solutions, because it supports extremely large data stores and scales easily from small to large user community deployments, depending on the intended usage, by preserving centralized control for systems and infrastructures.

Cognos 8 BI delivers powerful Business Intelligence capabilities to the powerful and reliable System z environment. Together with DB2 and Information Server, Cognos 8 provides an end-to-end Business Intelligence solution, as shown in Figure 1-1.

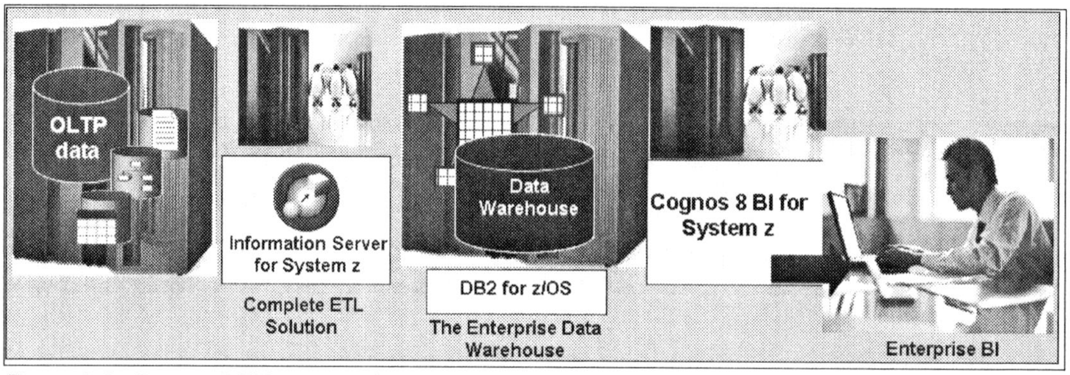

Figure 1-1 Cognos 8 BI leverages System z for end-to-end information management

BI solution consolidation allows IT to deliver better service, reducing the cost of maintenance of existing implementations and the efforts to answer new requests. By easing access to relevant information, IBM Cognos 8 BI facilitates BI solution adoption among the enterprise, and IBM System z elevates performance and reliability. Let us see how this strategy applies to different scenarios.

1.2.1 Data warehouse and operational data on System z

Operational data on System z are generally large centralized information stores of accurate information that support high performance and high availability. Operational data and data warehouses have resided on System z for many years primarily because of scalability and performance. It just makes sense to be able to leverage this vast amount of data without incurring the expense of moving it across a network. Additionally, new ETL and reporting technology on System z allows the enterprise to consolidate the operational data on System z into a dynamic enterprise data warehouse on System z. This enables the enterprise to leverage the strengths of System z to reduce the latency of data warehouse updates and provide BI analysis and reporting with timely accurate information.

1.2.2 System z strengths

System z has for many years proven its ability to manage mixed workloads successfully. This strength is especially evident when running at 100% utilization. The strengths of System z make it an ideal platform to run a BI workload.

Scalability

As businesses grow, their data processing needs also grow. Mergers and acquisitions mean you now need to get reports across different businesses with different technologies. New government regulations bring with them new reporting needs and auditing needs. As rapid growth occurs, companies need a way to scale their business successfully. When it comes to scalability, the System z has delivered 9,445 business transactions per second based on more than 380 million accounts with three billion transaction histories as part of the world's largest Core Banking Benchmark run by IBM and Financial Network Services (FNS), a subsidiary of Tata Consultancy Services, for the Bank of China.

With the new IBM System z10™ enterprise class machine, it is possible to have up to 64 processors in a single box. The System z10 offers a 70% increase in capacity over the largest System z9®. As an enterprise's workload grows, processors can be added without impacting the system (that is, no downtime). In addition, very large enterprises can grow further horizontally with System z Sysplex capabilities. Additional machines (Sysplex members) can be added to the Sysplex without impacting the existing production environment (that is, no downtime).

Availability

The System z hardware, IBM z/OS® operating system, and z/VM® are designed with reliability characteristics, such as self monitoring, redundancy, self healing, and dynamic configuration and management. For example, if a System z10 processor fails, it will be dynamically and nondisruptively replaced by a spare processor, and the users will never know it happened.

You can achieve unparalleled availability with System z Sysplex and DB2 z/OS Data Sharing at the core of a clustered deployment of warehouses or BI solution. When a Sysplex member experiences either an unplanned or planned outage, other members of the Sysplex are able to take on the workload. System z even provides the ability to bring online additional CPU resources that were dormant on those members.

Workload management

The Workload Manager (WLM) component of z/OS has proven its worth in many studies, demonstrations, and everyday work being done in systems around the world with its ability to maximize the use of available resources. WLM has the ability to manage widely, varying workloads efficiently and effectively using all available system resources. This means that you can run your data warehouse workload together with the transactional (OLTP) workload on the same DB2 subsystem or different DB2 subsystems on the same system. The distributed threads used by the Cognos 8 BI solution to access DB2 for z/OS are managed by WLM.

Hardware data compression

Using Cognos 8 BI with a data warehouse on DB2 on System z provides the added performance and space benefit of hardware compression, with minimal additional cost as compared to software compression. Compressing data can reduce the elapsed time of most data warehouse type queries. DB2 for z/OS compresses the rows on a page so that each data page is full of compressed rows. It uses hardware instruction along with a data dictionary to provide the most efficient compression available. The compressed data can also be encrypted, thereby saving space and implementing security requirements at the same time.

With a 50% compression rate (the rule of thumb), a compressed page contains twice the rows that an uncompressed page contains. This means that each I/O retrieves twice as much compressed data as it retrieves if the data is uncompressed. The data remains compressed in the buffer pool. DB2 for z/OS can cache twice as much compressed data in its buffer pool as it retrieves when the data is uncompressed. Finally, when data is modified in a row that is compressed, the information copied or logged about that data change is also compressed, thus reducing copy and log volume.

Specialty processors

IBM has developed three specialty processors for System z: the Integrated Facility for Linux (IFL), the System z Integrated Information Processor (zIIP), and the System z Application Assist Processor (zAAP). These processors execute specific workloads and do not add to software licensing cost of IBM programs running within the z/OS operating system.

- The IFL is a processor dedicated to Linux workloads on IBM System z servers. This processor can run Linux in a stand-alone fashion or shared through virtualization. The IFL hardware feature is isolated from general use. It is supported by z/VM, the Linux operating system, and Linux applications, and cannot run other IBM operating systems. Cognos 8 BI runs on Linux on System z, so all of the Cognos 8 BI CPU needs are met by IFLs.
- The zIIP processor is designed to help free up general computing capacity and lower the overall total cost of computing for select data and transaction processing workloads for Business Intelligence (BI), ERP, and CRM, and select network encryption workloads on the mainframe. This can be a major advantage to having a data warehouse on DB2 on System z, because it allows Cognos 8 BI running on Linux on System z to access DB2 data with little effect on the System z CPU.
- The zAAP processor provides an attractively priced execution environment for new, z/OS only, and Web-based applications and service-oriented architecture (SOA) based technologies, such as Java™ and XML.

By adding specialty processors to System z, the processing capacity is increased without any increase in z/OS licensing fees.

By teaming Cognos 8 BI with a dynamic enterprise warehouse on System z, BI consolidation can take advantage of IFL and zIIP specialty engines.

Regulatory compliance

Regulations, such as the Sarbanes-Oxley Act (SOX), Basel II, Data Protection Act (UK), and the U.S. Patriot Act, were created to protect investors' interests, to avoid fraud, and to improve financial reporting. Companies must comply with these regulations. Database administrators must ensure that data is secure, access is controlled, changes are audited, and disaster recovery is in place. Regulations also emphasize the growing need to reproduce versions of data, applications, and entire business states, which challenges companies to keep a long record of activities.

The System z platform meets the highest industry security certifications. Encryption support is built in, even at the hardware level. Authorization functionality is an integral part of the operating system. Detection services prevent intrusions and record intrusion attempts. Network communication encryption follows the highest standards.

Consolidating BI, warehouse data, and operational data on one platform, such as the System z platform, eases efforts to comply with regulation requirements. Centralized reporting using Cognos 8 BI with multiple data stores allows a single version of the truth. Cognos 8 BI offers enterprise customers a comprehensive foundation to address BI security concerns, including the areas of authentication, access control, data-level security, application firewalls, and encryption. Cognos 8 BI provides auditing capabilities, defined user roles, and lineage.

Disaster recovery

With the emergence of mission critical BI and dynamic enterprise warehousing, the disaster recovery requirements for a data warehouse environment are similar to that of OLTP. Therefore, it is important to consider disaster recovery scenarios before implementing a BI and data warehouse solution.

The following System z and DB2 for z/OS technologies help provide some of the best disaster recover solutions in the industry:

- Remote Copy Services

  Metro Mirror Synchronous (PPRC) causes each write to the primary volume to be performed to the secondary as well, and the I/O is only considered complete when updates to both the primary and secondary volumes have completed.

  Global Mirror for System z (XRC) combines supported hardware and z/OS software to provide asynchronous replication over long distances.

  DPS achieves the defined goals for disaster recover and high availability by simplifying and enhancing data management activities. For information about GDPS®, refer to *GDPS Family - An Introduction to Concepts and Capabilities*, SG24-6374, as well as the following address:

  `http://www.ibm.com/systems/z/advantages/gdps/index.html`

- BACKUP and RESTORE SYSTEM utilities of DB2 for z/OS

  These utilities use disk volume FlashCopy® backups and copypool z/OS DFSMShsm constructs to copy and restore volumes of DB2 data.

  Refer to *Disaster Recovery with DB2 UDB for z/OS*, SG24-6370*Optimizing Restore and Recovery Solutions with DB2 Recovery Expert for z/OS V2.1*, SG24-7606 for more information.

I/O connectivity

As the amount of data in a data warehouse environment increases every day, there is a requirement to provide fast data access to the processor unit, for example, building an *ad hoc report* that reads a large table space; fast data access to a CPU will determine how quickly that report can be built. The newest generation of FICON® features for the z10 EC and z10 BC servers, FICON Express8 10 KM LX and FICON Express8 SX, are designed to support a link rate of 8 Gbps with autonegotiation to 2 or 4 Gbps to support existing devices for added investment protection. FICON Express8 helps support increased CPU performance and meet the need for increased application performance while providing a manageable migration to higher speeds. FICON Express8 continues the tradition of a robust and balanced I/O system design on IBM System z.

FICON Express8 and other System z channel enhancements help improve channel performance, provide support for more devices, and support standards-based Fibre Channel Protocol (FCP) enhancements that help improve resource sharing and access control for Linux on System z environments.

FICON distance and bandwidth capabilities also make it an essential and cost-effective component of data high availability and disaster recovery solutions when combined with System z Parallel Sysplex® and GDPS technology. Parallel Sysplex provides resource sharing, workload balancing, and continuous availability benefits while GDPS provides system level automation that enables the most advanced, application-transparent, and multi-site disaster recovery solution with a fast recovery time. It offers two non-repeating distance options (4 KM and 10 KM) when using single mode fiber optic cabling.

All FICON Express features support the Modified Indirect Data Address Word (MIDAW) facility. MIDAW is new system architecture with software exploitation that helps improve channel utilization, reduce channel impact, and potentially reduce I/O response times.

With support for native FICON, High Performance FICON for System z (zHPF), and Fibre Channel Protocol (FCP), the System z10 servers enable you to position your SAN for even higher performance, helping you prepare for an end-to-end 8 Gbps infrastructure to meet the increased bandwidth demands of your applications.

For details about FICON, refer to the following address:

`http://www.ibm.com/systems/z/hardware/connectivity/news.html`

Parallel access DASD

High I/O delays from the data storage devices can lead to performance problems in data warehouse queries, which sometimes process a high amount of multiple reads from one particular volume, which in turn could cause issues for a BI system. System z has addressed this issue by using parallel access volume (PAV). PAV enables a single System z server to simultaneously process multiple I/O operations to the same logical volume, which can significantly reduce device queue delays (I/O Supervisor Queue (IOSQ) time). This is achieved by defining multiple addresses per volume.

With dynamic PAV, the assignment of addresses to volumes can be automatically managed to help the workload meet its performance objectives and reduce overall queuing. With PAV, reads are simultaneous. Writes to different domains (a set of tracks the disk controller is working on) are simultaneous as well; however, writes to the same domain are serialized. No double updates are possible to preserve integrity. Large volumes, such as 3390 mod 9, 27, and 54, benefit greatly from using PAV. Multiple paths or channels for a volume have been around for many years; however, multiple Unit Control Block (UCBs = MVS addresses) were only introduced with PAVs.

For more information about PAV, HyperPAV, and IBM System Storage™ DS8000® features, refer to *IBM System Storage DS8000: Architecture and Implementation*, SG24-6786.

Total cost of ownership

Studies[1] have shown that when operations, maintenance, and high availability costs are included in the cost of any system, System z costs become much more favorable and in some cases actually turn out to be less than those of other platforms. This is true mostly because many different applications can share a single System z and, in some cases, share the same DB2 subsystem. This allows the cost of administering System z to be amortized over multiple application workloads, while this may not be possible on other platforms.

This is also an important factor in BI consolidation with Cognos 8 BI. The Cognos 8 BI system running on Linux on System z allows the costs for BI to be amortized across all BI users and lines of business[2].

IBM also continues to introduce innovations that further decrease total cost of ownership (TCO), such as the zIIP, zAAP, and IFL specialty processors. These processors are priced less than general purpose processors and the MIPS they provide generally do not count toward the software costs of the z/OS system.

---

[1] Refer to "Step up to IBM Mainframe TCO Challenge", found at:
`http://www-03.ibm.com/systems/migratetoibm/systems/z/tco.html`

[2] See the IBM case study "IBM Cognos 8 BI for Linux on System z: 30,000 users in production in just four months" at `http://www.ibm.com/software/success/cssdb.nsf/CS/SANS-7WUJEV?OpenDocument&Site=default&cty=en_us`

1.2.3 When you should use DB2 for z/OS

Once you decide to use Cognos 8 BI for Linux on System z and some of the System z unique features, this question arises: When is DB2 for z/OS a good fit for implementing a data warehouse to support Cognos 8 BI?

When considering DB2 for z/OS for implementing the warehouse, keep in mind the following criteria:

- The majority of source systems are on z/OS within IMS™, VSAM, DB2, or sequential files, or there is a requirement for tight integration with existing resources and systems on the System z platform.
- The data warehouse, data marts, or operational data store already exist on System z.
- Existing skills and investments are on the System z platform.
- You already maintain a System z-centric IT solution because of the favorable cost of ownership and comfort.
- You are implementing an operational BI application with embedded analytics. These types of applications can leverage the System z transaction scalability capabilities.
- There is a requirement for a true real-time operational data store and
  - Operational data is already on the System z platform.
  - Data must be virtually in-sync with the operational data.
  - Availability, security, and resiliency requirements are high.
  - Auditable data warehouse requirements exist.
- Independent software vendor (ISV) packages offer both transactional (OLTP) and informational (warehouse and BI) systems.
  - These packaged applications, which have tightly integrated components, have always made it desirable for the operational data and the warehouse to be housed in the same environment. Co-location reduces operational complexity, allowing for the reuse of skills and infrastructure in the form of processes, tools, and procedures.
  - You want to consolidate distributed marts or data warehouses on an existing System z data serving platform and you may have spare System z capacity.
- The absolute best in reliability, availability, serviceability, security, and workload management is needed.

For details about DB2 for z/OS functions, refer to *Enterprise Data Warehousing with DB2 9 for z/OS*, SG24-76377.

1.2.4 Extract, transform, and load on the same platform

Extract, transform, and load (ETL) identifies the processes that extract information from any source, such as the OLTP system, transform it according to the needs of the data warehouse environment, move it to the platform that houses the data warehouse, and finally loads the data into the data warehouse. The process of extracting information from the OLTP system can run on the same platform as the OLTP system. The process of transforming it to conform to the needs of the data warehouse should be performed on the platform where the OLTP system resides. This is because many of the techniques used in the transformation process reduce the amount of data that then must be moved to and loaded into the data warehouse.

Regardless of where the transformational process is performed, it is necessary to move the data to the platform that is housing the data warehouse. Many methods can be employed in this movement of data. Regardless of the method that is employed, if the data warehouse is physically distinct from the platform that is housing the OLTP system, it is necessary to transmit this data over a communications path of some kind. Often, this is the single most time consuming and expensive component of the entire ETL process.

The solution is to house the data warehouse and the OLTP system on a System z server. The System z platform is capable of handling the different characteristics of OLTP and BI workloads within one logical database system. This can be achieved by DB2 subsystems that are optimized for different workloads within a data sharing group. Data sharing is a DB2 feature of exploiting System z Parallel Sysplex technology and, therefore, sharing the workload between multiple DB2 subsystems that access the same data.

If the OLTP data absolutely needs to be transformed for warehouse consumption, this can be achieved by doing in-database transformations that do not require the data to leave the DB2 subsystem. For those cases where the required transformations cannot be achieved by using only SQL functions, data can be efficiently delivered by way of DB2 Data Event publishing to a transformation engine like DataStage running on Linux for System z and efficiently inserted back into the warehouse. The linkage between System z and Linux on System z uses HiperSockets™. This is a special high speed, in-memory TCP/IP connection between System z and Linux on System z that results in a maximum transfer rate of 6 GBps. This is extremely more efficient than moving data from System z to a distributed platform for ETL and then moving the data back to System z.

Figure 1-2 shows the architecture of full implementation of InfoSphere Information Data Warehouse on System z and Cognos 8 BI for Linux on System z.

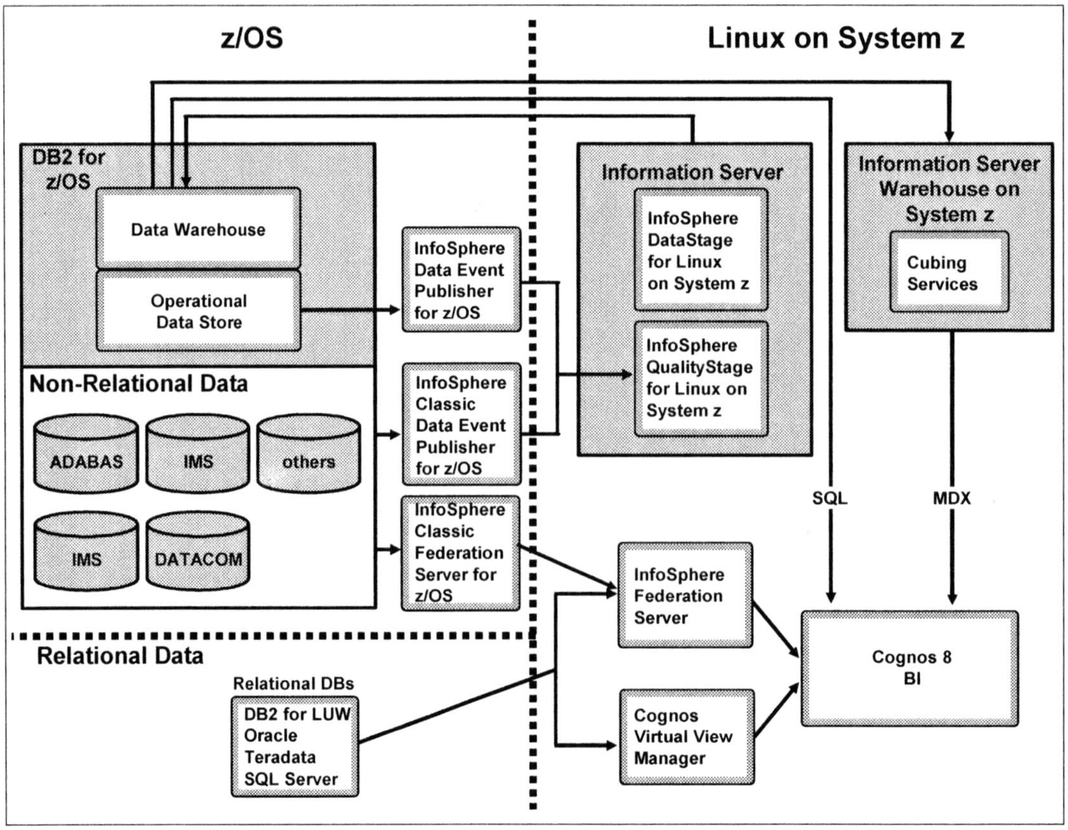

Figure 1-2 Architecture of InfoSphere Information Server Warehouse and Cognos 8 BI

This configuration of System z and DB2 is optimal for the different types of workload that occur if OLTP and BI data is mixed in the same system. It is highly scalable. Detailed data can be accessed in the same way as aggregates, which allows *in-database transformations*.

In addition to DB2 for z/OS, which is an essential core component hosting data in a data warehouse, System z also provides the other components required to build a comprehensive BI solution.

Table 1-1 summarizes the components by function and platform.

Table 1-1 BI solution components

Function	Product	Platform	Description
ETL	InfoSphere DataStage for Linux on System z	Linux on System z	Extracts, transforms, and loads data between multiple sources and targets on the mainframe.
ETL	InfoSphere Warehouse on System z	z/OS and Linux on System z	Designs, populates, and optimizes a DB2 for z/OS data warehouse to support BI applications.
Profiling	InfoSphere Information Analyzer for Linux on System z	Linux on System z	Profiles and establishes an understanding of source systems, and monitors data rules on an ongoing basis to eliminate the risk of proliferating "bad" data on the mainframe.
Data cleansing	InfoSphere QualityStage for Linux on System z	Linux on System z	Standardizes and matches information across heterogeneous sources on the mainframe.
Incremental updates	InfoSphere Data Event Publisher[a] for z/OS	z/OS	Captures incremental updates to DB2.
Incremental updates	InfoSphere Classic Data Event Publisher for z/OS	z/OS	Captures Incremental Updates to IMS, VSAM, CA-IDMS, or Software AG ADABAS.
Access to relational data sources	InfoSphere Federation Server	Linux on System z	Accesses and integrates diverse data and content sources as though they were a single resource, regardless of where the information resides.
Access to non-relational data sources	InfoSphere Classic Federation for z/OS	z/OS	Provides access to IMS, VSAM, CA-IDMS, ADABAS, CA Datacom, or flat files. For performance reasons, consider using simple basic queries in InfoSphere Classic Federation to feed ETL/Cube builds. Complex BI queries can create performance issues on non-relational data.

a. The Event Publisher function is also available as part of WebSphere Information Integrator Replication for z/OS (program number 5655-L88), which includes Q replication, Event Publishing, and SQL replication. Refer to *Publishing IMS and DB2 Data using WebSphere Information Integrator: Configuration and Monitoring Guide*, SG24-7132 for more information.

1.3 Standardized reporting using Cognos 8 BI

Standardized BI reporting has many benefits to the enterprise. First of all, standardized reporting provides productivity benefits to the enterprise. By having standardized reports, it is easier to correlate information across the different lines of business as well as different departments. This leads to less confusion and quicker, more accurate business decisions.

1.3.1 Why Cognos 8 BI

There are many reasons why you should run your BI system on Cognos 8 BI:

- Cognos 8 BI is a solution that provides BI consolidation and allows the enterprise to operate the BI system in close proximity to its data. In this case, we are talking about Linux on System z. With large warehouses and very large operational data stores, it makes sense to run your BI system on the same platform, in close proximity. This helps the enterprise avoid the performance implications of transferring vast amounts of data across their network.
- Cognos 8 BI delivers a broad range of capabilities that include reporting, analysis, dashboards, and event management. Cognos 8 BI also ensures that all user communities receive relevant information about how, when, and where it is needed. With Cognos 8 BI, you can also create a report once and deliver it in which ever method best makes sense for your users. This may be a PDF file, an Excel file, into a mobile device, or into a zero-footprint browser based interface, thereby eliminating software deployment headaches.
- Cognos 8 BI is flexible and can be tailored for different types of users from simple report consumers to sophisticated professional authors. This flexibility enables the enterprise to consolidate data on Cognos 8 BI and allows individual users or departments to maintain their existing level of control and function.
- Cognos 8 BI is part of the IBM Information on Demand (IOD) architecture and also participates in the SOA. When Cognos 8 BI is combined with other elements of the IBM IOD vision, such as Dynamic Data Warehousing, the enterprise has the ability to create a BI system that provides trusted information, with a single view of the truth, with time relevancy to the enterprise. The result: better and faster decisions.

1.3.2 Business Intelligence with Cognos 8 BI

By using IBM Cognos 8 BI, enterprises can make informed, faster, and more aligned decisions.

What is BI

BI is the process of gathering, consolidating, and analyzing data from multiple sources for strategic decision making. BI helps the enterprise:

- Derive new value from your transactional data
- Support strategic planning, monitoring, and efficiency
- Deliver knowledge of the customers, suppliers, and channels
- Unify the business with a single version of the truth
- Develop the insight and understanding needed to make informed decisions

Figure 1-3 shows the Business Intelligence architecture.

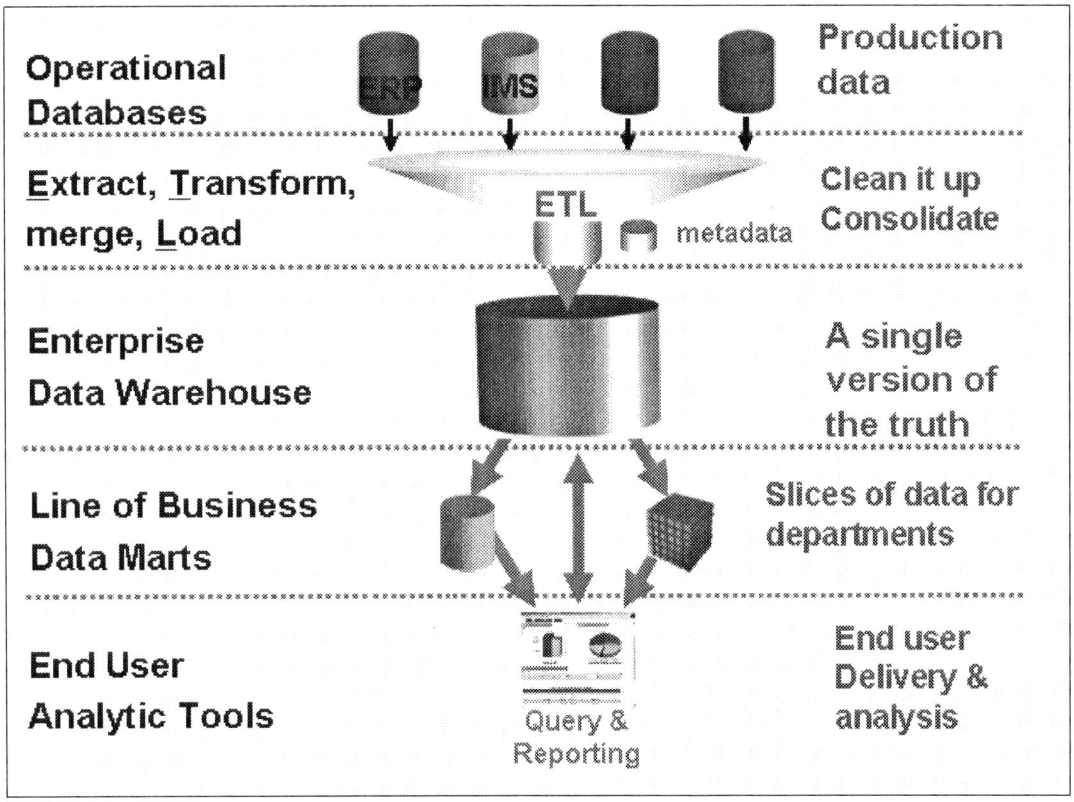

Figure 1-3 BI architecture

Cognos 8 BI offers a complete set of BI capabilities to help organizations address those vital questions about their performance: "How are we doing?" and "Why?". With reporting, analysis, dashboards, and scorecards, all accessible through the Web, office integration, search, and mobile devices, we can ensure all user communities in an organization gain the task-based capabilities to use information how, when, and where they need it.

In most organizations, the answer to "How are we doing?" is provided by scorecards and dashboards that are compiled manually. Because it is a manual process, it has to be repeated, but may be done a little differently each time. You must discover or remember definitions, how things roll up, how targets are set, how the calculations are formatted, and how objects such as revenue and customer are defined. As a result, this process may vary among the business community, which introduces risk and makes the process unauditable.

With Cognos 8 BI dashboards, an enterprise can:

- Translate complex information into high-impact presentations
- Easily spot changes
- Align decision makers
- Provide a highly intuitive look into the business

It is usually difficult for an enterprise to answer the question "Why?". The major challenge with BI in an enterprise is that tools have grown up regionally or functionally in a patchwork of different applications and tools. The result is that the enterprise has different interfaces, different time periods, and gaps in the critical information needed to make business decisions. The result is a lack of confidence in the information.

Additionally, from an IT perspective, there are huge costs to maintaining a host of different BI tools. It costs money and time, and it takes many people to maintain, administer, and support a patchwork BI solution.

Cognos 8 BI gives the enterprise powerful tools so that it can consolidate its BI systems and perform enterprise reporting and analysis.

Enterprise reporting:

- Supports multiple report types, such as production, managed, ad hoc, and financial
- Is adaptable to any data source
- Operates from a single metadata layer
- Can be personalized and targeted
- Can be distributed by way of e-mail, portal, MS-Office, search applications, and mobile devices

Analysis gives the enterprise:

- A guided exploration of information that pertains to all dimensions of the business
- The ability to perform complex analysis and scenario modeling easily and quickly
- The ability to get to the "why" behind an event or action to improve business performance
- The ability to move from summary level information to detail levels of information effortlessly

Figure 1-4 shows a high-level architecture overview of Cognos 8 BI.

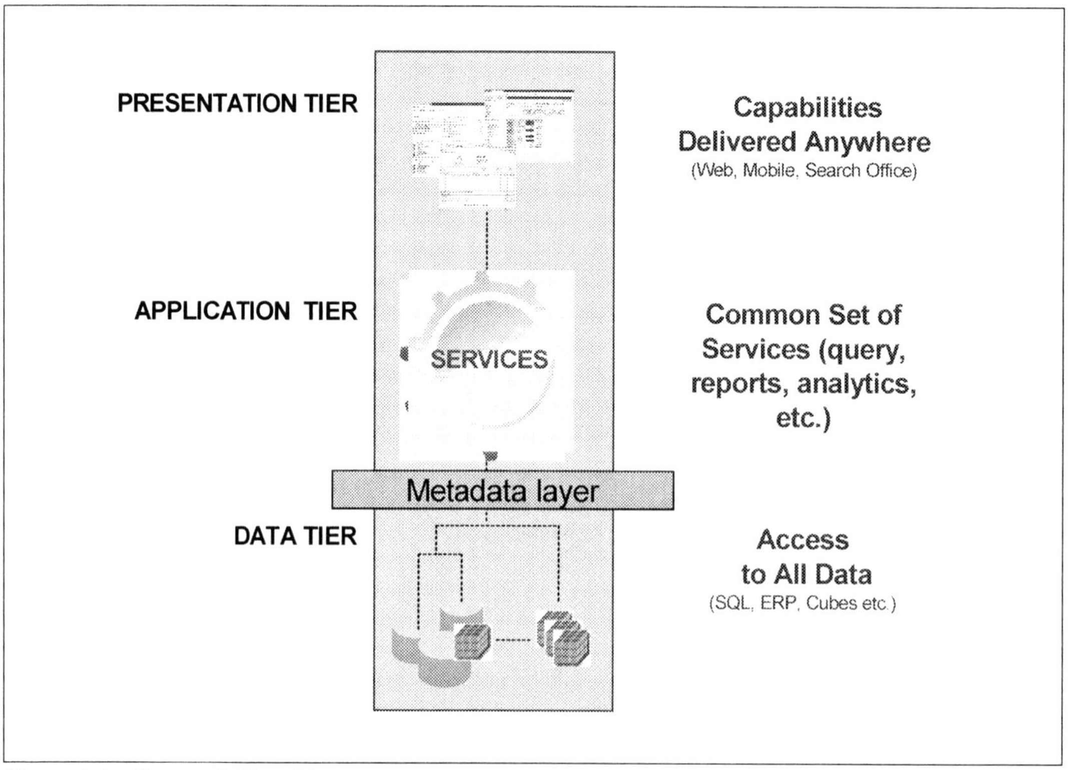

Figure 1-4 Cognos 8 BI architecture

Figure 1-5 provides a more detailed representation of Cognos 8 BI architecture showing Cognos components, their level, and relationship with each other.

The components are described throughout this book. Chapter 2, "Scenario for deployment" on page 23 includes the modeling tools, such as VVM Studio and Framework Manager, Chapter 3, "Reporting and analysis" on page 75 describes Go! Office, Go! Dashboard, Go! Mobile, and so on), Chapter 4, "Information on Demand integration" on page 113 includes the InfoSphere products, and Chapter 6, "Online Analytical Processing processing comparisons" on page 151 mentions the Cognos Transformer.

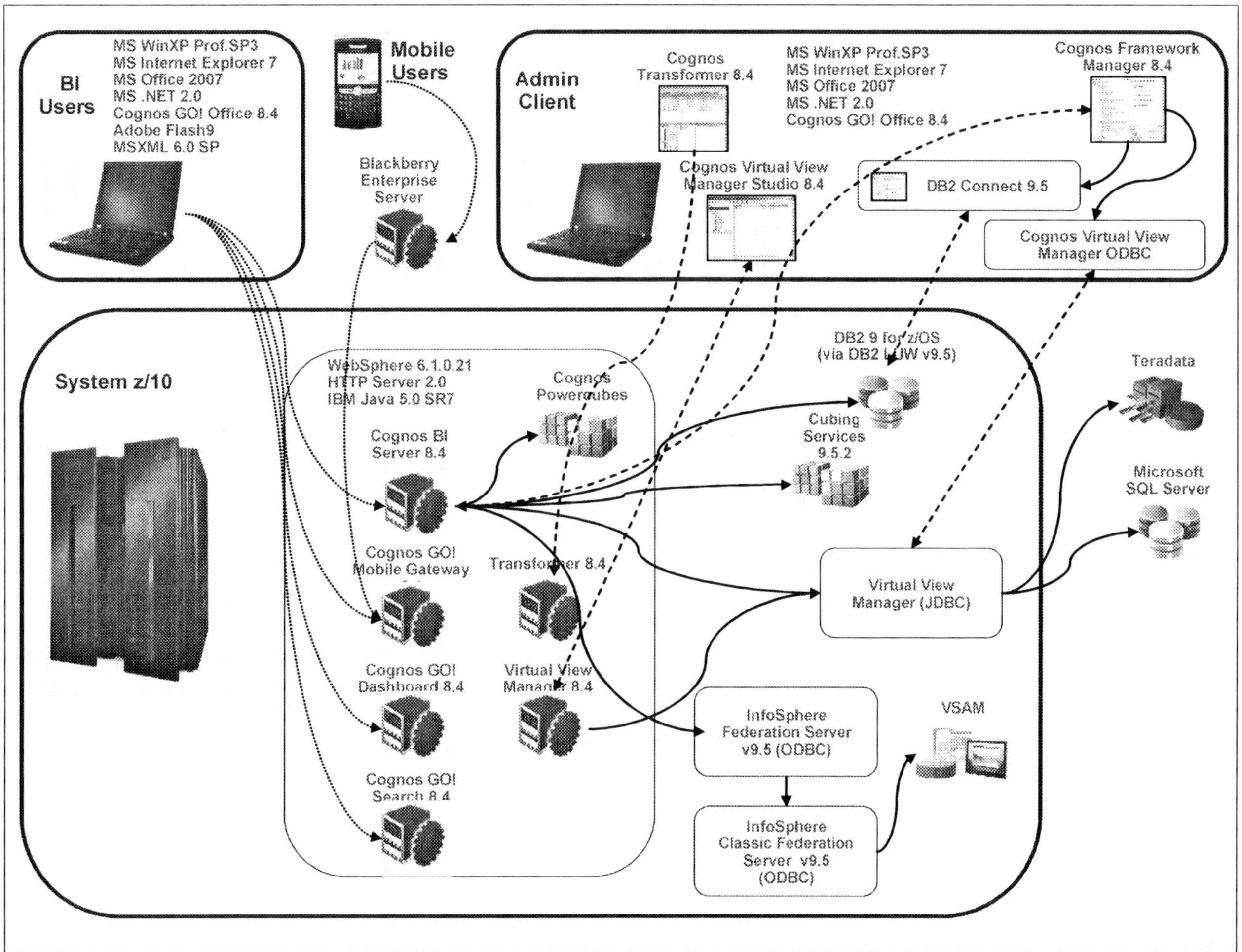

Figure 1-5 Cognos components and interfaces

1.3.3 Cognos 8 BI Performance Management platform

Delivering performance management capabilities to users throughout the organization requires a single system for Performance Management. A system that delivers consistent, timely accurate information to users when and where they need it. The system has three core components:

- An enterprise-class platform that provides the technical underpinning of the system. The platform is architected from the ground up as a modern, open, Web services, and services-oriented platform. The platform sits on top of your existing infrastructure investments and provides one single solution for your Performance Management requirements.

- Universal capabilities to deliver targeted information to decision makers in the organization whenever and wherever they need it. These capabilities enable users across the organization so that regardless of where individuals sit, they have the information they need to actually impact performance.
- Solutions of packaged know-how and expertise to quickly address business and technical challenges. Cognos and its partners have taken know-how from the best performance management initiatives from around the world and distilled that know-how into head-starts, proven practices, services, training, blueprints, and analytic applications. You can use these accelerators to avoid common pitfalls and get your solutions running quickly and successfully.

  For more information about IBM Cognos Analytic Applications, refer to the following address:

  `http://www.ibm.com/software/data/cognos/products/cognos-analytic-applications/`

Cognos 8 BI offers these capabilities in role based packaging, allowing customers to start with one or more capabilities and add incremental capabilities over time as needed. Performance management solutions can automate and monitor finance specific key performance indicators, but they can easily be extended to include any of the data and metrics that an organization uses to measure itself, such as human resources, finance, workforce planning, and so on.

The Cognos 8 BI Performance Management platform is comprised of three major components:

- Measuring & Monitoring: Answers the question of "Why?"
- Planning: Answers the question of "What should we be doing?
- Reporting & Analysis: Answers the question of "How are we doing?"

Figure 1-6 shows the relationship between the three areas of performance management. In this book, we focus on Measuring & Monitoring a well as Reporting & Analysis.

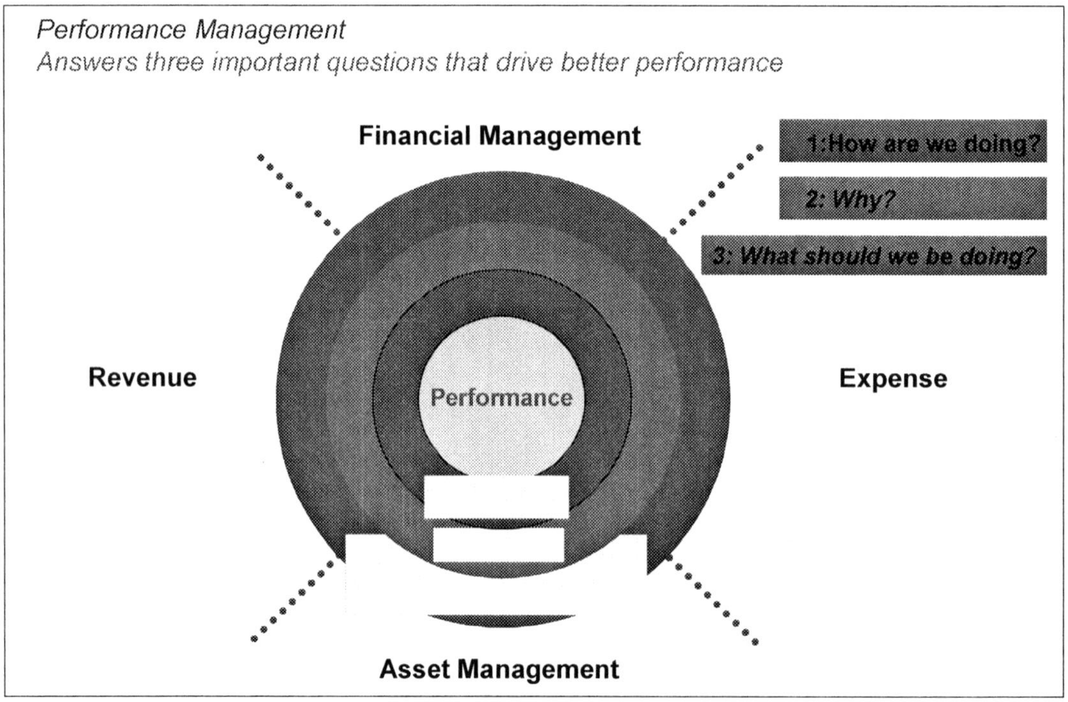

Figure 1-6 Performance Management areas

Cognos 8 BI addresses the four critical requirements shown in Figure 1-6 on page 16 in eight major ways:

1. The ability to reach all information reliably and timely on all supported data sources.

   The Cognos 8 BI platform, which includes the Virtual View Manager V8.4 Software Environments, allows you to access all supported data sources regardless of their structure while insulating business users and metadata modelers from their complexity. The single query service provides predictable and consistent results across all your capabilities while simplifying management and maintenance for IT. It provides these abilities:

   - Native interfaces or adapters to many data sources.
   - Access to relational data sources exploiting advanced features of SQL, including SQL-OLAP, common table expressions, derived tables, and so on.
   - Optimized access to Cognos 8 BI PowerCubes.
   - Access to modern data sources, including XML and collaboration sources.

   The Cognos 8 BI platform gives IT the flexibility to combine data sources or change sourcing strategies over time without disrupting the user experience. It provides these abilities:

   - Direct access: Enables immediate access to your existing data sources.
   - High-performance federated access: Combines data from multiple sources on the fly to create virtual views from current and historic data as a single, easy-to-query view.
   - Integration with additional tools: Includes IBM InfoSphere Information Server and DataStage, Informatica PowerCenter, and change data capture (CDC) technologies, such as IBM InfoSphere Change Data Capture.

2. Deliver information to business users quickly and efficiently without impacting the performance of your source systems by using these functions:

   - Multi-dimensional cube building lets IT and business analysts reshape data without the need for costly and time consuming changes to back-end systems.
   - Build new OLAP cubes quickly using existing data, queries, or reports.
   - Business analysts can publish new OLAP cubes directly into the Cognos 8 BI environment without IT intervention.
   - Virtual caching lets IT reduce the load on the source systems by re-using existing views and caching data to a disk or database.

3. Identify problems before they happen. Scale up and out as needed.

   The Cognos 8 BI platform lets you predict your system performance to minimize risks and plan accordingly for the capacity required when you deploy your solution by using these functions:

   - Peer-to-peer services: Deploy peer-to-peer services across the network without a single point of failure.
   - Automatic load balancing: Built-in round robin load balancing with self-aware, self-starting, and self-spawning peer-to-peer services.
   - Proven linear scalability: Services can scale up or scale out for a predictable, linear response to workloads. Administrators can proactively reallocate resources when scaling the solutions.
   - Completely Web-based deployment, including administration and authoring: Deploy and expand user communities across geographies, platforms, or where capability is required.

4. Get a complete view of system activity for administrators to take action before business impact by using these functions:
   - Task-oriented system monitoring: Reduce the time and effort you need to monitor system activity, assess the status, and take appropriate actions. Administrators can view all system activity, from scheduled and interactive reports to servers and dispatchers, from a single location.
   - Proactive administration: Detailed system metrics and custom thresholds reduce the time you need to troubleshoot, identify anomalies, and resolve performance issues before they negatively impact system performance or the user experience.
   - Integration with third-party enterprise management systems (EMS): Expose metrics within EMS solutions, including IBM Tivoli® products.
5. Shorten the time you need to upgrade and minimize user disruptions by using these functions:
   - Visual upgrade manager: Streamline the upgrade process with the ability to visually compare report results between versions.
   - Automated environment validation: Test, compare, and record report results between environments to validate the impact of making changes to your solution.
6. The Cognos 8 BI platform provides a comprehensive foundation to manage all aspects of your security, including authentication, access control, data-level security, application firewalls, and encryption. You can reduce the complexity, time, and costs of administering and maintaining multiple security systems with best of breed security providers and in-place application security. You have these functions;
   - Full support for LDAP and Custom Java Provider.
   - Authentication: Pre-built integration with leading security providers, which are fully documented API for custom authentication.
   - Access control: Centralized authorization and support for granular user access rights from within Cognos 8 BI or a third-party security provider reduces the burden of managing multiple security schemes. IT can grant or deny permissions and track/audit usage for select users and groups.
   - Data-level access rights: Simplify your security scheme with granular-level security for all objects and information, including folders, subject areas, individual reports, portal pages, data connections, and so on.
   - Application firewall: Prevent unauthorized access to performance management services. An application firewall monitors and interprets protocol traffic between services to help prevent hostile attacks and service interruption, and logs any denied traffic.
   - Encryption: Protect data and transmissions with industry-standard encryption algorithms, such as Triple DES and AES. The Cognos 8 BI platform features standard 56-bit encryption.
7. Deliver results more quickly using the IBM Cognos 8 BI System Management Methodology, a proven and systematic approach consisting of:
   - Metadata models that accelerate your ability to administer your deployment.
   - Tools that automatically establish performance thresholds in your specific environment.
   - Sample administration models and reports, built using Cognos 8 BI, that help administrators understand performance trends and tune system performance.

8. Leverage your existing infrastructure and adapt quickly to change.

   The Cognos 8 BI platform gives the enterprise the ability to leverage existing investments in platform, security, portal, and Web environments. The enterprise can also deploy any Cognos 8 BI service and make it accessible from anywhere. In addition, Cognos 8 BI performance management capabilities can be added to other applications, such as your Web applications, business process management (BPM), or enterprise search. The enterprise also has the capability to add new functionality across the capabilities to keep pace with future business demands.

1.3.4 How does Cognos 8 BI fit into the Information On Demand solution

The IBM vision for the Information On Demand (IOD) solution is to empower the enterprise to make better business decisions and to gain a competitive advantage by giving the enterprise timely access to trusted information from across the enterprise. However, timely access to trusted information alone does not give the enterprise a competitive advantage; the enterprise must have the capabilities to use, analyze, and report on the information. This is the value Cognos 8 BI adds to the IBM IOD vision, that is, to “Unlock the Business Value of Information for Competitive Advantage”.

Cognos 8 BI is an integral part of the IBM IOD vision. In Figure 1-7, you can see that the IBM Cognos 8 BI functions are critical components for a solution built from the ground up on the principles of SOA, which can be deployed across the enterprise and address the changing requirements in business and IT.

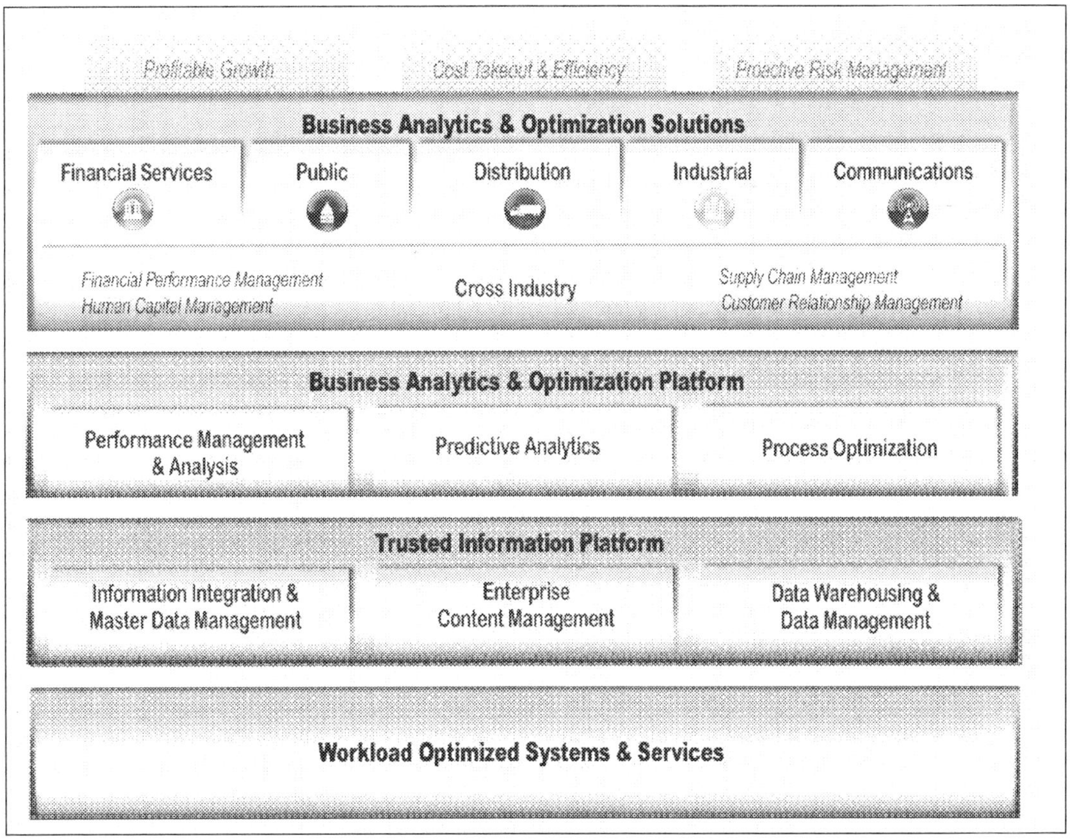

Figure 1-7 Information On Demand

The Cognos 8 BI architecture is based upon these requirements and enables an enterprise to:

- Maximize the value of their information
- Optimize their business processes
- Deliver trusted information in real time
- Achieve higher performance across the enterprise

Cognos 8 BI supports enterprise deployments that are flexible, allowing a solution that can scale across the enterprise and meet the needs of all the users as well as the needs of IT. This is all possible because Cognos 8 BI is based on SOA.

Cognos 8 BI fully leverages SOA for its platform architecture to achieve industry leadership in Business Intelligence and performance management. By adopting SOA as its foundation, the Cognos 8 BI architecture enables customers to have efficient solutions that fit within fast-changing environments, the reliability needed to function effectively in the face of diverse and changing business requirements, and the agility to respond quickly to rapidly changing business needs.

1.3.5 Metadata and information integration

Being able to integrate Cognos 8 BI into your environment is very important. There are several ways that Cognos 8 BI can make this easier for you. Analysis enables the guided exploration of information that pertains to all dimensions of your business, regardless of where the data is stored. The ability to analyze and report against online analytical processing (OLAP) and dimensionally aware relational sources is vital to your business. Discovery of data sources as well as being able to import the metadata from these sources will give you faster access and the ability to provide Trusted Information. Additionally, the ability to easily integrate other data sources is also key to your success.

Metadata

Metadata can be imported and published directly into Cognos 8 BI from the source data store by way of the Cognos Framework Manager. Importing metadata simplifies or eliminates the need to model the data source in Cognos 8 BI. Cognos 8 BI supports the following sources for importing metadata:

- Architect models and Impromptu® catalogs
- DecisionStream or IBM Cognos 8 BI Data Manager models
- Third-party metadata sources
- XML as a data source
- IBM metadata sources, such as InfoSphere DataStage
- Relational databases, such as Oracle, DB2, and Microsoft® SQL Server

Information integration

There are multiple ways to integrate information in Cognos 8 BI. Cognos 8 BI can integrate data directly from multiple data sources if the data sources are supported for direct connection to Cognos 8 BI. Otherwise, it is necessary to federate the data source.

Federation is a data virtualization technology that allows a collection of different data sources to be viewed and manipulated as though they were a single relational database. You can do this with either IBM Cognos Virtual View Manager[3] (VVM) or IBM InfoSphere Federation Server[4], depending on the type of data you need to federate. Federating the data source opens up new integration opportunities. Both VVM and InfoSphere Federation Server provide for data integration closer to the data sources as well as optimized access capabilities to retrieve the data. It is important to federate as close to the data source as possible in order to provide the best performance.

[3] Virtual View Manager is the component that makes additional data sources available to IBM Cognos 8 and improves performance when using heterogeneous data sources.

[4] IBM InfoSphere Federation Server, together with InfoSphere Replication Server and InfoSphere Data Event Publisher, expand the capabilities of the IBM enterprise information integration solutions for virtualized integrated access of heterogeneous data, high availability of data, and high-speed, low-latency data replication.

2

Scenario for deployment

A common approach to Business Intelligence (BI) for many organizations often involves departmental deployments that provide basic answers in terms of operational reporting and basic analysis needs. But if you are looking at a BI platform as a strategic support for driving business and performance, streamlined technologies and solutions are the most efficient ways to orchestrate the distribution of information at the right time.

In this chapter, we discuss how you can couple the power of Linux on IBM System z and the complete BI capabilities of Cognos to consolidate and standardize an existing BI solution, improving performance and data consistency.

All the described solutions have been proven in an environment that simulates a real life scenario based on an IBM Cognos sample application. This case study is called The Sample Outdoors (SO) Company.

This chapter discusses these items:

- Extracting and consolidating data for BI solutions
- Techniques for consolidation
- Implementation considerations

2.1 Extracting and consolidating data for BI solutions

Because market and business needs change rapidly, strategies must consequently evolve, and the effectiveness of a new business plan is related to the quality of information on which it relies. Getting information on time and ensuring data consistency are key to success. It is clear that standardizing on a single BI platform means more than reducing system complexity and streamlining IT investments in terms of education and infrastructure maintenance.

By improving business processes, a single standard BI platform increases the perception of IT as a valuable engine for the enterprise, ensuring the delivery of consistent information. While multiple BI tools address single project needs, adopting a standard BI tool allows an enterprise economy of scale and consistent interfaces. Even though BI tools are needed to address different needs, having a common approach to information facilitates the achievement of the much sought after "single version of the truth".

Considering the costs of non-standardization, fragmented systems confine BI to a poor tactical role, rather then supporting the executives in high level strategy decisions. This behavior prevents organizations from performing cross-departmental analysis, spotting trends, and identifying relevant information.

By combining the power of Linux on System z and the complete range of capabilities and ease-of-use of Cognos 8 BI, IBM maximizes the quality and efficiency of Business Intelligence and ensures a pervasive adoption through the enterprise.

2.1.1 The topology

With Business Intelligence becoming more pervasive in enterprises, there has been a proliferation of different tools addressing specific needs, with purchases driven by project specifications. BI vendor markets have consolidated in the past few years, and the main leaders have provided customers with complete suites of products. Unfortunately, the merging of companies did not mean a real merging of technologies in a seamless way, so it is often the case that the same vendor's software requires separate installations and more hardware to be dedicated to BI platforms. This scenario increases complexity from an IT point of view, and increases the volume of costs related to know-how, ownership, maintenance of data integration jobs and consistency of data.

An ideal Business Intelligence platform should include these three pillars:

- State-of-the-art technology for simplified maintenance, rapid deployment, and wide distribution
- Completeness and easy usage for pervasive adoption
- Maximized adaptability to minimize impact and leverage existing assets

The architecture of IBM Cognos 8 BI meets the standards of "state of the art" software technology, because it has been developed according to standards such as service-oriented architecture (SOA) and Web Services that enable an efficient approach to Business Intelligence, with a native propensity to scale for future requirements.

IBM Cognos delivers all BI tools through a unique platform, with special attention to simplicity, for both user and IT administration. Cognos provides a complete set of BI tools, such as OLAP Analysis, Dashboards, Scorecards, and Query & Reporting on a unique standards based platform. It also allows users and IT administrators to improve the delivery of meaningful information by activating personal scheduling and alerts with only one click.

Having all the BI tools in one platform is the first step towards streamlining systems and keeping all the users' needs satisfied.

Being platform independent is not just a matter of running on different operating systems. Cognos 8 BI deployments can easily be promoted to an enterprise large scale environment based on a different OS (for example, Windows to Linux on System z) as well as move from small deployments to larger deployments as needed. Additionally, with IBM Cognos, you can also leverage existing or new acquired standards in terms of Web platforms, authentication providers, data sources, and so on, as shown in Figure 2-1.

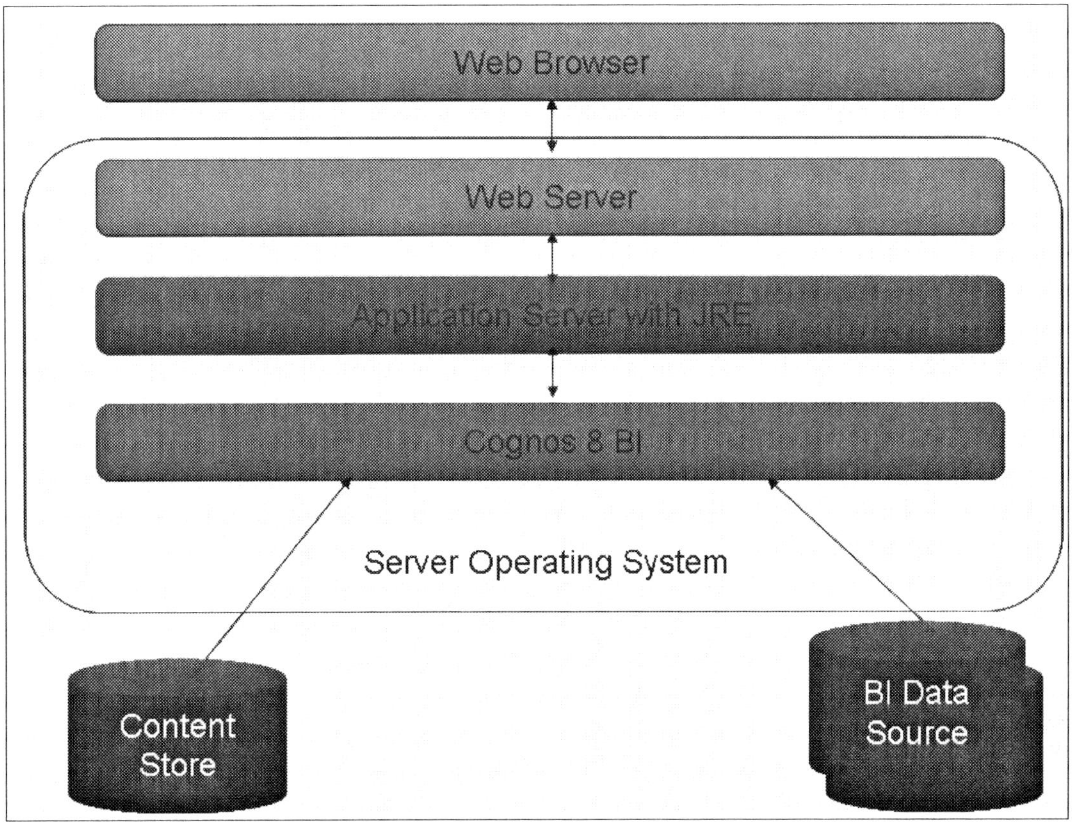

Figure 2-1 Cognos 8 BI installation requirements

Conformance information for all Cognos product versions in all platforms is available at the following address:

`http://www.ibm.com/jct01003c/support/docview.wss?rs=3528&uid=swg27014782`

2.1.2 Existing BI solutions

Depending on how markets, business, and technology evolve, organizations may need to replace applications on different systems. Mergers, acquisitions, corporate visions, new technology standards, or simply the changing of a key account often leads to the proliferation of platforms.

Also, a need for flexibility or lack of knowledge can push users to develop nonstandard, stand-alone solutions. For example, a large company producing commercial vehicles developed a large multipurpose data warehouse on a standard database platform. However, other departments, such as marketing, sales, logistics, and others, still needed information that was not available in the central warehouse. As a result, there was a proliferation of small data stores (mainly desktop databases and spreadsheets) managed by individual departments containing both empirical data as well as data from the data warehouse. These departments built a plethora of reports and dashboards that were completely out of control in terms of maintenance, data quality, and cost of development.

To rectify this situation, IBM produced a suitable strategy for users by applying IBM Cognos as a standard front end. Cognos allows you to organize data sources and therefore reduce unnecessary corporate data proliferation and distribution, as well as retaining data kept in spreadsheets and desktop databases. This data, due to its nature, could not be classified in the corporate data warehouse.

However you modernize your IT systems, you must manage the transition to a standard platform, or be forced to keep multiple standards or small enclaves to store specific data. The good news is that you can easily manage these data sources with a complete Business Intelligence platform. IBM Cognos 8 BI can leverage any of the data sources commonly used in the market and deliver high performance access to data by using native formulas and generating a native query language for each data source shown in the Data Model definition in Figure 2-2.

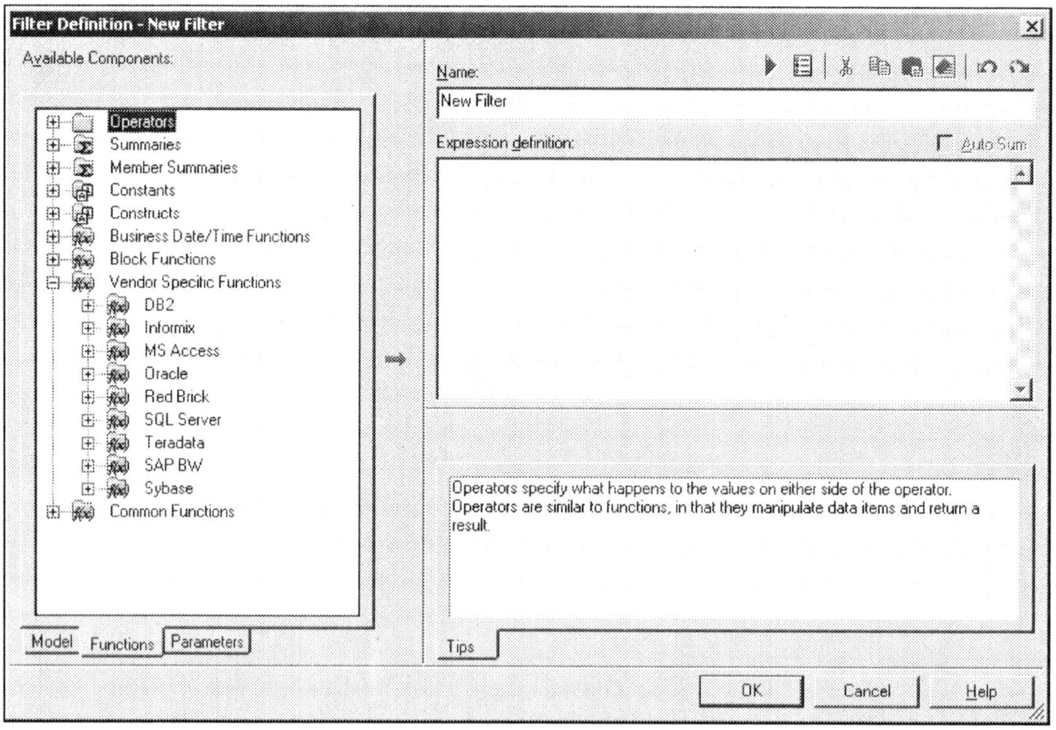

Figure 2-2 IBM Cognos 8 BI using native language in a Data Model definition (Framework Manager)

Report and dashboards developers can also take advantage of native formulas to reduce the workload requested by query processing, as shown in Figure 2-3.

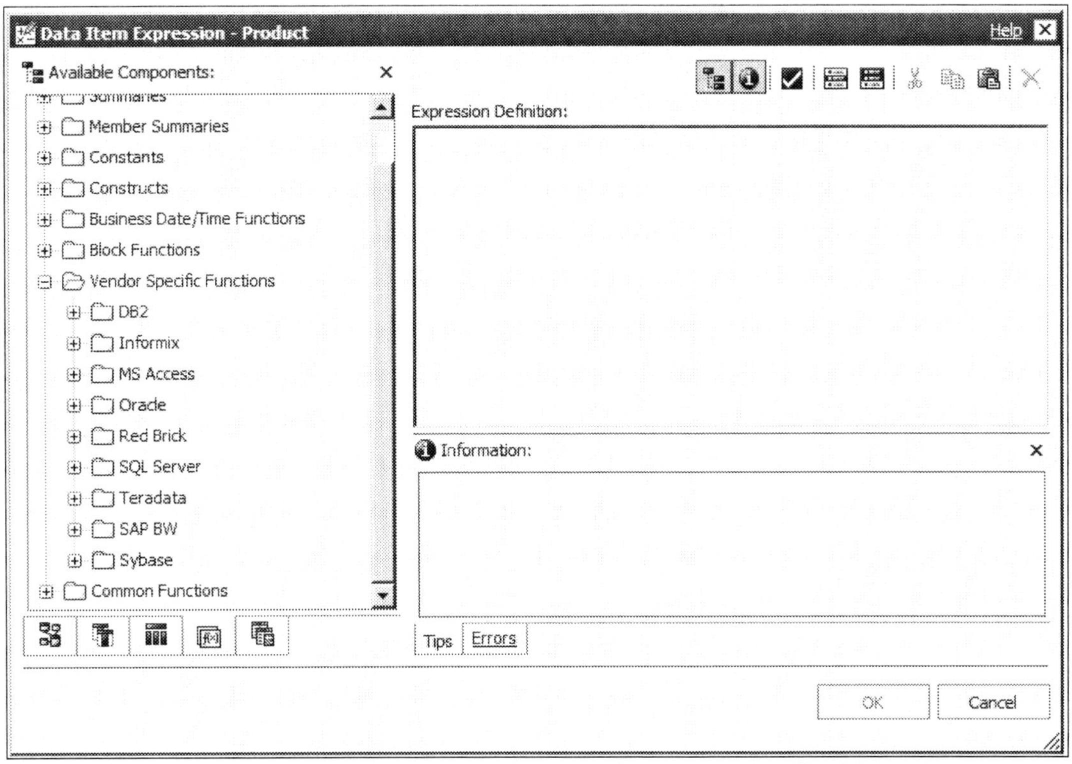

Figure 2-3 Cognos 8 BI leverages native query language functions (Report Studio)

In this section, we talk about data sources that can be accessed by IBM Cognos 8 BI using a fictitious company called *The Sample Outdoors Company*. You can get a detailed list and definition of all supported data sources and software environments from the Cognos 8 BI Software Environments Web site at:

`http://www.ibm.com/support/docview.wss?rs=3442&uid=swg27014432`

The Sample Outdoors Company is a group of companies specializing in outdoor products. Revenue for The Sample Outdoors Company comes from corporate stores and from franchise operations. The revenues are consolidated from the wholly-owned subsidiaries. There are six distinct organizations, each with its own departments and sales branches. Five of these are regionally-based companies, as shown in Figure 2-4.

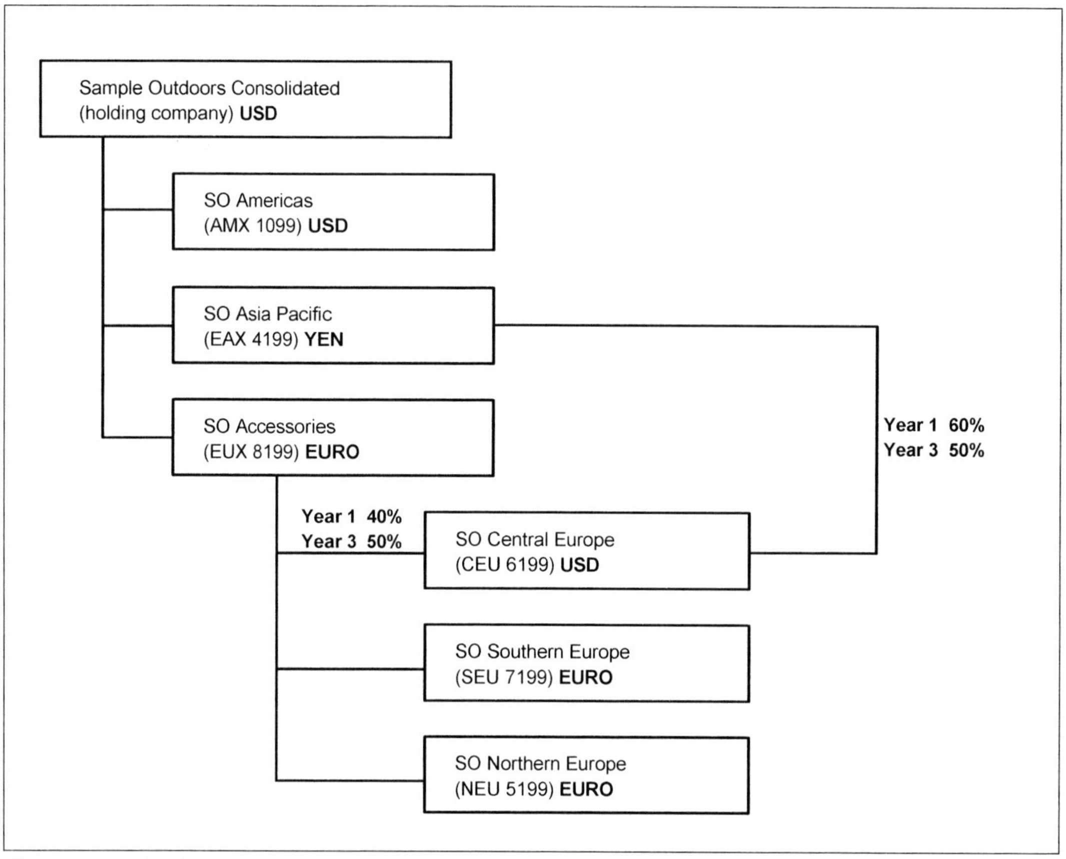

Figure 2-4 The Sample Outdoors Company group of companies

The sixth company, SO Accessories, has its own collection of products, which are differentiated from the other SO companies by brand, name, price, color, and size. SO Accessories sells from a single branch to all regions and retailers and also functions as both an operating company based in Geneva and part owner of three SO subsidiaries in Europe.

Because some of the companies were acquired, part of the corporate data resides on different data sources. The Sample Outdoors Company's employee data contains a full list of employees in all divisions, departments (see Figure 2-5), and locations. Data is available for reports about bonuses (Global Bonus report), sales commissions (Sales Commissions for Central Europe report), training (Employee Training by Year report), performance reviews, and employee satisfaction surveys (Employee Satisfaction 2006).

Division (GL)	Department (GL)
Corporate (1700)	Sales (1720)
	Marketing (1750)
	IS&T (1760)
	Human Resources (1730)
	Finance (1740)
	Procurement (1710)
Operations (1800)	Production and Distribution (1820)
	Customer Service (1820)

Figure 2-5 The Sample Outdoors Company department organization

Data about sales and marketing is available for all of the companies in The Sample Outdoors Company group. Marketing and sales campaigns are tied to The Sample Outdoors Company regional companies. Overall, the SO companies have experienced solid growth across most product lines (Sales Growth Year Over Year), in all regions (Revenue by SO Subsidiary 2005), because of factors such as an increase in repeat business and new or improved products, such as the high margin sunglasses product line. In the product lines sold by the five regional companies (all but SO Accessories), promotions have had mixed success (Promotion Success by Campaign, Bundle, and Quarter).

Revenue from the corporate outlets is available at the transaction level. Revenue from the franchise outlets is available at the consolidated level only (Sales and Marketing cube). Metrics about retailers show that the number of new retail outlets has dropped over the time period covered by this data.

SO Accessories sells worldwide, and sells only accessories. Transaction data for SO Accessories is the primary source for analysis of product by brand, color, and size. The other five subsidiaries in the group of companies are regional and sell all product lines for retailers in their region.

All of the corporation's information is based on two different databases: the SO data warehouse and the SO sales transactions database. The SO data warehouse contains data about human resources, sales and marketing, and finance, grouped into business areas. The SO sales database is structured as a transactional database. It contains principally sales data.

Some information is collected in multi-dimensional PowerCubes, enabling user to perform quick, *ad hoc* analysis or create, from simple to advanced, reports based on sales marketing activities, expenses management, and financial reporting for each subsidiary.

The Sample Outdoors Company decided to invest in IBM Cognos 8 BI in order to provide a common interface to key users so that they could access all the information they need, wherever it is stored, according to IT standards in terms of security and consistency of information. We list the type and number of data sources that are part of the information assets in the SO group, shown in Figure 2-6, in the next sections.

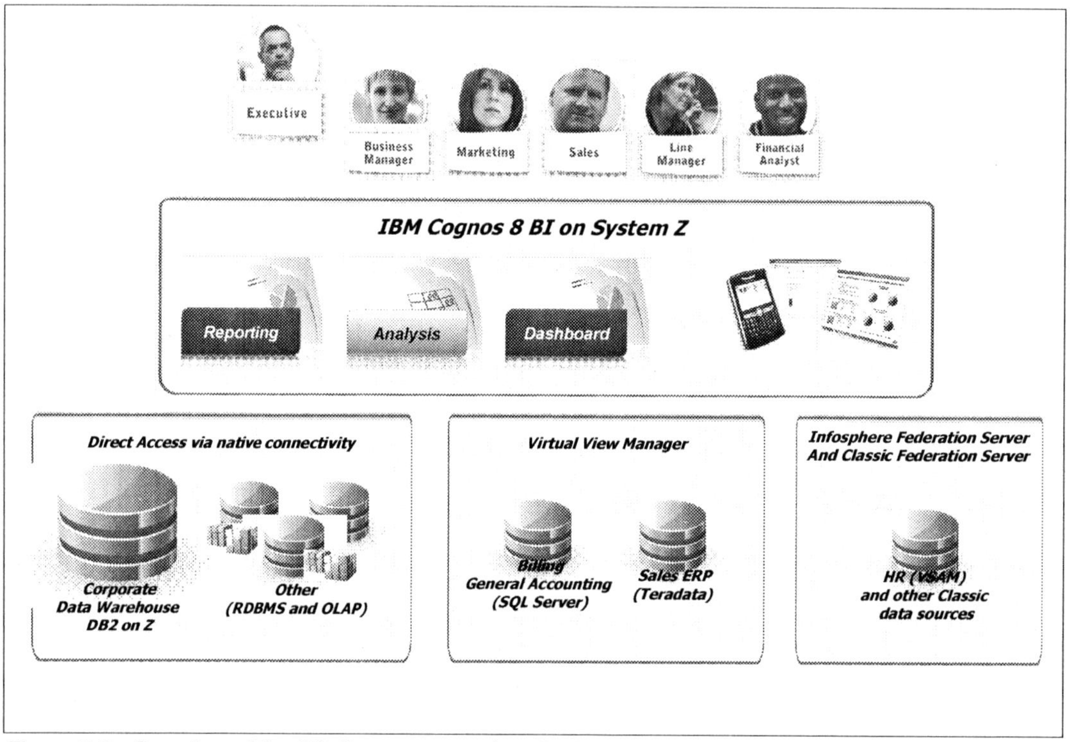

Figure 2-6 Overview of the SO Group approach to Business Intelligence

DB2 for z/OS

Mainframes have always been an integral part of The Sample Outdoors Company strategy. Due to their secure and stable infrastructure, they are often used to run business critical applications and manage transactional data stores. Even though these kinds of data stores are configured to track and store up to billions of transactions, they can play a relevant role in BI.

Online operational reports usually run on transactional data sources: They collect detailed and updated information. But sometimes it is useful to view summaries with fresh data to check trends. DB2 for z/OS delivers excellent performance for managing transactional data stores and large data warehouses.

By using native query language, IBM Cognos 8 BI sets up high performance access to the transactional data, while the power of System z accelerates in-memory transformation. Cubing services also plays an important role in defining an OLAP approach to a large volume of relational data, giving a perfect balance of performance and volume of data to analysts. The cubing services are enabled with drilling and slicing options for a wide selection of information.

In our example, the data warehouse for The Sample Outdoors Company (SO Datawarehouse) is mainly stored in DB2 for z/OS, leveraging the high level of performance in collecting data into storage areas, in performing extractions, transformations, and loads, and in query response time. IBM Cognos 8 for Linux on System z provides native access to DB2 for z/OS.

Teradata

Teradata is a long standing hardware and software vendor for data warehousing. IBM Cognos 8 BI leverages Teradata's technology across clients, servers, and the Web on Windows, UNIX®, and Linux platforms.

From a performance point of view, IBM Cognos 8 BI can leverage Teradata Optimizers to generate version-specific, optimized, and native SQL. It also supports optimizing techniques, such as Soft Referential Integrity, Join Indexes, Aggregate join Indexes, and Partitioned Primary Indexes.

From a user's point of view, the format of the data sources does not matter, so there is no need to write SQL code. IBM Cognos is schema-neutral (3NF, Snowflake, and STAR) and take advantage of Teradata's normalized models. Users analyze interactively data through multidimensional models with high performance and predictable response times. Dashboards and scorecards add meanings to information through a wide variety of graphical elements.

Teradata Metadata Services (MDS) are leveraged to propagate metadata to IBM Cognos 8. The Secure Socket Layer (SSL) protocol ensures secure data transmission through a firewall, using any combination of Lightweight Directory Access Protocol (LDAP), operating systems, (OS), or Relational Database Management Systems (RDBMS) security.

The Sample Outdoors Company collects transactions and summary results related to retailers' activities on Teradata; for Business Intelligence purposes, there is a need to merge information from Teradata and other sources, so we will federate them using Virtual View Manager.

Microsoft SQL Server

Microsoft SQL Server is another common application in the market. IBM Cognos 8 makes it easy to merge information stored in SQL Server with other data sources. The complex sources that provide the data are hidden from the user, and using native code maintains performance. IBM Cognos 8 BI leverages OLAP sources or allows you to map relational sources in a Dimensional Model. SQL and MDX functions, calculations, stored procedures, views, and synonyms can be used as well.

SQL Server has been used by The Sample Outdoors Company to store data collected by the Financial Department. It has a dedicated point of view of the enterprise branches organization. Virtual View Manager optimizes the usage of SQL Server 2005 as a data source for reporting on System z by way of a JDBC driver.

VSAM

In The Sample Outdoors Company, some HR applications leverage VSAM performance and reliability. As with other classic data sources, they will be mapped for reports and dashboards on IBM Cognos 8 BI, combining the usage of IBM InfoSphere Federation Server and IBM InfoSphere Classic Federation Server.

OLAP sources

The Sample Outdoors Company also provide some departments with OLAP tools that are directly accessed from IBM Cognos 8 BI on System z; those sources are described in Chapter 6, "Online Analytical Processing processing comparisons" on page 151.

2.2 Techniques for consolidation

In a perfect world, the perfect approach to information for an enterprise's data assets would not be independent of a corporate data warehouse implementation. Nevertheless, because the market changes and organizations evolve quickly, data mart delivery often cannot keep pace with these changes. Analysts and executives cannot wait for information. So, we must identify at least two different ways to deliver information through a BI deployment:

- Merge and organize data in a corporate warehouse.
- Merge and organize different data sources.

It is essential that a good business process definition drives the accuracy and reliability of a corporate data warehouse, from the very beginning of its implementation to the setup of its maintenance procedure. Large volumes management, indexes, aggregated views, and ETL tools play key roles.

Business needs drive the need for information. As we have noted before, sometimes not all information can fit into a data warehouse; moreover, some online data is often indispensable. These reasons are why we want to retain the option to merge different data sources in a BI deployment.

IBM Cognos 8 BI can deliver this second approach by accessing data sources through IBM Cognos direct access and federating data sources through InfoSphere Federation Server or by using IBM Cognos Virtual View Manager.

Using InfoSphere Federation Server is a good option for two main reasons:

- You maintain a cleaner BI environment by reducing the number of data sources and drivers for client connectivity with a cost driven solution for cross-database queries.
- You can distribute workloads, using InfoSphere Federation Server for cross-product joins by way of standard JDBC access and, optionally, leverage the local functions, such as materialized query tables (MQTs).

Similarly, IBM Cognos Virtual View Manager enables data source federation inside the BI environment. As an Enterprise Information Integrator, it provides benefits in terms of connectivity (by way of JDBC) and improves performance in multiproduct joins.

Both InfoSphere Federation Server and Virtual View Manager play a similar role in BI deployment, but, as mentioned earlier, they enable Cognos 8 BI to access different data sources; for a quick list of the available data sources, refer to Table 2-1 on page 73. In terms of workload, query processing will be executed in different places, stressing an InfoSphere or VVM machine. In terms of cost, consider that IBM Cognos Virtual View Manager currently comes in the box with IBM Cognos 8 BI.

None of these approaches limit data availability in the front end. Federated data sources mapped in InfoSphere Federation Server or in Virtual View Manager need to be set up and validated centrally in a Framework Manager Model. IBM Cognos 8 Framework Manager allows you to develop and propagate certified meta models to the BI front end. Through Framework Manager, the administrator orchestrates the way in which any data sources will be exposed in dashboards, reports, and interactive analysis. Therefore, a Cognos package could include data sources from InfoSphere Federation Server, Cognos Virtual View Manager, and other forms of direct access data sources in a way that enables you to merge all relevant data in a single dashboard environment.

It is up to the administrator to define a security policy in order to define which level of detail, and what kind of sources or subset of models, are delivered to users and groups. By controlling each packages' settings, the cross-product joins and the number of entities and rows retrieved are delimited by each BI function to keep complete control over data privacy.

2.2.1 Cognos direct access

By using proper connectivity software, an IBM Cognos 8 BI server allows you to connect to several data sources. As we have seen already, this approach applies to data sources that provide specific client connectivity on Linux for System z.

Setting up a model based on directly accessed sources is simple and fast and only has a few steps.

Link to the data sources

Once client connectivity has been properly configured at the environment level, IBM Cognos can access the data source. New data sources are established in Cognos Connection (the Cognos 8 BI Web interface) or in Framework Manager (the Cognos metadata modeler that enables the creation of models that can be used with any style of BI) by using the same procedure and set of parameters.

Data source definition for direct access usually require a few parameters, such as a database name, connection string, and type of sign-on (see Figure 2-7).

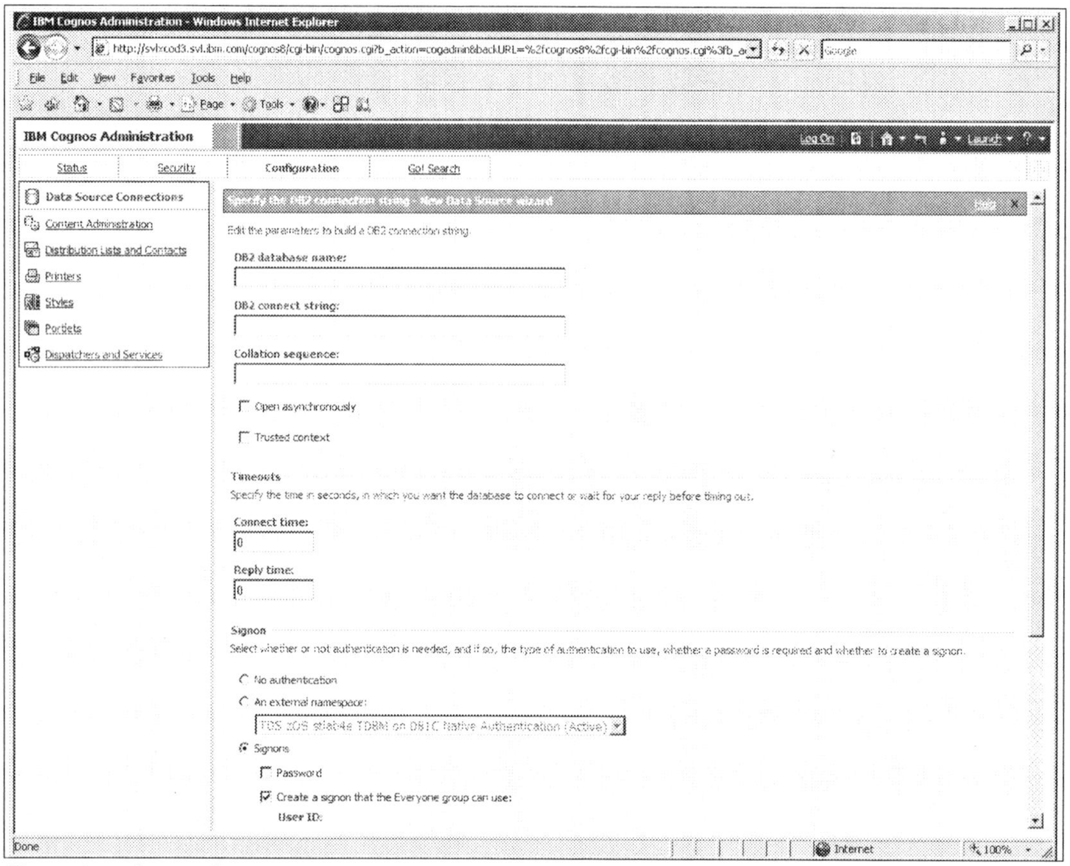

Figure 2-7 Setup of data sources connectivity

Security aspects

Access to a data source can be secured. With an authentication provider such as System z LDAP, it is possible to define database users and map groups, profiles, and security filters on the database side. Cognos can leverage this kind of security configuration: BI users inherit profiles and filters on data and you do not have to rewrite them in Cognos.

IBM Cognos can also map a data source to a single, general purposed user. Usually, this kind of use enables a complete viewing of all the information stored in the data source. In this case, you have to set access privileges on database items and security filters on data (row-level, column-level, or table-level) while modeling in Framework Manager.

Leveraging existing security and authentication provider facilitates login maintenance. For example, you do not have to maintain users' passwords and expiration policies in Cognos.

Moreover, a Cognos instance may support multiple authentication providers simultaneously: for example, a user can authenticate simultaneously on LDAP or another security provider, cumulating profile privileges in terms of data access, in a single session.

Once a data source link is created, it is visible in the IBM Cognos Administration window of Cognos Connection (the Cognos Web portal environment). The data source link can be found in the Data Source Connection list under the Configuration tab. If the database server, the database schema, or other connection options change (for example, there is a new platform standard, software upgrade, or server substitution), all of those parameters must be updated.

Even though a modeled package has not been created yet, according to the profile's capabilities, advanced users could enable an instance of the new data source in Report Studio (see Figure 2-8).

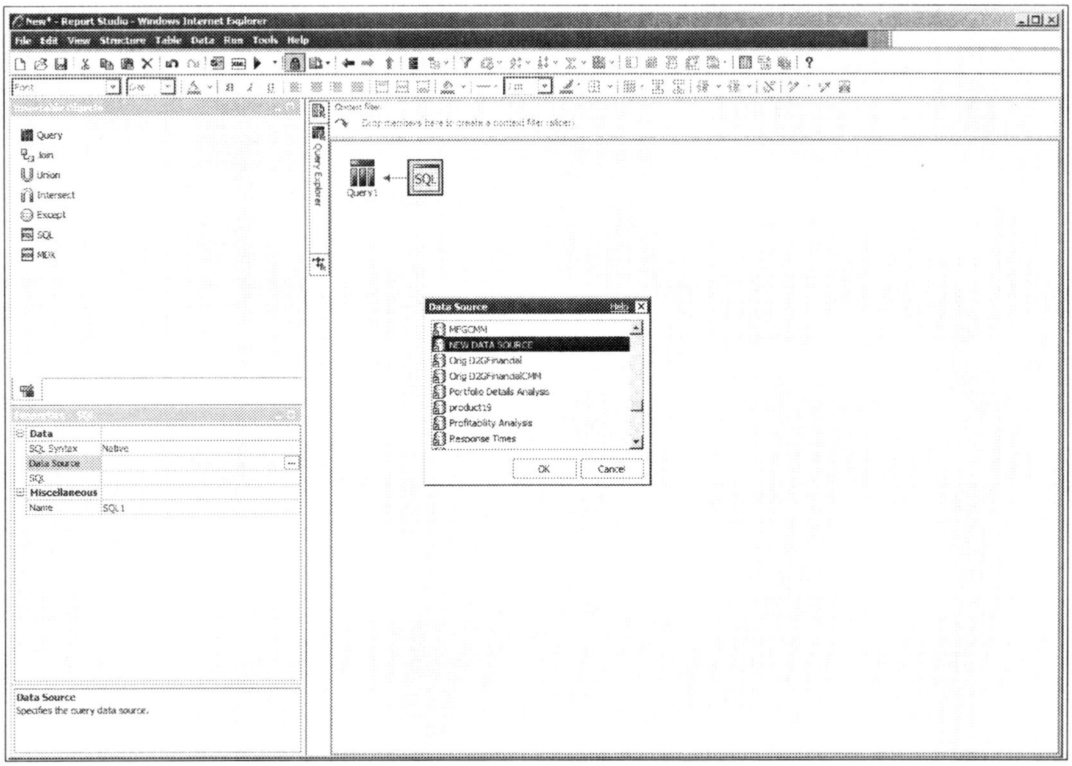

Figure 2-8 New data sources are immediately available for usage in Report Studio

Report integration

New data sources that are not modeled in a Cognos package can be invoked in Report Studio through an SQL statement. With the statement validated, the content of the new data source can retrieve data or be merged with an existing report's content.

This option is intended to provide immediate access to a new data source for fast delivery of BI solutions. However, in order to achieve the best data consistency, we strongly suggest using this solution only in a controlled time frame. As a best practice, defining the data elements in a Framework Manager Model and publishing a package for user access provides predictable and homogeneous results.

Import metadata

Framework Manager increases the speed of model definition by way of using wizards. When creating a new project, the modeler must connect to an available repository to manage objects.

Cognos prompts you to select the base language for the model: if the database contains data in multiple locales, the model embeds a macro to deliver the content in the proper language to each user. A lookup table and specific macro language enable automatic detection of a user's localization parameters.

In the next step, the wizard prompts you to derive metadata from a data source or from an existing metadata provider (see Figure 2-9).

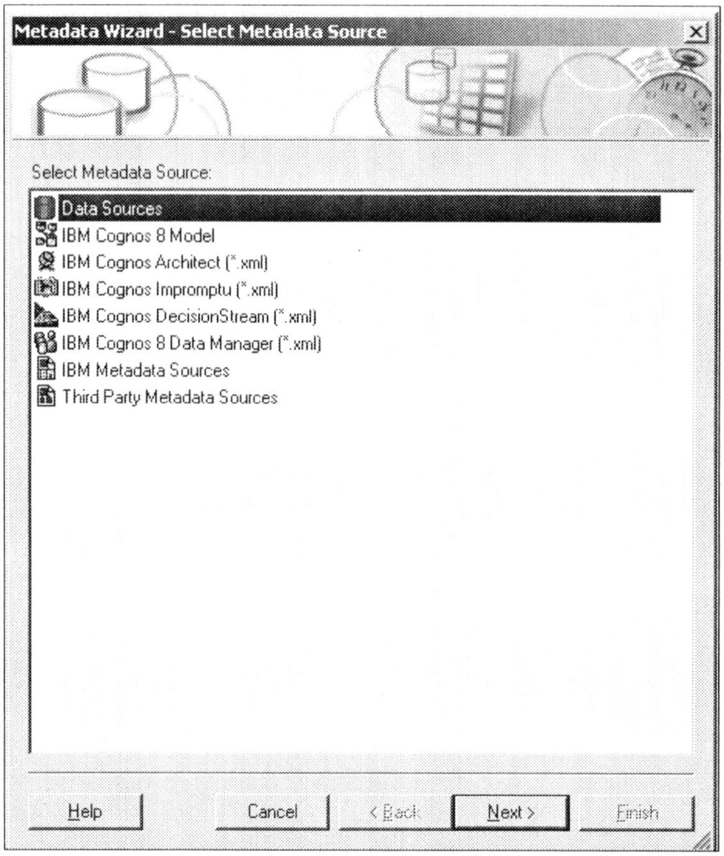

Figure 2-9 Data Model wizard: importing or deriving metadata

IBM Cognos 8 BI supports several metadata providers, such as IBM DB2 Cube Views® (by way of XML), IBM Rational® Data Architect, IBM Rational Rose®, IBM InfoSphere DataStage, and many others. The purpose is to save time by reusing what is already provided in terms of metadata definitions; this means mapping entities, semantic layers, relationship definitions, measure formatting, dimension levels, and so on. In Framework Manager, it is still possible to enrich existing metadata by applying new formatting, creating data contexts by grouping tables, adding tips, descriptions, and embedded and stand-alone filters and calculations to save more time in creating reports, analyses, and dashboards.

Data model maintenance can be also managed through a metadata wizard; this wizard is available by right-clicking the main project namespace.

A modeler may have access to many data sources. It is possible to select an existing one or create a new one.

The client on which Framework Manager is executed has to be aligned with the IBM Cognos server in terms of data source connectivity, that is, the same driver and same descriptions are requested. For example, if you are modeling a DB2 data source, you need the DB2 Client Connectivity installed and configured to access that database on the BI Server and in every workstation in which Framework Manager will be used to model that data source. The typical user will not require the client installation, because a Web interface will be used connected to the Client Connectivity component.

Each data source may have multiple schemas. There are several objects that Framework Manager can import, such as tables, views, synonyms, procedures, and functions. While interaction with pure MOLAP objects can be limited (because they usually have a proprietary metadata definition), importing metadata from relational or near-relational sources require the interpretation of indexes and foreign keys to inherit or define existing and recognizable relationships (see Figure 2-10).

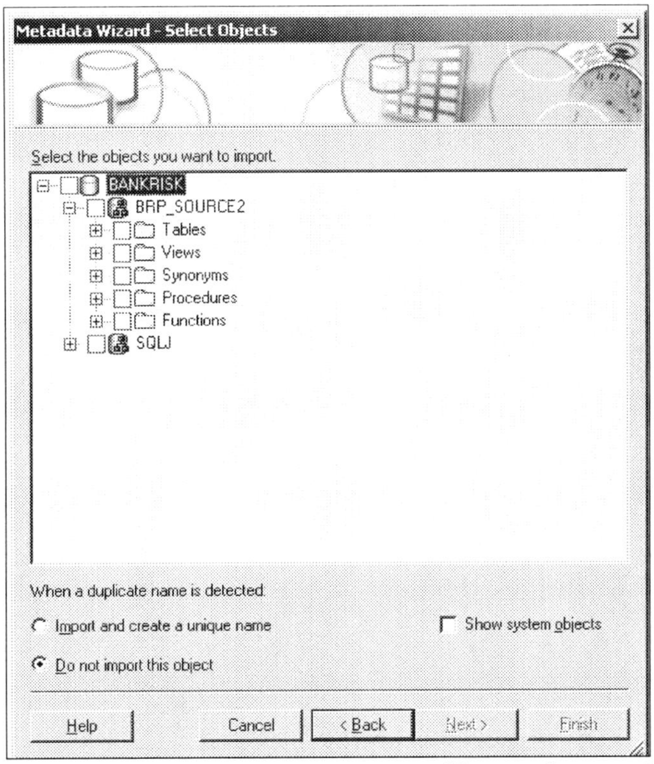

Figure 2-10 Metadata Wizard importing different schema and object types

Primary and foreign keys, matching field names, and indexes are used to identify relationships among newly imported or existing objects; an inner join can be converted to improve performance, and a fact detection feature can drive join granularity.

Finally, each import returns the number of items imported and the relationships detected.

Model data sources

Framework Manager improves data modeling by providing a number of tools and functions that help organize content. Its interface is organized to deliver a commonly used developer environment. There are four basic areas of interaction: List of Objects, working area, a Properties window, and a Statistics and Tools section. The Properties window and the Statistics and Tools section can be hidden. The working area could display diagrams, list of objects, or dimensional views.

In our sample environment, The Sample Outdoors Company data warehouse on DB2 for z/OS, tables and queries are grouped into folders that deliver specific contents, which can be easily shared in a secure environment and used in reporting.

Creating a data model mainly involves four objects: main namespace, lookup table, data sources, and packages.

A lookup table and data sources have been mentioned already. The main namespace is used to collect imported objects. A developer may use a number of tools to create a sophisticated metadata definition.

While *namespaces* are useful for organizing objects according to best practice (they prevent naming duplicates), *folders* may be used to collect reporting tools, such as predefined filters and calculations. These classes are also useful for gathering objects that come from different data sources.

Right-clicking an object shows the available tools for that object. Properties and functionalities are always subject to contextual selection of items. Query items refer to logical views of entities within a data source; query items are single fields within a table or a query. Prompts, filters, calculations, and parameters can be embedded in a query subject definition.

Lookup tables and macros can be useful when applying a multi-language approach; macros could also be used to apply a single data model to multiple dynamic data sources. When you face a similar schema, session parameters, such as user locale or user department, can drive the selection of a specific data source (see Figure 2-11).

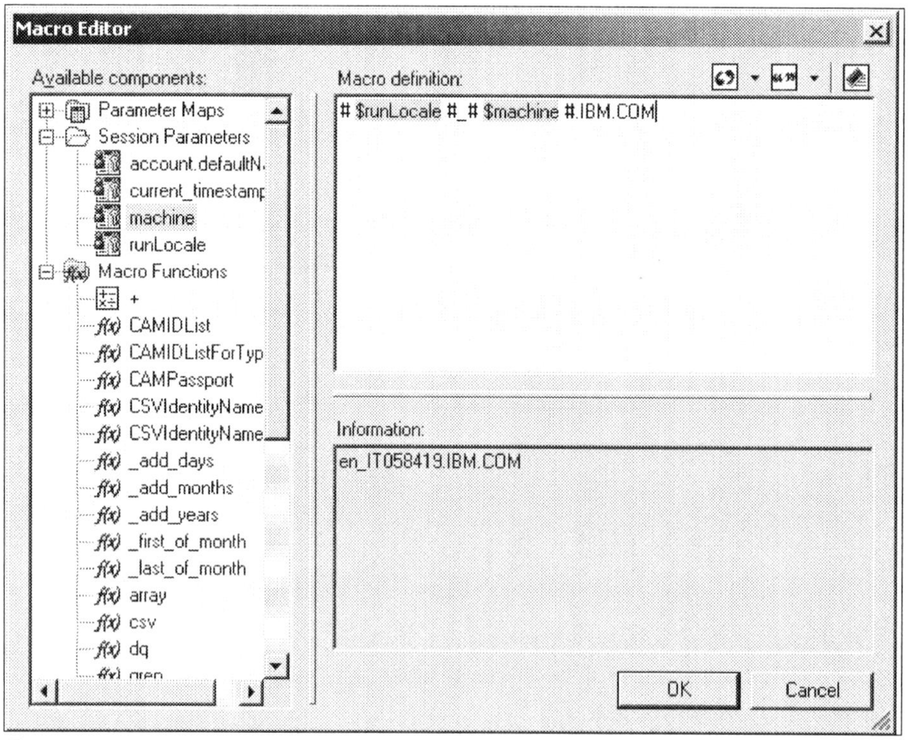

Figure 2-11 Macros for conformed model selected through session parameters

The model developer can set up relationships among different data sources or different schemas; there is also the option to limit and govern the usage of this relationship from the user's side by editing the governor's parameter (see Figure 2-12).

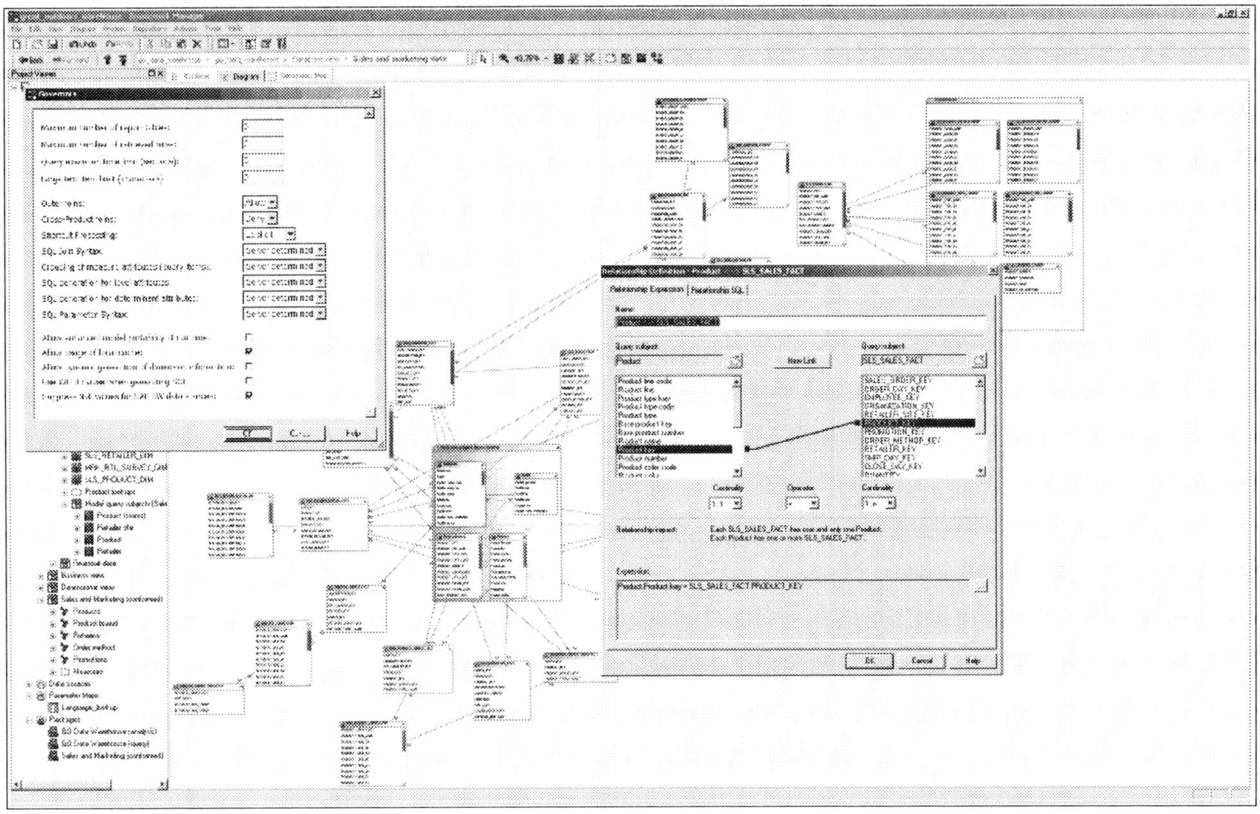

Figure 2-12 Framework Manager keeps control over multisource relationship settings

Large multi-source models could be easily developed in parallel; the different models can be merged later by using the functionality to link or incorporate a model or a part of it. A relationship and intersection can be set up later (see Figure 2-13). This also implies that an existing BI deployment could be easily consolidated into a single IBM Cognos model by performing these steps:

- Importing metadata from a data source or inheriting metadata from metadata providers
- Merging models by linking segmentation

This option is useful for moving projects from disparate systems onto IBM Cognos 8 BI for Linux on System z platforms.

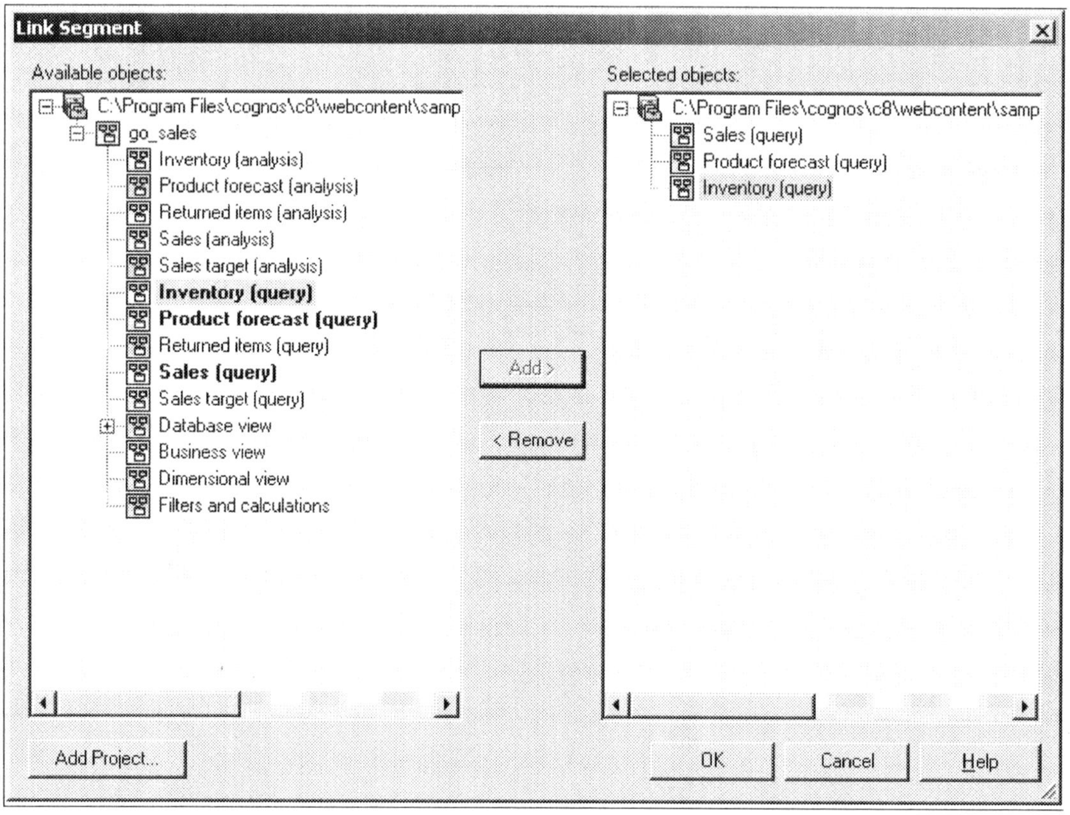

Figure 2-13 Multisource parallel model development

Package a model

The last step in model creation is to deliver a packaged data source. Again, creating and publishing a package can be done by using a wizard.

Publishing places a package into the IBM Cognos content store and makes it available for BI purposes. A single publication enables users to produce reports, dashboards, and analyses (if a dimensional model is provided).

During the package publishing process, there is the option to secure administrator and consumer access to a package. To streamline the usage of a package, defining multiple linked packages is a valid option.

A package can be published into specific folders within IBM Cognos Connection Portal, and it will only be visible to those users that have relevant access privileges (see Figure 2-14).

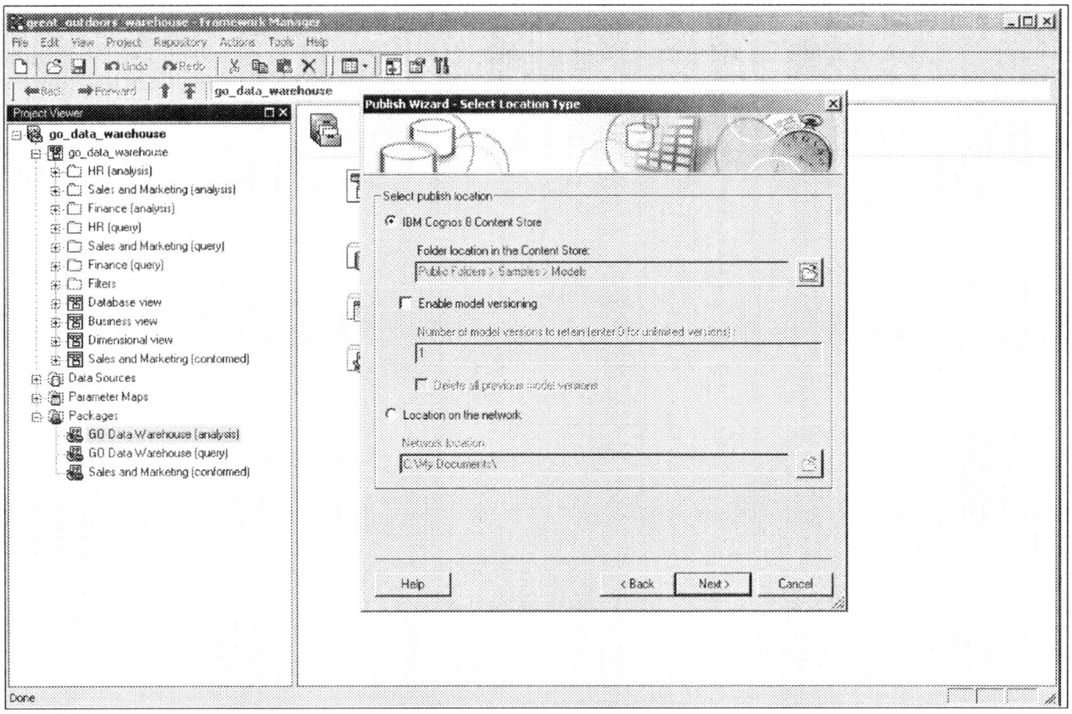

Figure 2-14 Sections of a model are packaged to streamline security and usage management

Reporting using single or multiple packaged data sources

Once a package containing multiple data sources has been successfully published, multiple data sources may be used to produce any type of BI application. Data source complexity is completely hidden from the users, analysts, and report developers. Users are not notified when running queries against multiple data sources unless a governor setting set by a modeler allows this function.

You should be aware that because IBM Cognos is doing a merging job solely on its own, there might a performance impact.

2.2.2 IBM Cognos 8 Virtual View Manager

Virtual View Manager is the primary tool used to access multiple data sources and define, publish, and manage resources. Virtual View Manager allows you to:

- Create, edit, and manage data sources, transformations, views, SQL scripts, parameterized queries, packaged queries, definition sets, triggers, Virtual View Manager databases, and Web services.
- Publish data sources, transformations, views, SQL scripts, parameterized queries, packaged queries, definition sets, triggers, Virtual View Manager databases, and Web services.
- Archive Virtual View Manager resources and deploy them back to a desired location with the export/import options. This function is based on Composite Information Server technology, and it delivers standard JDBC drivers to deliver high performance connectivity.

More information about Virtual View Manager software environments can be found at the following address:

http://www.ibm.com/support/docview.wss?rs=3442&uid=swg27014427

Virtual View Manager creates views of the database, optimized for IBM Cognos 8, and Framework Manager is then used to model the database view and create a single business view. IBM Cognos 8 components, including Framework Manager, use an Open DataBase Connectivity (ODBC) interface to access a Virtual View Manager data service. The Virtual View Manager Server accesses the data sources through Java Database Connectivity (JDBC), a Java API, ODBC, the OS File System, or SOAP (see Figure 2-15). JDBC drivers must be installed in the Virtual View Manager folders (`installation folder\apps\dlm\cis_ds_datasourcename\lib\driverJDBC.jar`).

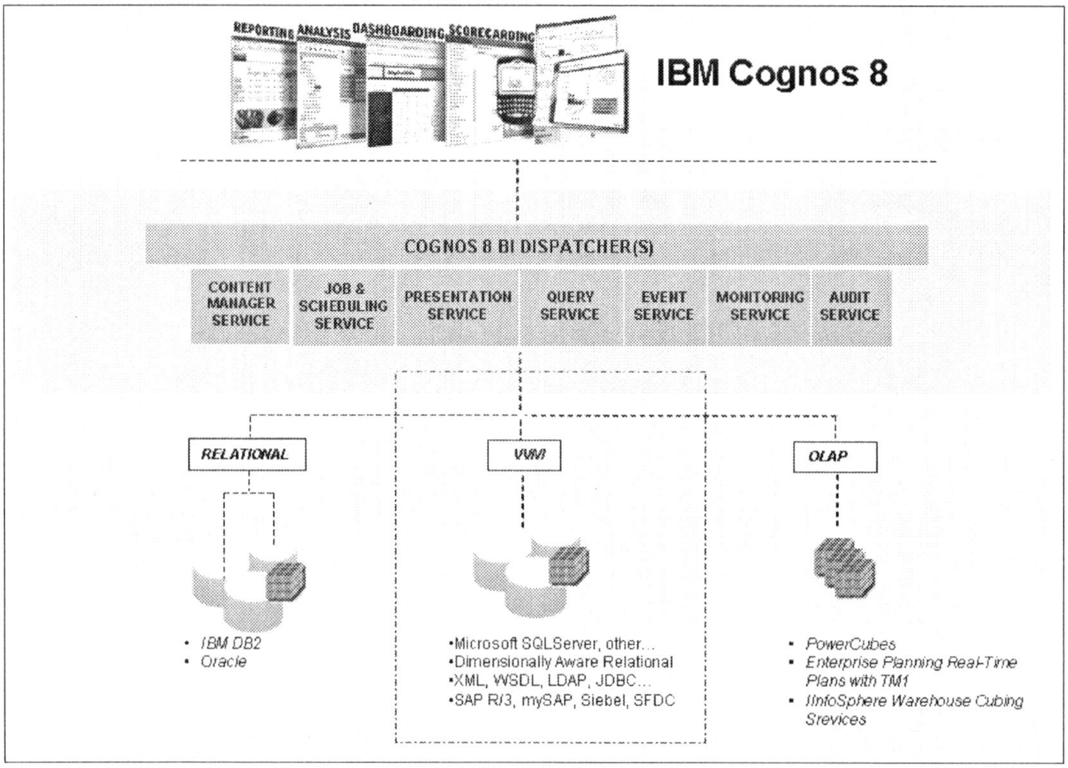

Figure 2-15 Virtual View Manager in the IBM Cognos 8 architecture

Virtual View Manager is composed of two main components: Virtual View Manager Server, which is the main engine that runs processes, and Virtual View Manager Studio, which is a client console that is used to connect, model, and expose data sources.

Basic concepts of Virtual View Manager

The workflow for using Virtual View Manager is separated into three processes:

- Setting up the environment by installing and configuring the appropriate software and drivers. The installation also installs IBM Informix® and creates a repository to contain your Virtual View Manager content.
- Creating a data source using Virtual View Manager Studio, which includes accessing and simplifying the metadata using Virtual View Manager Server.
- Accessing Virtual View Manager views using IBM Cognos 8 and preparing metadata for reporting in IBM Cognos 8.

Virtual View Manager Server can be installed in the same environment as Cognos 8, but an installation on a separate computer gives better performance and availability. The installation creates a Virtual View Manager repository and starts both the Virtual View Manager process and the Virtual View Manager Server.

Because IBM Cognos 8 uses the Virtual View Manager ODBC driver to access Virtual View Manager data sources, the ODBC driver and driver manager must be installed on each instance of the IBM Cognos 8 report server (refer to Figure 2-16) and the Framework Manager. The driver manager routes all IBM Cognos 8 requests to the appropriate ODBC driver to access the data sources. When you add an ODBC Data Source Name (DSN) using the ODBC Data Source Administrator, you identify an ODBC driver for the driver manager. The driver manager then knows that the data source associated with this DSN is accessed through a particular ODBC driver.

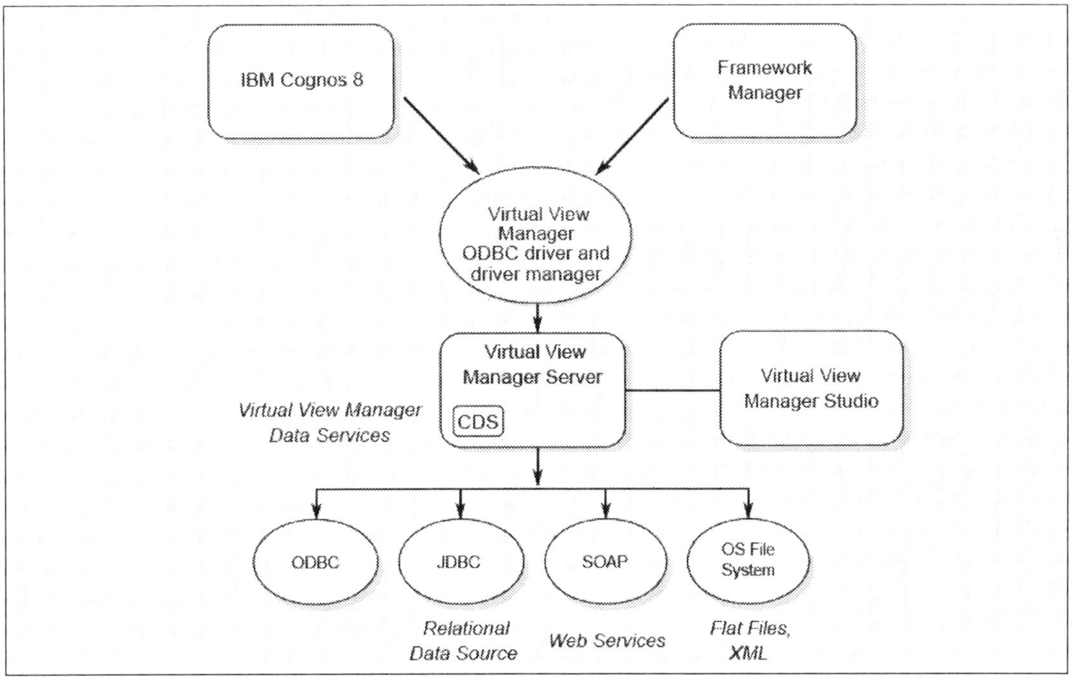

Figure 2-16 IBM Cognos Virtual View Manager architecture

Security considerations

When working with IBM Cognos 8 and Virtual View Manager, it is possible to specify security at different levels. By default, Virtual View Manager provides a domain named "cognos" to secure the application. An administrator can add other users and set their access permissions. It is also possible to specify metadata and data security in Framework Manager.

You can also limit access by using IBM Cognos 8 to secure a DSN that was created using the administrator user ID and password. By using pass-through logins, you ensure that Virtual View Manager users have user IDs and passwords that are valid on the underlying data source(s).

An ODBC DSN must be created to provide all users connectivity to the Virtual View Manager data source through an ODBC driver. These data sources are local to a computer. All users with the appropriate privileges can access the ODBC data source. The data source name must use fewer than 32 characters.

Virtual View Manager Studio

Virtual View Manager Studio serves as a data view design and development area. It provides three important functions: resource management, modeling, and publishing. Figure 2-17 shows the Virtual View Manager Studio interface.

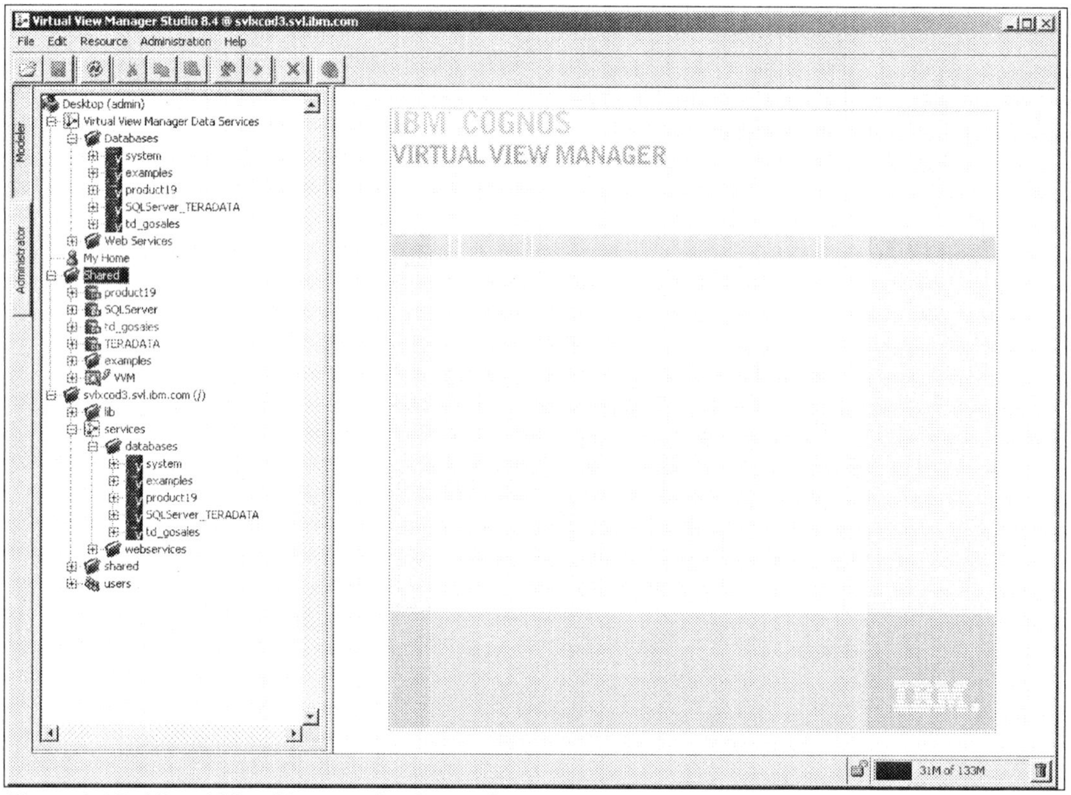

Figure 2-17 Virtual View Manager Studio interface

Resource management

The term *resources* in Virtual View Manage collectively refers to the resources that are used for data modeling and building business solutions. These resources are data sources, views, parameterized queries, SQL scripts, Java procedures, packaged queries, transformations, and Virtual View Manager data services (which are available as Virtual View Manager databases and Web services). Data stored in these resources are available in tabular or hierarchical format, and are noted accordingly as either tabular data and hierarchical data.

The resource management process includes several tasks that you can perform on a resource, for example, create, edit, save, move, copy, rename, export, import, delete, execute, and publish. To manage resources, Virtual View Manager provides context menu options, toolbar buttons, and menu bar options. Virtual View Manager also provides several editors with which you can define and refine the properties and parameters of a resource at anytime.

Modeling and publishing

These processes include several tasks, such as data source introspection and metadata modeling, as well as creating Virtual View Manager databases and Web services. To accomplish these goals, Virtual View Manager provides workspaces, named My Home and Shared, for modeling, and an area named Virtual View Manager Data Services to hold published resources.

Metadata simplification in Virtual View Manager can make modeling easier in Framework Manager. In some situations, we recommend modeling data in Virtual View Manager Studio, before exposing them, to:

- Combine heterogeneous data sources
- Drive predictable results
- Improve data caching
- Publish stored procedures
- Resolve SQL traps
- Create keys on all views published to IBM Cognos 8

Federate data sources: an example using SQL Server and Teradata

By using the sample environment provided by The Sample Outdoors Company set of data sources, we explain how it is possible to access and integrate data from multiple data sources, such as SQL Server, which collects branch data for financial reporting, and Teradata, where all sales transactions are stored.

Before modeling metadata, links between the modeling tool and the databases are created by adding a data source in Virtual View Manager Studio (see Figure 2-18).

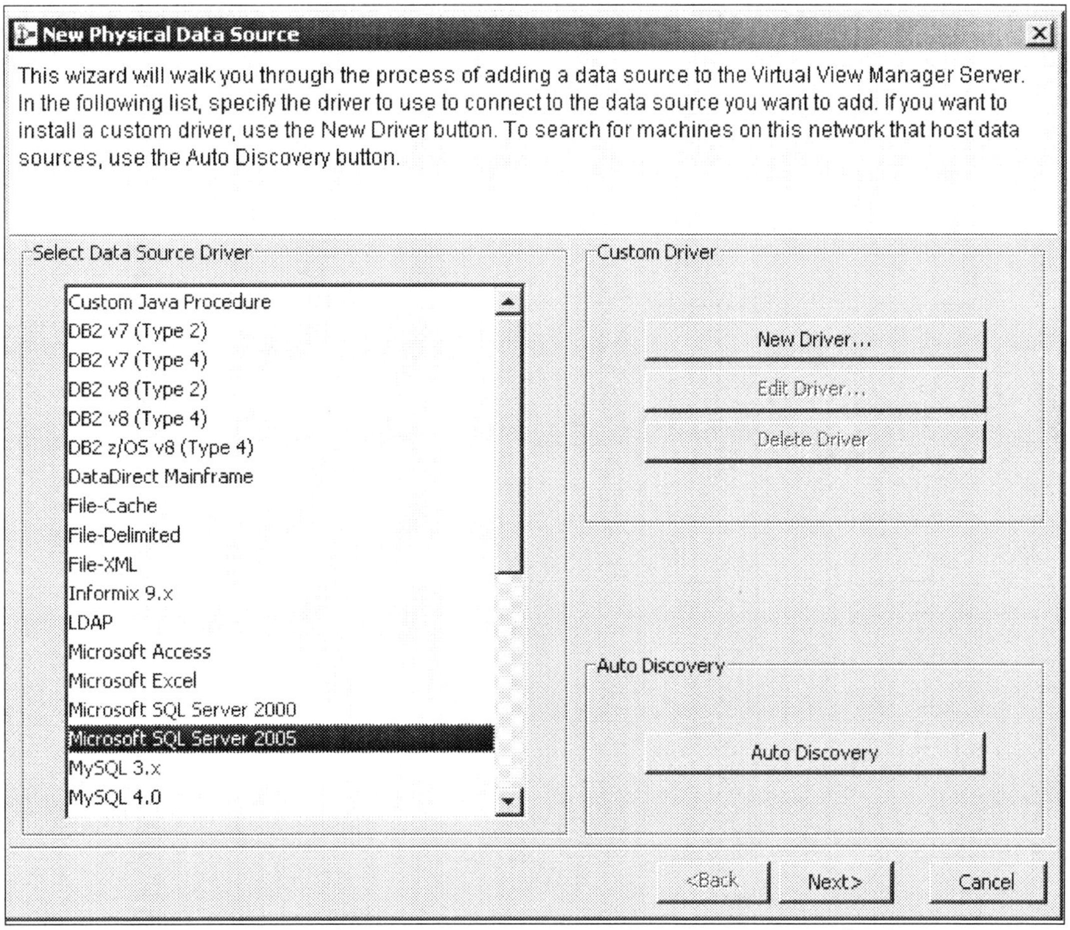

Figure 2-18 Mapping an SQL Server 2005 data source in Virtual View Manager Studio

A data source is the Virtual View Manager representation of the external, physical data source that is available to the Virtual View Manager Server. Mapping a data source requires authentication, as shown in Figure 2-19. In order to access different data sources, for example, Teradata and SQL Server, two different connections are created, in order to link tables, views, and other entities that exist in the original databases.

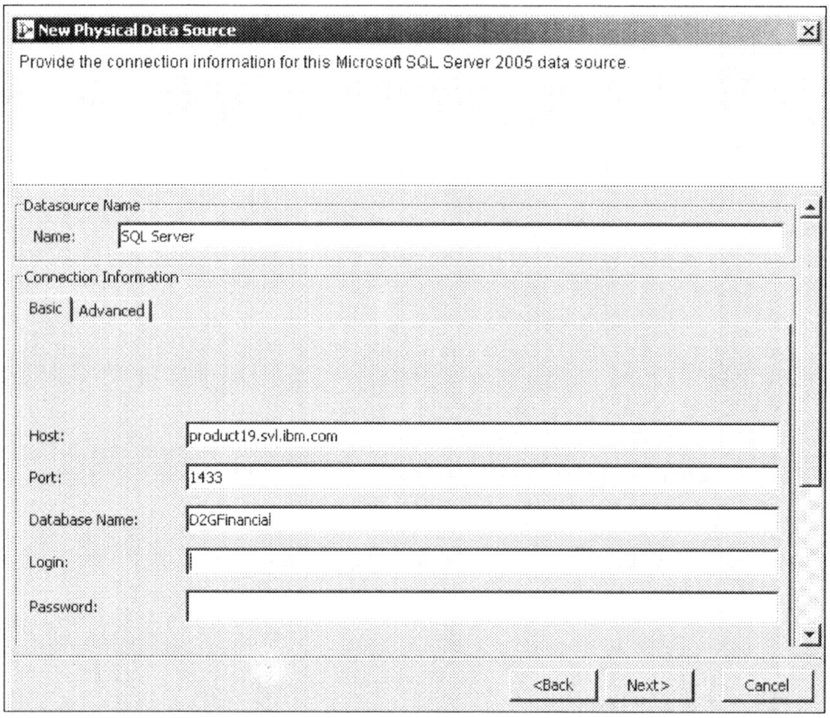

Figure 2-19 Authentication is required to access data sources

The data source is exposed by publishing it to a Virtual View Manager data service. A Virtual View Manager Data Service represents tabular data and procedures that were published as a relational schema. Figure 2-20 shows some tables selected to be published from a Teradata data source.

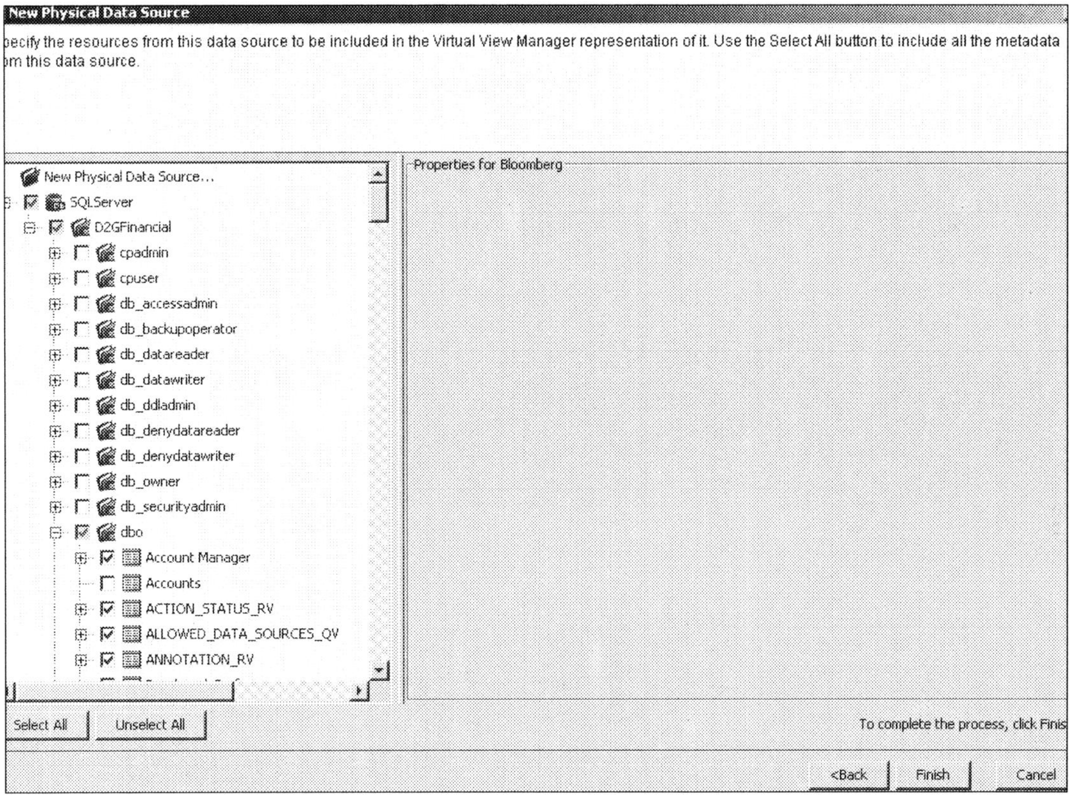

Figure 2-20 Catalog and schema will be created to collect all data sources entities

A catalog and a schema must be created to import views into Framework Manager. Publishing a data source to a Virtual View Manager data service makes it available to Framework Manager and IBM Cognos 8.

Object references that are published to a Virtual View Manager data service are exposed to IBM Cognos 8 using ODBC. They appear in Framework Manager as views. Because published Virtual View Manager data services are actually references to the published Virtual View Manager objects, any change in the Virtual View Manager data source is automatically reflected in the published Virtual View Manager data service.

Different data sources can be federated by creating a view. Figure 2-21 shows a view that merges branch information stored on a Teradata database with an Order Fact table, Channel, and Sales staff dimension stored in SQL Server. The view will be published to a Virtual View Manager data service, making it available to IBM Cognos 8. It is more difficult to detect usage properties because of the absence of index or key information about views. Index and key information could be defined with data type information to set usage properties automatically. Determinants specification will be required when there are multiple joins to the query subject at different keys/key combinations. Determinants must be available to ensure that rollups are calculated properly.

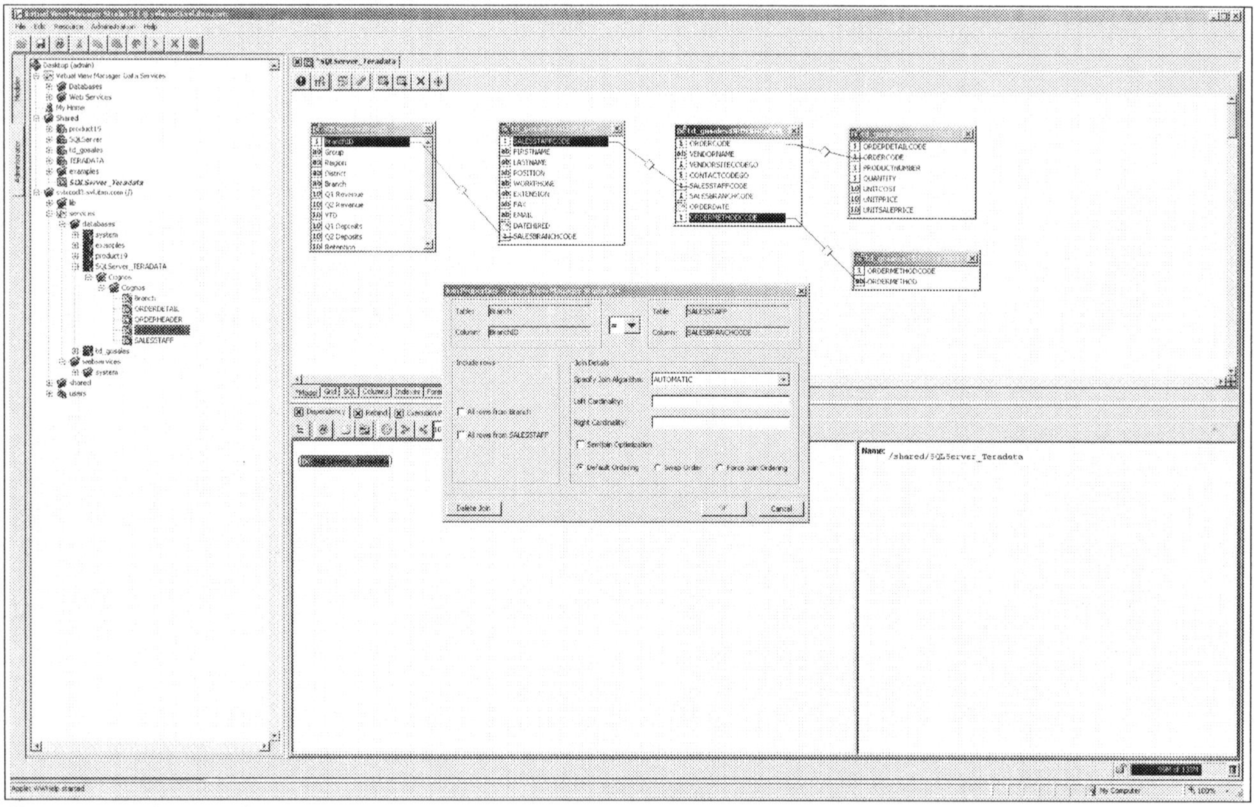

Figure 2-21 Creating federated views in Virtual View Manager

For views to be accessible for import into Framework Manager, they must be published in the schema level of a Virtual View Manager data service (see Figure 2-22).

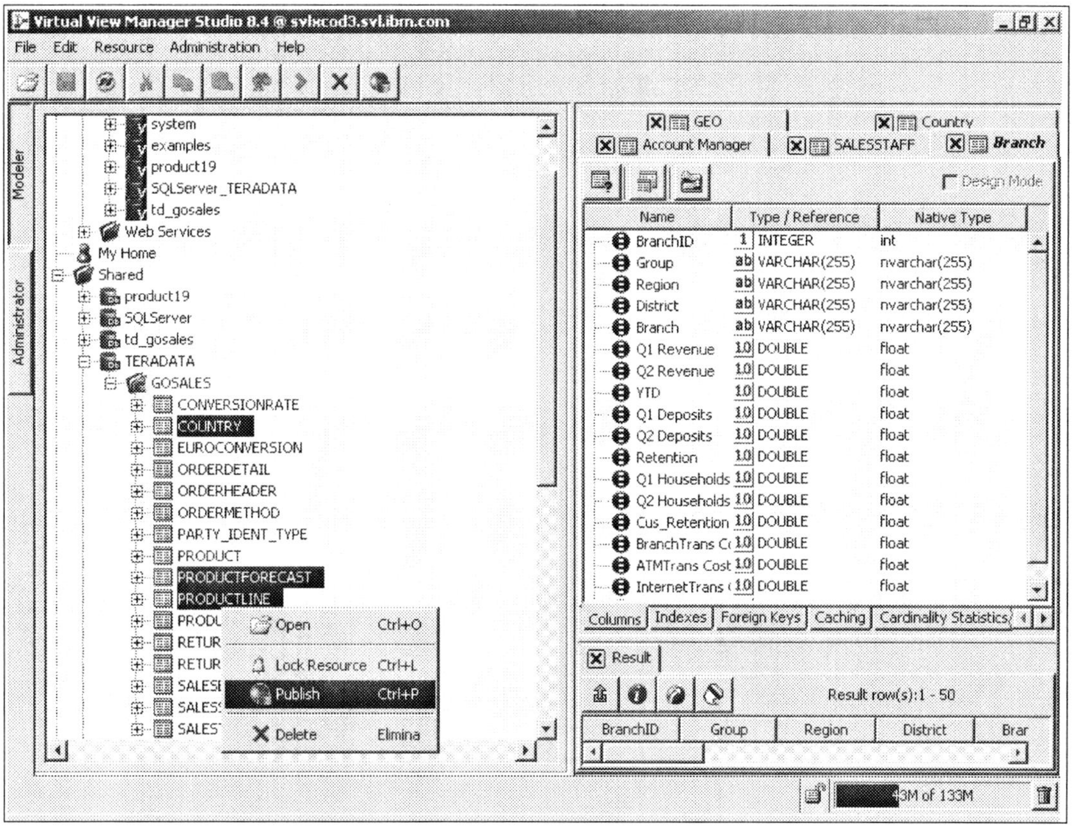

Figure 2-22 Exposing a view by way of Virtual View Manager Data Services

This task is accomplished by selecting the view to publish, clicking the Virtual View Manager Data Services in the resource tree in Virtual View Manager Studio, and navigating down the Database tree to select the proper data service, catalog, and schema (see Figure 2-23).

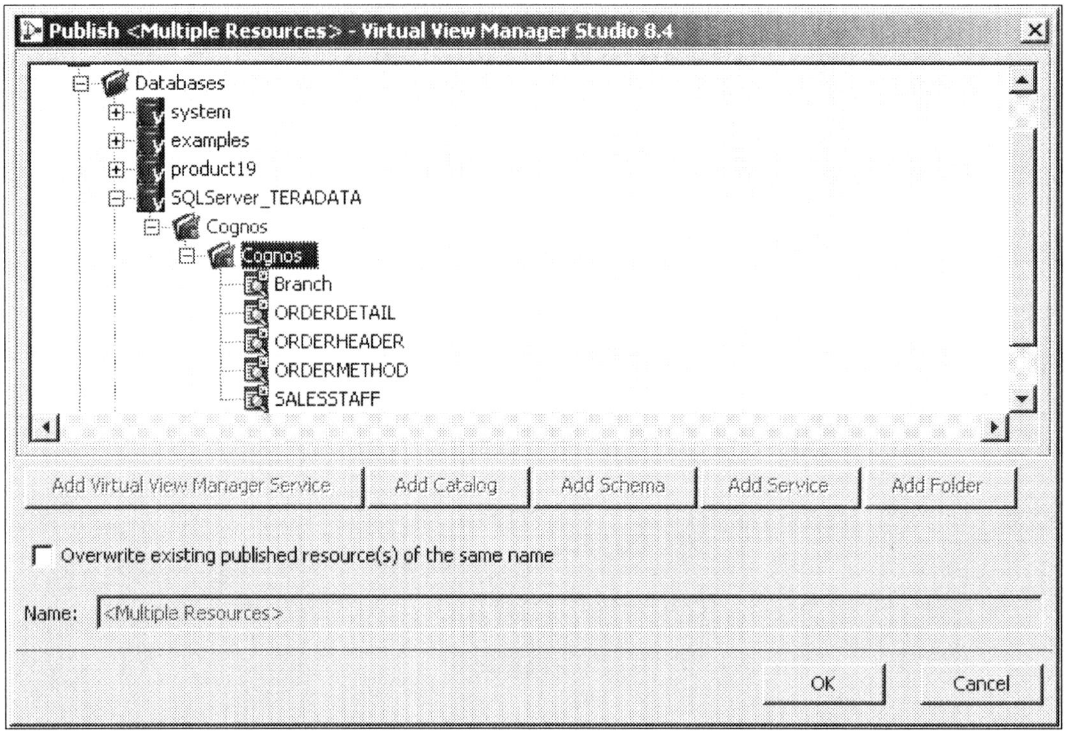

Figure 2-23 Published objects are related to catalog and schema

Virtual View Manager tuning

There are different ways to improve Virtual View Manager performance by providing access to federated data sources.

Persistent caching

Virtual View Manager can be configured to enable persistent caching. With persistent caching, the query result set is cached to improve performance or lighten the load on an underlying data source. The cache persists even after the session ends. The Virtual View Manager Server optimizes the running of queries by having the underlying data source do the query computations (see Figure 2-24).

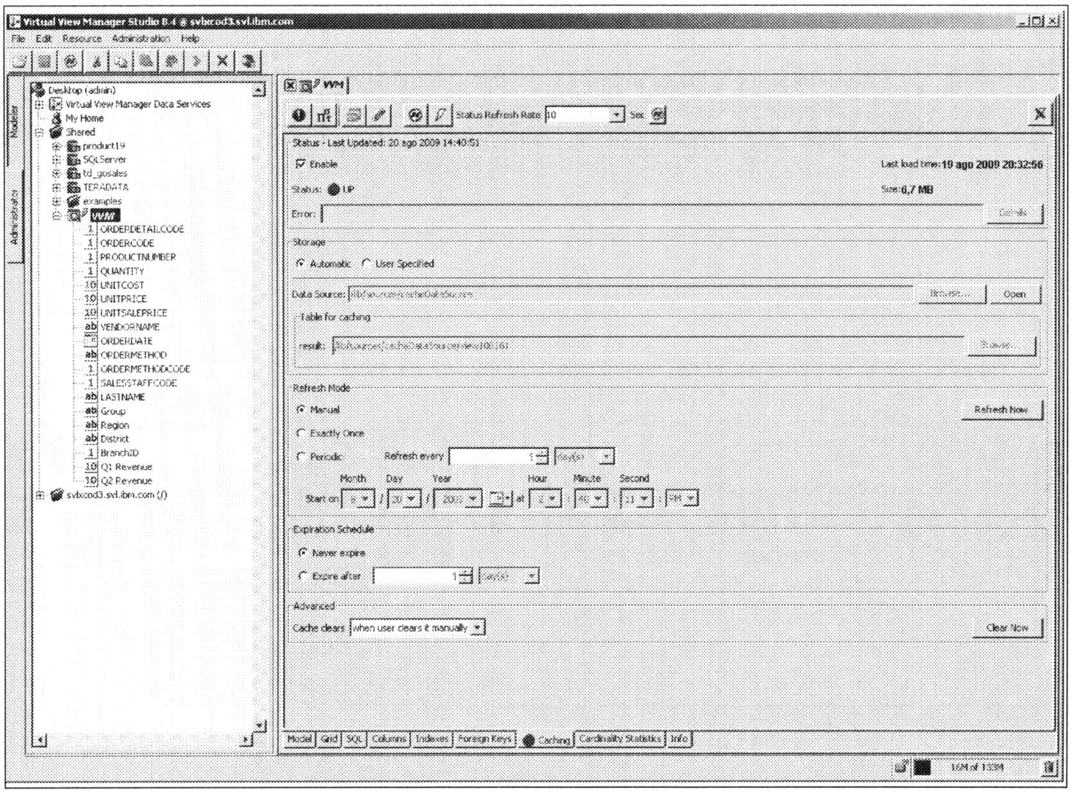

Figure 2-24 Performance could be optimized by setting cache parameters

You may want to cache data if:

- The query is complex.
- The query takes a long time to run.
- The same data is being queried repeatedly.
- The data source is not always available.
- The data changes significantly during peak periods.

Caching at a specific time means that users can see a consistent view of data when it is changing rapidly. By default, caching is not enabled. If you enable caching, you can cache the data to a local file or to a database. If you cache the data to a file, the file and the directory where the file is located are not encrypted. Therefore, you may want to consider other methods to secure the folder where the cache file is located.

Only views can be cached. Stored procedures and tables taken directly from the data source cannot be cached unless they are wrapped in a view. Virtual View Manager Server can generate a persistent cache for views that can be refreshed manually from Virtual View Manager Studio or on a scheduled basis. A user may not be able to identify whether the cached data is current. If the cached data is not current, the query results retrieved from the cache can be meaningless or misleading. Therefore, we recommend that you include a time stamp, such as CURRENT_TIMESTAMP, in the Virtual View Manager view to indicate when the cache data was last refreshed.

If you want to cache an entire data source, create views for each table and apply caching to each view. You can then publish these views to a Virtual View Manager data service, making them available to IBM Cognos 8.

File-based caching

Depending on your usage, file-based caching is typically sufficient. With file-based caching, the query result set is saved in a local file. The file does not require an administrator to manage it because it is managed automatically on the Virtual View Manager Server. If a cache refresh cannot complete, the data is rolled back. Local caching is not recommended for queries with large result sets. When the query makes a call to the cached data, the file-based cache must scan the data and read every row. If the cache is large, this may detract from the performance enhancements that are typical when using cached data.

The cached data in system files cannot be shared by multiple Virtual View Manager server installations. You can customize the location of the cached file. The directory where the system file is located is not encrypted. To secure the cached data, use folder permissions or an encryption file system. For more information, refer to the Microsoft Windows help.

Database caching

We recommend database caching if your SQL query makes selections against the cached view or when result sets are large. A database cache can contain indexing, which speeds up data selections. If the cached data is used in a join, the query is processed by the original data source, resulting in improved performance. If you store a cached view in a database, you must manually create the database table to match the column names and types of the view. Any available data source with permissions can be a cache container. The account used to update the database table must have insert, update, and delete privileges. The cache should be optimized by your database administrator. If you want to cache an entire data source, you must create views for each table and apply caching to each view. If the data in a table is volatile, you can schedule automatic or manual updates to refresh the cached data so that users see a consistent view of data.

Optimize a query

A query causes data to be fetched from the appropriate data sources. Letting the underlying data source process as much of the query as possible minimizes the amount of data returned and improves performance and speed of data retrieval. Virtual View Manager Server examines the query and optimizes the relationships in the data source before running it. These optimizations can be viewed in the query plan. Understanding how a query is processed is crucial to writing good queries. This becomes especially difficult when using queries that span multiple data sources. You may face some of the following issues:

- Network latency
- Limited capabilities of disparate data sources, such as the fact that comma-separated values (CSV) files do not support joins
- Limited access to data sources, which is dependent on the driver capabilities
- Inability to monitor fluctuations in the amount of available data

Virtual View Manager applies rule-based optimizations automatically, requiring no user input. This reduces the number of rows fetched from the data source, which reduces the amount of work done by Virtual View Manager Server and returns the result set as quickly as possible. Cost-based optimizations analyze the join algorithms to explore the nature of the data. These statistics are used to develop the best possible query plan.

Query plans

Query plans are generated when any query runs. Query plans are relationship-based and not flow-based. This means that views can be used to represent business processes, but when the query is run, the view is flattened. The relationships are examined and, using the rules of the underlying data source, an optimized query plan is reassembled before accessing the data source. When two queries have the same signature, Virtual View Manager Server attempts to reuse the previous query plan, thereby improving performance and decreasing the time to process the query.

Change connection pool properties

When you add a data source, you can change the properties of its connection pool. A connection pool is a set of database connections that are available for an application to use. There is one connection pool for each data source, and the pool is created on demand. Before running a command, a connection to a database must be established. Sometimes creating and removing the connection is more costly than running the command. For this reason, connection pools are created to maintain connections. After a connection is created, it is placed in the connection pool for future use. If all the connections in the pool are being used, new connections are automatically created and made available through the pool.

Each data source always has configurable connections open (the connection pool minimum size), a maximum number of allowed connections (the connection pool maximum size), and a timeout period (the connection pool timeout). Connection pools are never removed.

Modeling a Virtual View Manager data source

Use ODBC to access the Virtual View Manager data source from IBM Cognos 8 using the command-line utility named driverConfig to add an ODBC DSN. The data source associates a particular ODBC driver with the data you want to access through that driver. In order to be able to create an ODBC DSN, the user publishing the views must have the appropriate permissions for the Virtual View Manager configuration files and libraries. The ODBC DSN could be configured this way:

```
[SQLServer_TERADATA]
host = localhost
port = 9401
uid = admin
password = ********
domain = cognos
datasource = SQLServer_TERADATA
catalog = Cognos
```

The ODBC DSN must be configured with the same parameters on the client in which Cognos 8 Framework Manager is used to model and publish BI contents (see Figure 2-25).

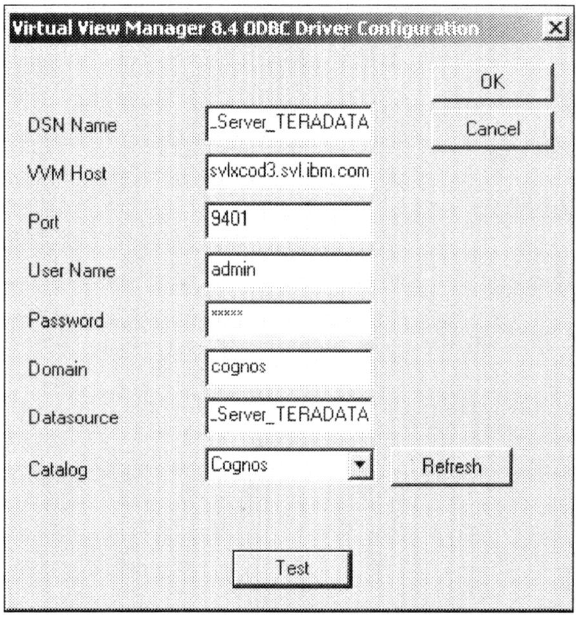

Figure 2-25 The Virtual View Manager ODBC set up on the Framework client

In IBM Cognos 8 BI, a data source is a named set of connections to a physical database or other data source. Cognos 8 BI connects to Virtual View Manager data sources using an ODBC data source connection. Again, data source authentication is needed when adding a data source.

A data source connection supplies the parameters that Cognos 8 BI needs to connect to the database, such as the location of the database and the timeout duration. A connection can also include credential and sign-on information (Figure 2-26).

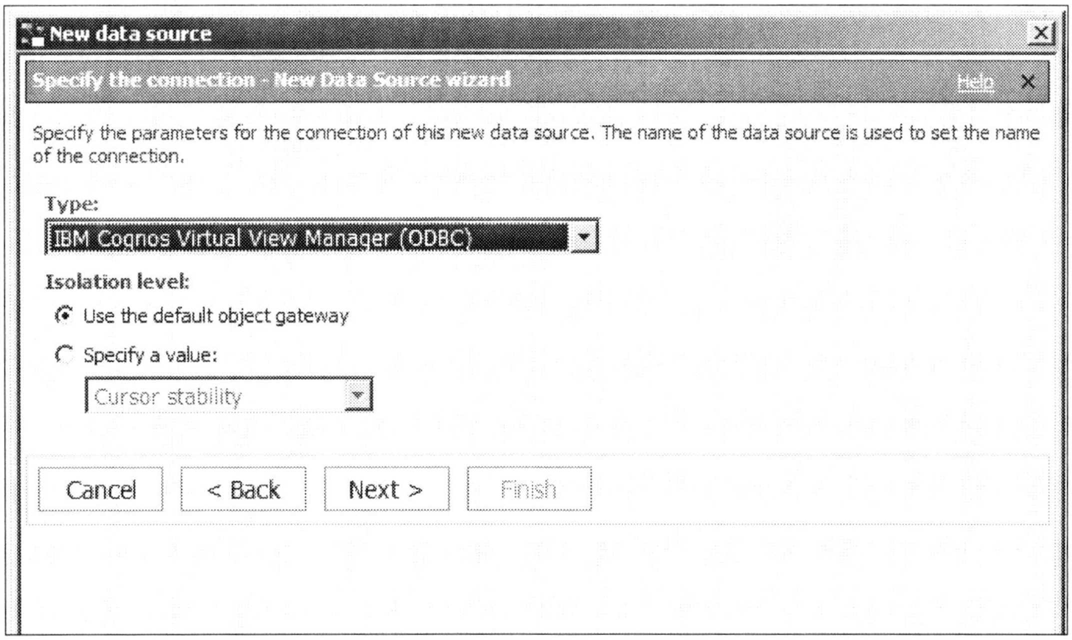

Figure 2-26 Defining a Virtual View Manager data source in IBM Cognos 8 BI

The data source appears as an entry in the Directory tool in the portal, and can be selected by using the Import wizard in Framework Manager. Framework Manager can use the metadata from external data sources to build a project. You can import metadata into a new project or an existing project.

All objects that are published by Virtual View Manager appear as views in Framework Manager. The index and key information for these views is not published by Virtual View Manager. For this reason, you cannot import joins and do not need to specify criteria in the Generate Relationships window. Although you can generate relationships using query item names, we do not recommend this action because there is insufficient metadata to generate cardinality correctly.

After importing the metadata, all numeric codes appear as measures. This is because the rules that Framework Manager uses to determine the Usage property are based on numeric fields having keys or indexes as identifiers. Numeric fields without keys or indexes are treated as facts.

Framework Manager sees Virtual View Manager data sources as collections of views that do not contain key or index information. After the Virtual View Manager data source is available in Framework Manager, examine the metadata carefully to ensure that it is ready to be modeled by performing the following steps (see Figure 2-27):

1. Set the usage properties.
2. Specify dimensional information.
3. Verify the relationships and create joins.
4. Create the star schema grouping.

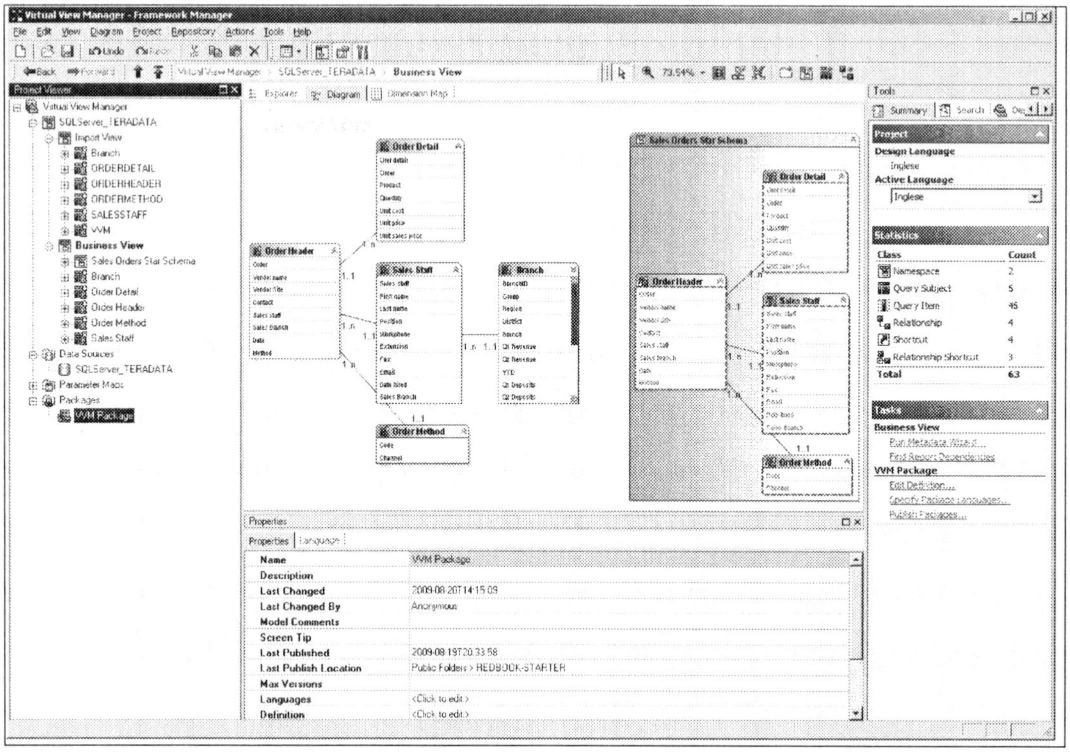

Figure 2-27 Federated Teradata and SQL Server data sources that are available in Framework Manager

Set the usage properties

The usage properties must be set for each query item. The usage property identifies the intended use for the data represented by each query item. Because the key and index information is not imported for views by Framework Manager, the usage properties may be set incorrectly. For example, all numeric and date codes without key and index information appear as facts. All character data types are set as attributes.

Specify determinants

Determinants define unique sets within the data and assist in the prevention of double counting. For example, days roll up to months and months roll up to years. Under normal circumstances, determinants are defined during import using keys and indexes. In the absence of index and key information, determinants ensure that rollups are performed correctly.

Verify relationships and create joins

Relationships should be verified and joins created accordingly. A relationship defines the connection between two query subjects. Without relationships, query subjects are isolated pieces of information. Under normal circumstances, keys, indexes, and names can be used to detect relationships. In the absence of key and index information, only names can be used.

Create the star schema grouping

A dimensional model often uses a star schema design. One common form of a star is quantitative, where transactional data is contained in a central fact table. Related dimension tables radiate out from the fact table.

Reporting against a package based on federated data sources

After the creation and publication of the Framework Manager package containing the Virtual View Manager federated data sources, it is possible to use any IBM Cognos 8 BI front end against the Virtual View Manager views. The example shown in the images provide federated views merging data from Teradata and SQL Server 2005.

From a BI user point of view, the complexity of the model is completely hidden; Figure 2-28 shows, for example, how the model appears to a Report Studio author.

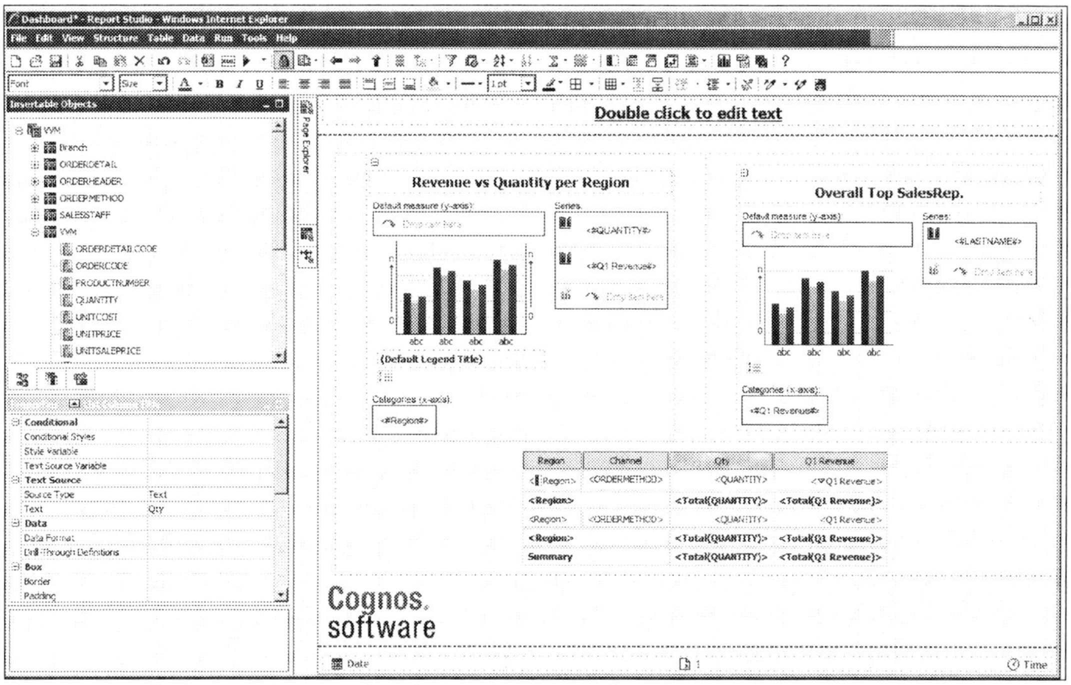

Figure 2-28 Federated views ready to be used in Report Studio

The package can now be used to create analyses, reports, and queries according to the attributes it has. For example, it could be used in Analysis Studio only if it was designed with hierarchical dimension and measures. Figure 2-29 shows how the federated views appear in a simple dashboard.

Figure 2-29 Federated views from SQL Server and Teradata in a dashboard

2.2.3 InfoSphere Federation Server

InfoSphere Federation Server, a key component of InfoSphere Information Server, is a data federation or Enterprise Information Integration (EII) solution that provides virtualized access to heterogeneous data sources as though they were a single database. Data federation helps organizations bridge information gaps, obtain high value insight into operational processes, and make more informed decisions by combining disparate data into a single view.

Virtualized access to disparate systems also enables significant cost reductions, as it eliminates the need for new servers and databases, system administration, and manual data integration processes. As a result, organizations can better manage their data while simplifying IT infrastructures.

Like Enterprise Information Integrator, InfoSphere Federation Server creates a consolidated view of your data to support key business processes and decisions by accessing and integrating diverse data and content sources as though they were a single resource, regardless of where the information resides (see Figure 2-30).

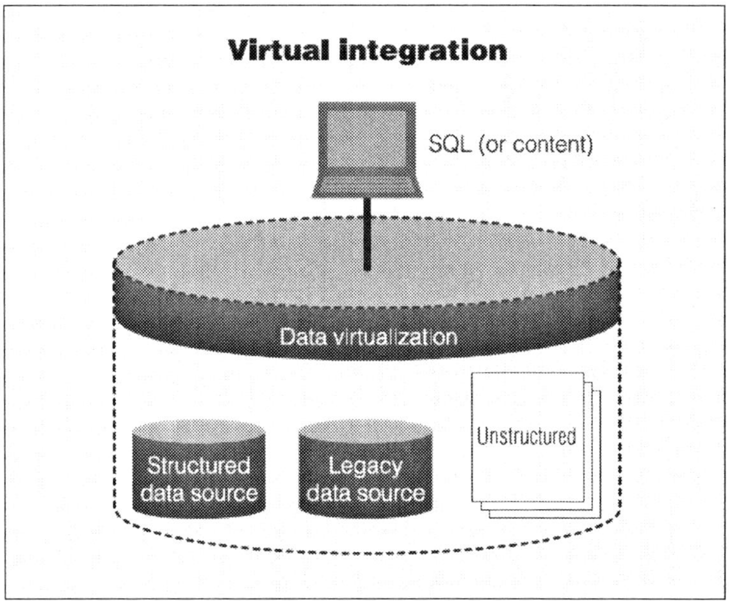

Figure 2-30 Federation creates a virtualized view of multiple sources

Therefore, it is possible to combine data from disparate sources, such as DB2, Oracle, and SQL Server, into a single virtual view. You can access, join, and manipulate data of different formats, such as relational, non-relational, and XML, from the same interface, with standard SQL tools, development environments, portals, and other standard IT infrastructure components.

InfoSphere Federation Server can incorporate data from multiple sources, such as up-to-the-minute inventory, sales, and customer information, into reports and analytics with a single query, but it also able to insert, delete, or update multiple data sources simultaneously no matter where the information is located.

Moreover, as an enterprise oriented solution, InfoSphere Federation Server enables security policies throughout the unified view of the complete data asset and provides a concrete hybrid data warehousing approach by collating up-to-date information from production systems with historical information from enterprise data warehouses.

The key benefits of using IBM InfoSphere Federation Server are:

- Gain virtualized real-time access to disparate data sources.

  Since data is accessed virtually, businesses do not need to create redundant replicas of enterprise information, set up new hardware for new databases, or make changes to the existing infrastructure, which reduces IT costs and risk. This increases business productivity and visibility by having a complete view of mission-critical data without having the development costs of having to build separate queries for each data source. For example, the information in data warehouses can be extended through federating other data sources to provide a unified enterprise view of the business.

- Speed time to market for new projects.

  InfoSphere Federation Server creates a virtual, consolidated view of data from multiple, disparate sources that does not require configuration or maintenance of a new database. That means low cost and fast development of applications by simplifying access to multiple data sources.

- Access more data sources.

  InfoSphere Federation Server keeps the value of existing investments by supporting all major data sources, including XML on DB2 and System z, therefore taking advantage of existing procedures without requiring additional databases or hardware on existing infrastructure. It is also useful for extending data warehouses or marts by way of remote data, and building holistic, unified financial, customer, or product views.

IBM InfoSphere Federation Server provides powerful features, such as:

- A federated, two-phase commitment to advance data integrity and accuracy by allowing the update of multiple data sources simultaneously within a distributed system
- Federated stored procedures to avoid redundant and unnecessary development costs by leveraging previously developed procedures for heterogeneous data sources
- A cost-based distributed query optimization that dynamically enhances queries for high performance
- XML support for transparent integration of XML data, from DB2 TrueXML and XML files, with SQL data from data sources, allowing users to create a simpler view of their information infrastructure, reduce programming costs, and quickly deliver information to users
- Powerful security strategies implemented throughout the unified view of the enterprise for secure federated query and federated updates processing
- An SQL-based access paradigm that enables federation across a wide range of data and content sources
- An application program interface to address the business needs of companies that require federated access to unstructured data sources

InfoSphere Classic Federation Server

In a computing environment that includes System z, it is important to have an information infrastructure that helps leverage the power of the critical data stored on System z. IBM InfoSphere Information Server and its companion products provide critical components for your IBM z/OS integration infrastructure. IBM InfoSphere Classic Federation Server for z/OS provides high performance, dynamic access to mainframe data sources driven by a standardized structured query language (SQL). The result is robust mainframe integration that addresses the needs of today's on demand environments (see Figure 2-31).

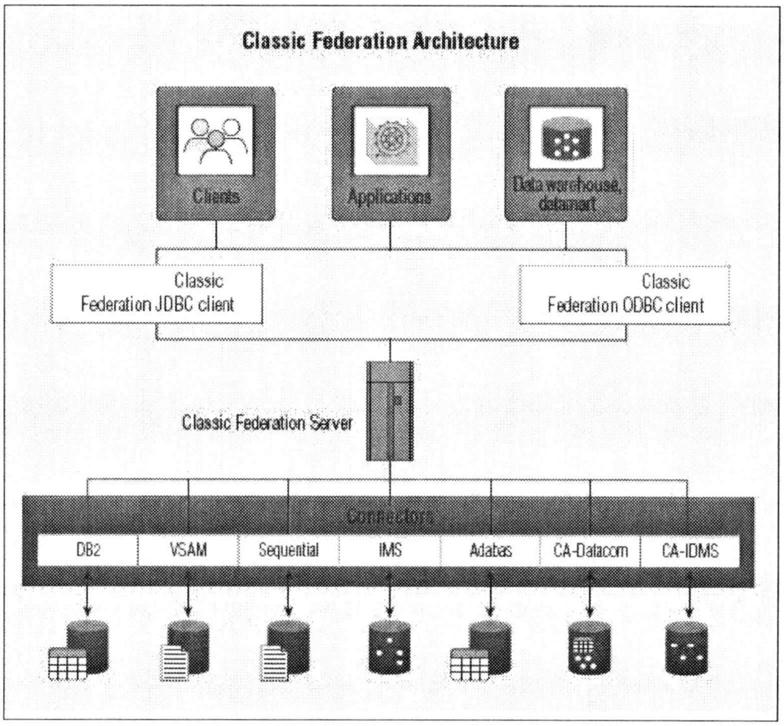

Figure 2-31 InfoSphere Classic Federation Server architecture

InfoSphere Classic Federation Server allows real-time integration of z/OS data with UNIX, Microsoft Windows, and Linux platforms for Internet, client/server, and desktop environments. It provides robust read/write data access and federation with transaction speed and enterprise scaling. Using a metadata driven approach, it dynamically translates SQL select/insert/update/delete statements into native data access commands that are optimized for each data source. Results are reformatted into standard relational row-column answer sets. The result is seamless integration of mainframe data without specialized or proprietary programming.

Dynamic data integration is viable only if it handles workload. InfoSphere Classic Federation Server accesses mainframe data at transaction speed so that Web sites can service thousands of users and transactions per second. InfoSphere Classic Federation Server has proven that it can handle large z/OS throughput requirements. Building applications using InfoSphere Classic Federation Server requires no mainframe programming and no earlier database skills. SQL-literate application developers using their existing development, reporting, and portal tools are productive immediately, building everything from a simple read-oriented, customer self-service Web site to a complex multi-database read/write e-commerce solution.

The InfoSphere Classic Federation Server solution:

- Accepts and validates SQL statements from a server, client, or desktop tool or application
- Communicates the SQL and result sets between distributed tools and applications and mainframe data platform(s)
- Accesses the appropriate data using all available native file and database access aids, such as indexes and keys
- Translates results into a consistent relational format regardless of source data type

Tools and applications issue Java Database Connectivity (JDBC), Open Database Connectivity (ODBC), or call-level-interface SQL commands (SELECT, INSERT, UPDATE, DELETE, and procedure CALL) to clients of InfoSphere Classic Federation Server. SQL is delivered by these clients to the InfoSphere Classic Federation Server z/OS based data server, whose subcomponents read from and write to the earlier data sources using native database I/O commands. This process maximizes the native performance profile of these mainframe data sources, minimizes the potential for errors during processing, and helps ensure the integrity and security of the underlying databases and files.

Processing an SQL data access request for a pre-relational data source, such as a VSAM file or an IBM IMS database, requires a mapping between the physical data layout and one or more logical relational tables. These logical tables must also contain information about the underlying file or database structures, such as the hierarchy of an IMS database, the set relationships of a CA-IDMS database, or even the redefined record layouts of a VSAM file. This metadata mapping enables the operational components of InfoSphere Classic Federation Server to efficiently navigate the databases and files.

InfoSphere Classic Federation Server is a metadata driven implementation that leverages a dynamic metadata discovery process to accelerate the implementation process. The Classic Data Architect, an Eclipse-based GUI, automates the process of mapping earlier file and database content to logical relational tables and views using the physical definitions (IMS DBDs, CA-IDMS schemas and subschemas, Software AG Adabas Predict, and COBOL Copybooks) that you already have. This foundation enables InfoSphere Classic Federation Server to deliver the power of SQL for everything from a simple VSAM file to a complex IMS database.

IBM InfoSphere Information Server helps business and IT personnel collaborate to understand the meaning, structure, and content of any type of information across any source. It also provides breakthrough productivity for cleansing, transforming, and moving this information consistently and securely throughout the enterprise, so it can be accessed and used in new ways to drive innovation, help increase operational efficiency, and lower risk.

Supported databases include:

- Software AG Adabas
- CA Datacom
- Advantage CA-IDMS/DB for z/OS
- DB2 for z/OS
- IMS Version 8 or higher
- VSAM for z/OS
- Sequential files for z/OS

InfoSphere Classic Federation Server has multiple uses:

- It delivers operational data to customer self-service environments. For example, using ODBC SQL, an insurance company connects its policy holders, medical providers, and agents with IMS, VSAM, and IBM DB2, and connects accounting, policy, and claims data through an interactive voice response (IVR) system and self-service Web sites.

- It connects e-commerce sites with current mainframe order-processing data. Using JDBC SQL with IBM InfoSphere Application Server, a catalog retailer connects its Web sales site with the mainframe Computer Associates CA-IDMS inventory data and critical shipping algorithms that also are used by its mainframe COBOL call-center order-processing applications.
- It integrates Business Intelligence systems with enterprise data. Using ODBC SQL, a leading motor craft manufacturer cut data mart development time in half while also empowering credit analysts to evaluate dealer credit requests based on up-to-the-second operational data.
- It empowers IBM Information Server with robust mainframe data delivery for a dynamic customer data cleansing service, a bulk extract-transform-load (ETL) of an operational data store, and everything in between.

Merging a VSAM file in an IBM Cognos 8 package

Much like a Business Intelligence consolidation process, it is possible to create a virtual warehouse by using InfoSphere Federation Server, which allows you to integrate quickly many data sources that handle enterprise strategic information.

VSAM data management is a high performing option that is used to manage a huge load of transactions, so it has been adopted by The Sample Outdoors Company to handle HR transactions. Because this operational data gives you the latest update about ongoing business, it can be useful to see how the data fits into the IBM Cognos 8 BI platform. To merge a VSAM file into IBM Cognos 8 packages, you must:

- Create a federated database
- Configure and register the ODBC for VSAM wrapper
- Register the server definitions for the ODBC VSAM data source
- Create a user mapping for the data source
- Test the connection to the data source server
- Register nicknames for ODBC VSAM

A database should be created in order to collect or federate all incoming instance to disparate data sources. The creation follows the standard wizard (see Figure 2-32).

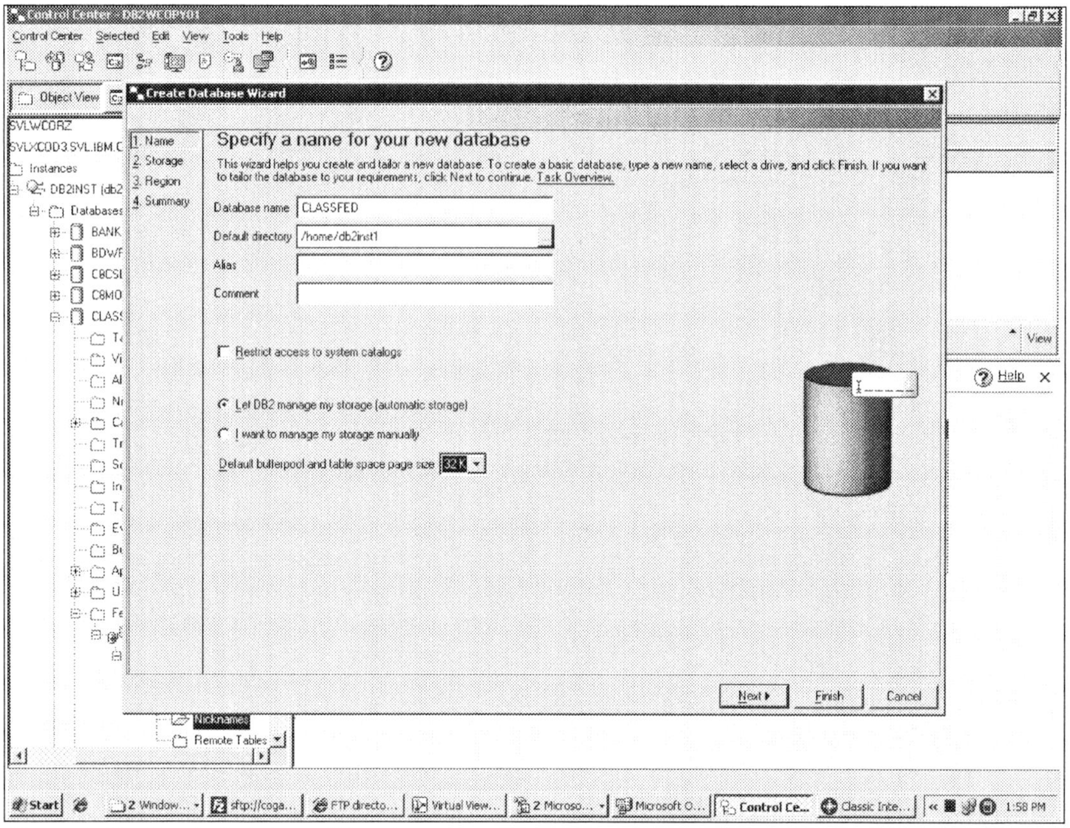

Figure 2-32 Create Database Wizard

While creating a federated database, you should use a code set, territory, and collating sequence (see Figure 2-30 on page 59). This information controls the language in which data is stored and the sequence in which character data is sorted. A code set is a set of unique bit patterns that map to the characters of a specific natural language. IBM products use the term *code page* as a synonym for code set. A territory identifies a locale and specifies region-specific information for the specified code set. If not specified, the database uses the language and collating sequence of the DB2 client used to create the database. The code set for the federated database should corresponds to the code set that the remote data sources use. If multiple data sources are used, and code sets are not compatible, Unicode would be the code set for the federated server.

Any ODBC server that will be used for federated databases should be registered. The server definition for an ODBC data source is registered through a wizard in the DB2 Control Center. The process for configuring access to data sources is the same, regardless of the data source. What differs in the process are the particular settings that you apply as you complete each configuration task for each data source.

Register the wrapper

The federation installation program installs support for data sources, but the corresponding wrapper must be registered and configured. A wrapper is a set of library files that the federated server uses to communicate with the data source and to retrieve data from it. For each type of data source that you want to access, a wrapper must be registered. For example, to access one table in DB2 for Linux, UNIX, and Windows, one table in DB2 for i, and one table in Teradata, you register two wrappers: the DRDA® wrapper for the DB2 data sources and the Teradata wrapper for Teradata data sources. You have the option to use the default wrapper name or assign a different name to the wrapper, and review the wrapper options that are available for each data source that is configured. Each data source has one or more required wrapper options to be set (see Figure 2-33).

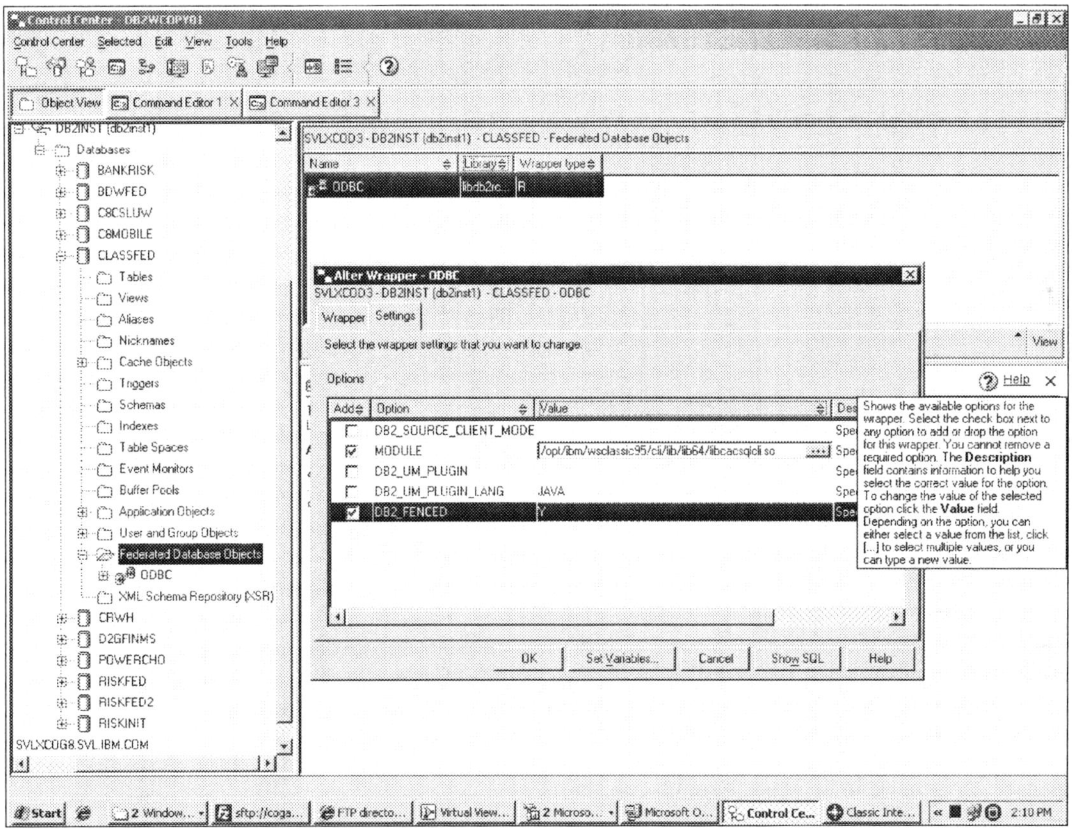

Figure 2-33 Create Wrapper wizard

In order to get access to VSAM files, in our example we have specified the path to the ODBC library for VSAM files:

```
/opt/ibm/wsclassic95/cli/lib/lib64/libcacsqlcli.so
```

The parameter DB2_FENCED is also set to Yes, which is a mandatory option to access InfoSphere Classic Federation Server data sources.

Register the server definitions

If you want your setup to be enabled for specific data source objects, you must provide one or more server definitions. For a relational data source, a server definition represents a remote database, a database partition, or a node. For a non-relational data source, a server definition often maps to other types of external data objects. Each data source has required and optional parameters that must be specified when registering the server definition. Each data source has one or more required server options to set (see Figure 2-34).

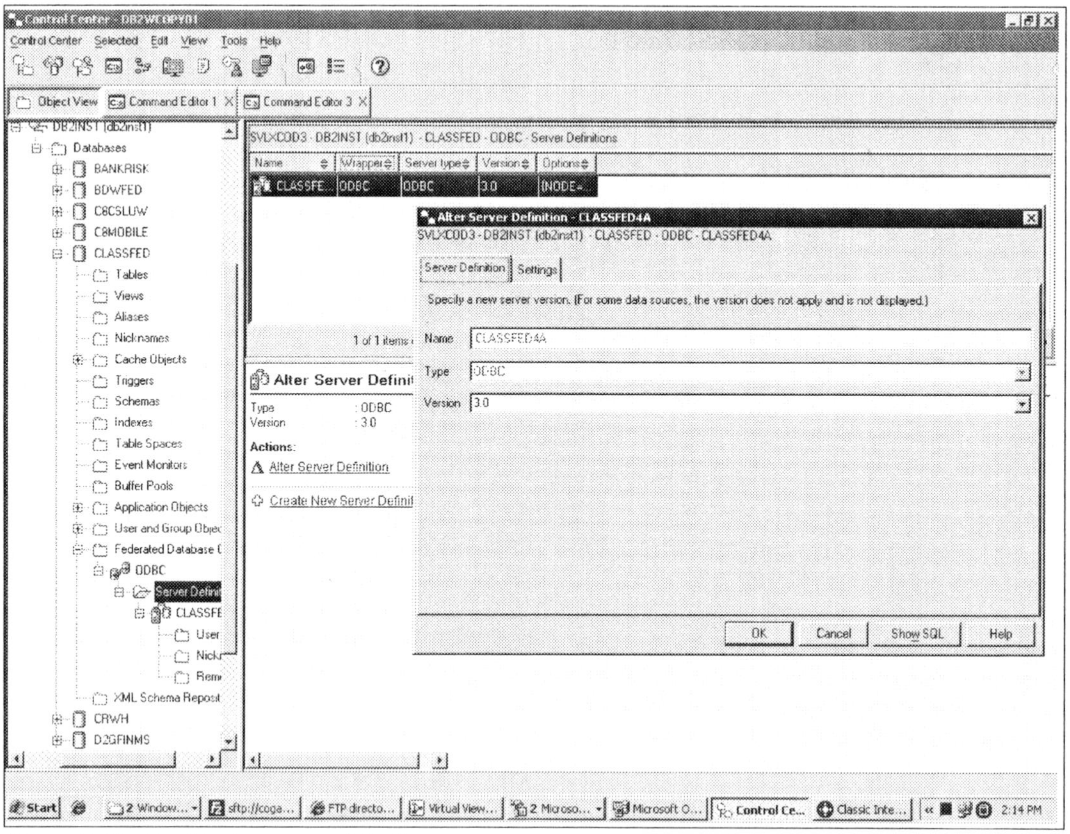

Figure 2-34 Registering server definition

NODE, CODEPAGE, and DBNAME are required to map a VSAM ODBC data source. In our sample configuration, the NODE server option have been set to the data source specified by the DATASOURCE keyword in the `cac.ini` file (DATASOURCE = CACSAMP tcp/150.45.37.49/5000). Then the NODE option is set to CACSAMP.

The CODEPAGE server option must be set to the codepage number of the client codepage specified in the `cac.ini` file. In our example, the `cac.ini` file specified CLIENT CODEPAGE = IBM-850, and then we set the CODEPAGE option should to 850.

The DBNAME server option must be set to the name of the data source database that you want to access; in our example, we used ‘CLASSFED4A’.

Register user mappings

If a remote data source requires user authentication and if a user's remote user ID and remote password are different from the ones that the user uses to connect to the federated database, user mappings are required. A user mapping is an association between a federation server authorization ID and a data source user ID and password. By default, user mappings are stored in the catalog on the federated server. User mapping information could be stored in an external repository, such as on an LDAP server or in a file. To use an external repository, you must use a plug-in that provides the federated server with the interface to the repository (see Figure 2-35). In our sample environment, we created a user mapping for a remote user named 'cacuser' with the password '1234'.

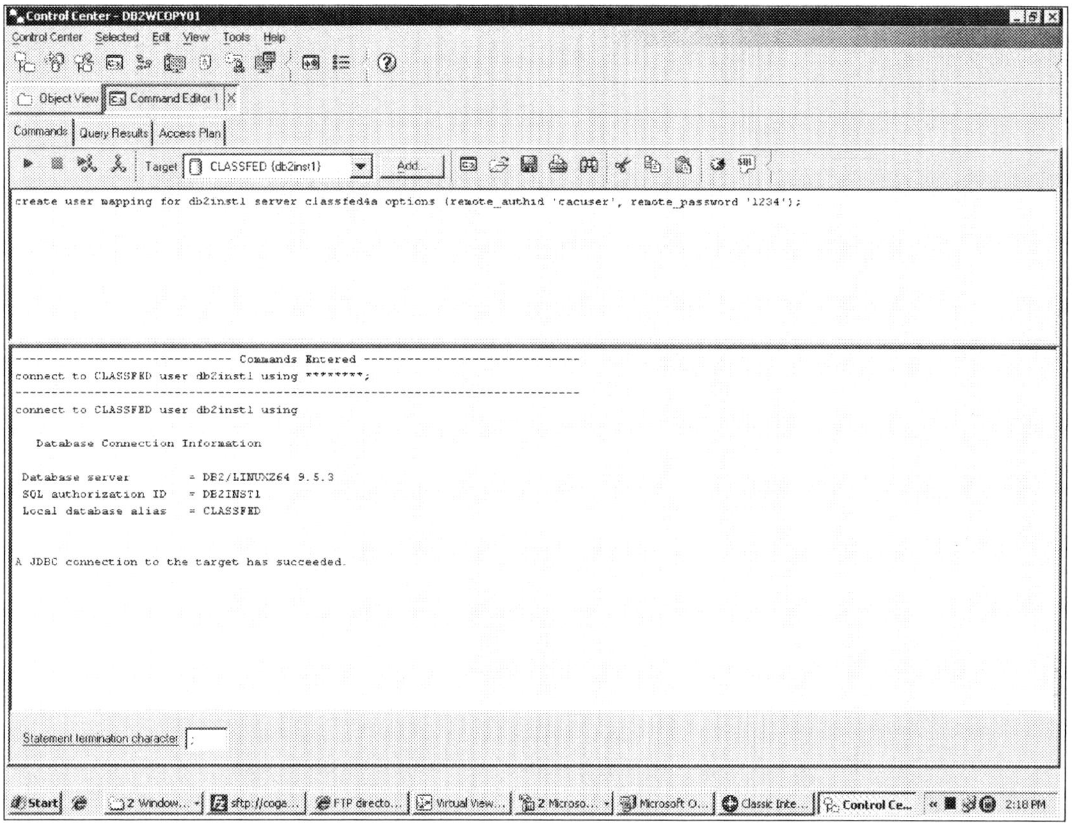

Figure 2-35 User mappings registration

Update data source statistics

For each relational data source to be accessed, a command that is equivalent to the DB2 RUNSTATS command updates the statistics at the remote data source. Then, once nicknames have been created, the most up-to-date statistical information is added to the system catalog in the federated database. Later, when running a query on the data source, the query optimizer uses this information to determine the most efficient way to perform the query.

Statistics at the data source might change after the nicknames are set. When statistics for a relational data source change, the SYSPROC.NNSTAT stored procedure is used to update the statistical information in the system catalog. When statistics for a non-relational data source change, it could be necessary to manually update the statistics in the SYSTAT catalog views.

Register nicknames

It is necessary to create a nickname for each data source object to be accessed. For some non-relational data sources, there is a fixed list of input and output columns when registering the nickname. Each column is mapped to a particular field, column, or element in the data source object. Some data sources have required nickname and column options to be set. In our example, we start the wizard in DB2 Control Center by right-clicking the **Federated Data Objects** folder and then selecting **Create Federated Objects**. While creating the nickname, the federated server queries the data source catalog using the nickname. This query tests the connection to the data source table or view, eventually reporting errors if the configuration does not work. In our example, the nickname was set to EMLPLVSAM, which is the employees list in the VSAM data source (see Figure 2-36).

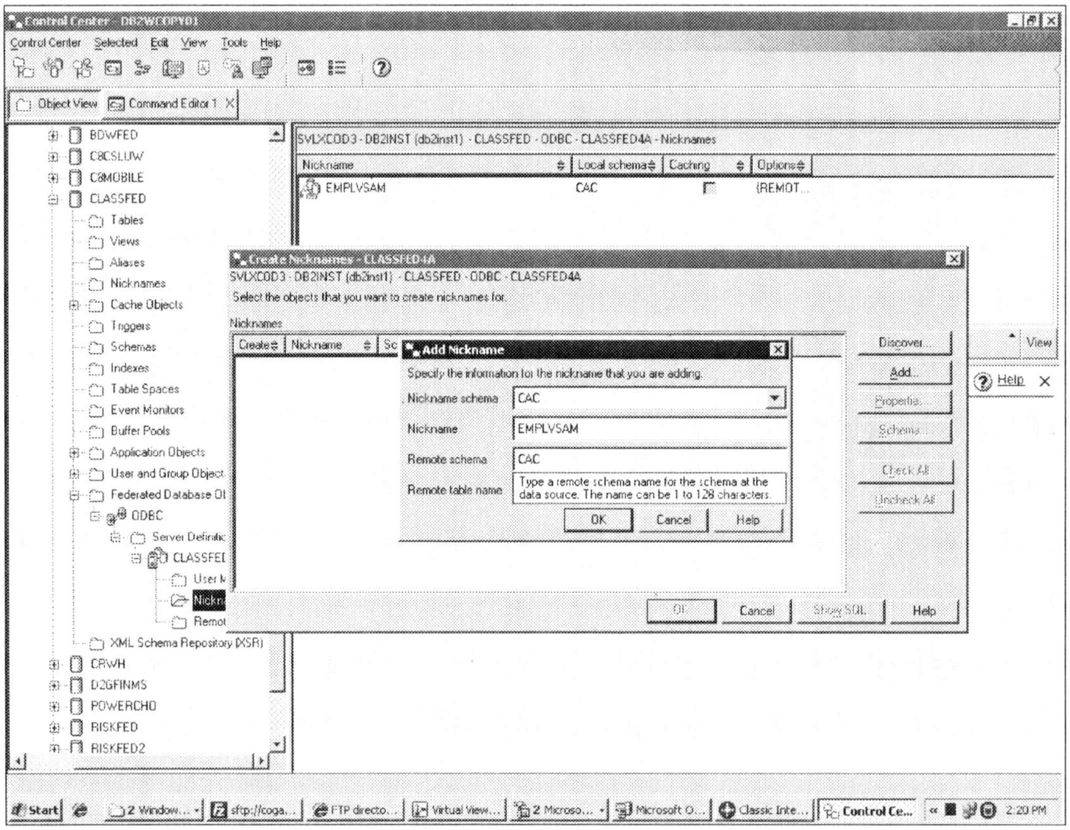

Figure 2-36 Registering the nickname in DB2 Control Center

Depending on your needs, additional configuration tasks can be performed:

- Create index specifications: An index specification could be defined for objects, such as views, that do not have indexes.
- Define alternative data type mappings: In the federated system, there are default mappings between the data source data types and the federated database data types. For relational data sources, it is possible to define alternative data type mappings.
- Define alternative function mappings: In the federated system, there are default function mappings between the built-in data source functions and the built-in federated database functions. For relational data sources, it is possible to define alternative function mappings when a new built-in function or a user-defined function, which is available at the data source, is needed.

IBM Cognos modeling and reporting on a federated VSAM data source

Delivering Business Intelligence solutions on a VSAM source is very easy. Perform these three steps:

1. Create a link to the new data source.

   Connect to the federated data source with the necessary parameters, such as the name of the sources defined in DB2 Control Center. In our example, the name of the source is CLASSFED (see Figure 2-37).

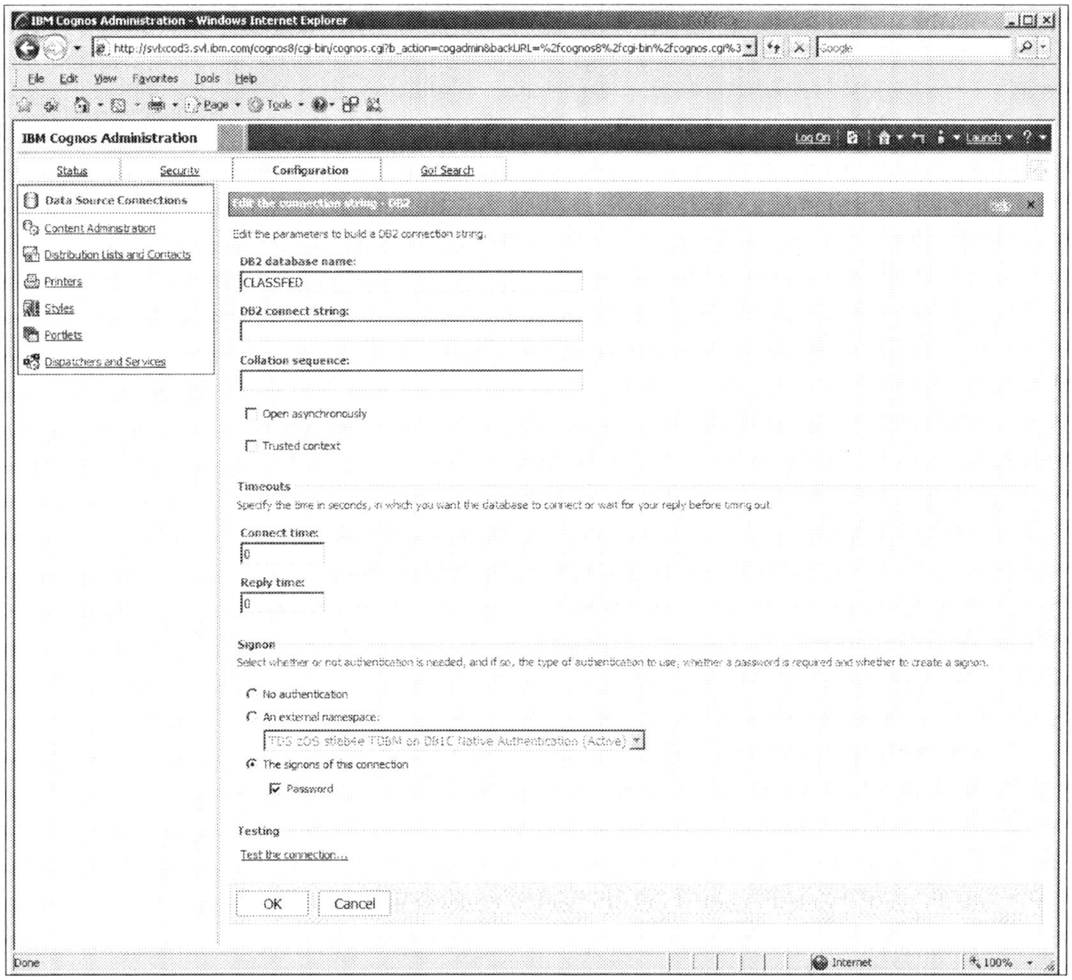

Figure 2-37 Mapping of an InfoSphere Federation Server data source

2. Model the data source in Framework Manager.

   The Import Metadata Wizard shows all the items available for reporting purposes (see Figure 2-38).

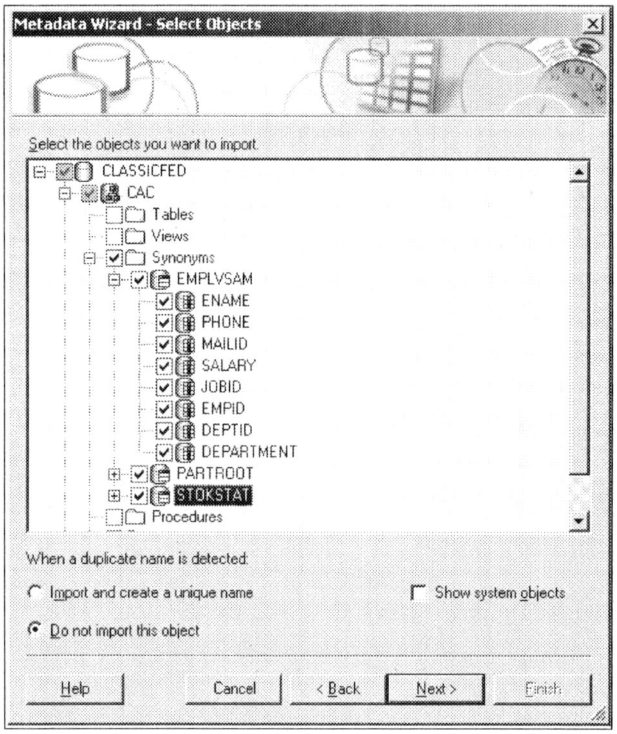

Figure 2-38 Federated data sources in the Synonyms folder

3. Create and publish a package with Framework Manager.

   It is also possible to deliver useful objects, such as predefined filters and calculations. In our example, the employee's list appear as a satellite of a predefined star schema (see Figure 2-39).

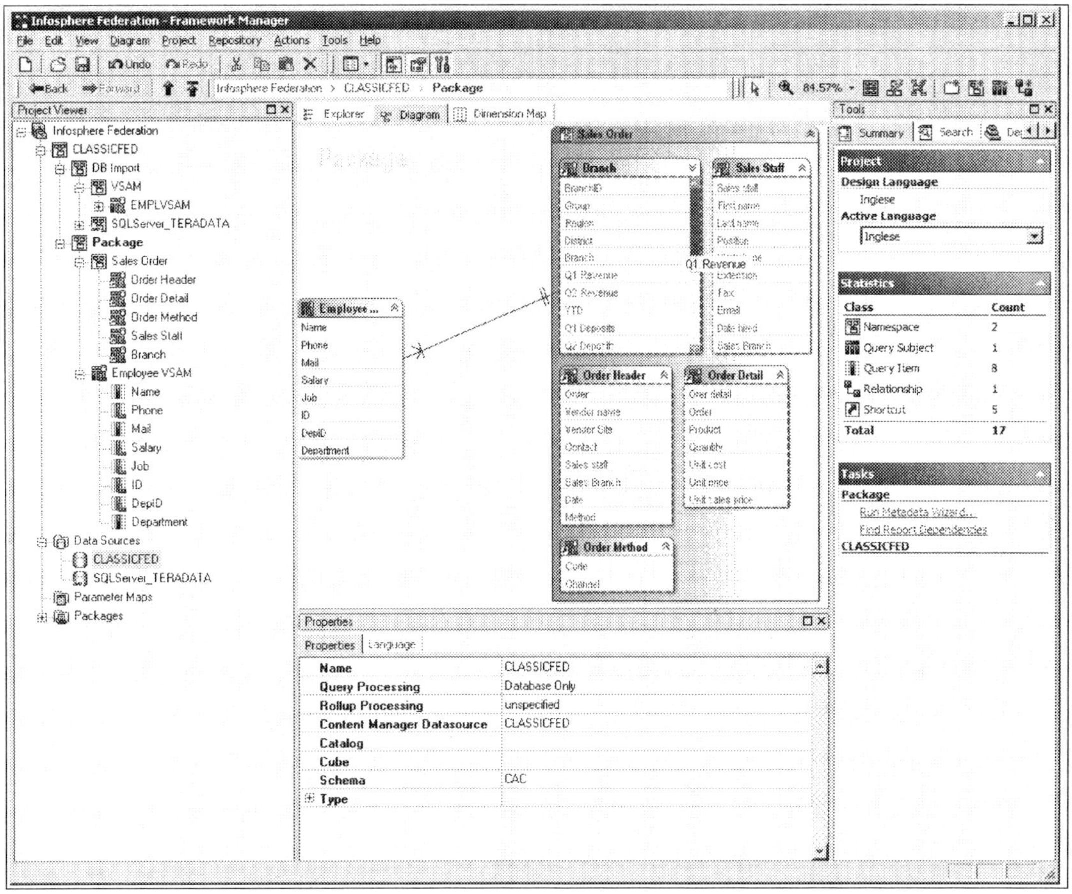

Figure 2-39 VSAM table in a Framework Manager mode

Once the model is completed, it will be packaged and published through the publishing wizard. The model can be updated at any time; any modification may impact the reports and analysis, if the package has already published. In this case, we suggest performing an Impact Analysis before publishing the new version of the package. If many reports need to be updated because of the update, you can opt to keep previous versions of the package until all the reports are updated to the new version.

Reporting on a federated data source does not show any peculiar behavior; the report author does not know what data source is being used. In our example, we modified an existing dashboard by adding information to a list, for example, an employee's name, that comes from the VSAM file. This information is combined with other data sources that contain Branch information and Sales summaries (see Figure 2-40).

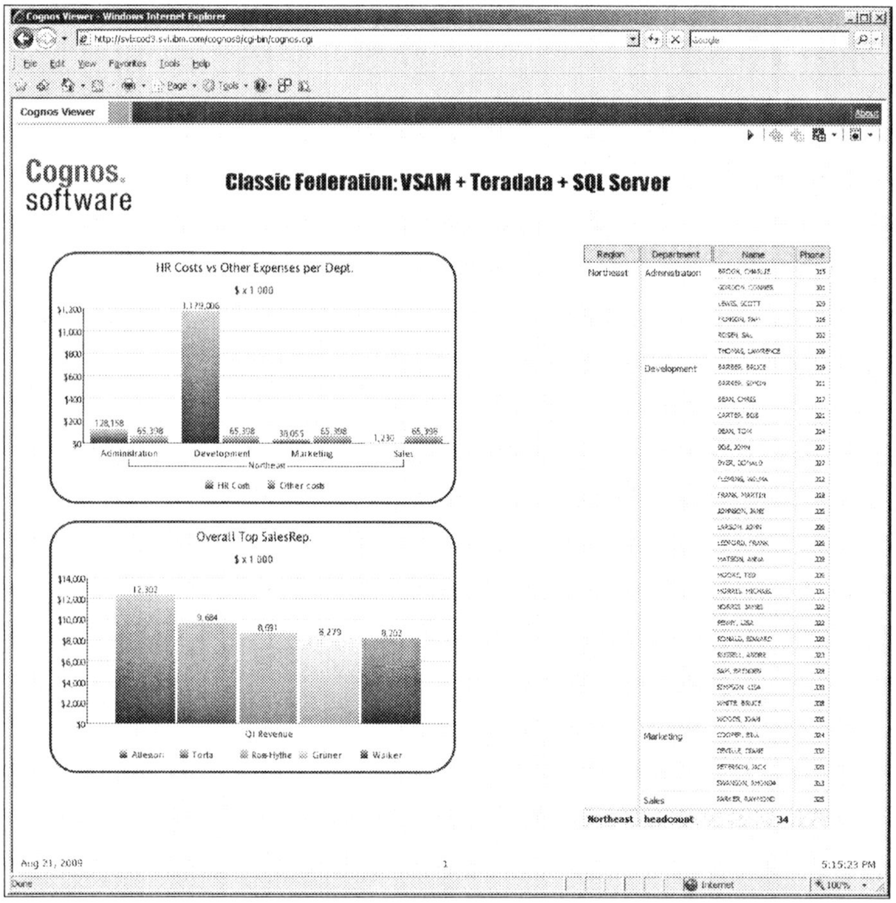

Figure 2-40 VSAM, Teradata, and SQL Server merged in an IBM Cognos 8 BI dashboard

2.3 Implementation considerations

We have described a potential scenario of Business Intelligence consolidation. Using The Sample Outdoors Company as a sample case, we applied different techniques for consolidation. Now we summarize and provide some basic suggestions and general points of discussion to discover, case by case, the consolidation strategy that best fits your needs. We develop the discussion around three main points:

- Data sources
- Deployment and maintenance
- Performance

2.3.1 Data sources

The three consolidation options we discuss in this chapter differ in terms of the data source they can access. IBM Cognos Framework Manager direct access usually requires installing client connectivity on both the server and client sides. It usually can access several sources, but some of them do not provide drivers for the Linux on System z environment.

IBM Cognos Virtual View Manager provides access by way of a standard JDBC driver and supports more data sources on Linux on System z; it also supports some specific data sources, such as Enterprise Resource Planning (ERP).

InfoSphere Federation Server and Classic Federation Server cover some relational and non-relational data sources accessed by Virtual View Manager, and support some other ones, such as sequential files on System z. This fact means that the data source conformance list should help determine which implementation you should use. As mentioned before, a detailed list of available data sources is available on the IBM Support Web Site.

Table 2-1 summarizes the types of data sources available for each one of the three federation approaches.

Table 2-1 Compare federation approaches by data source type

Data sources	Framework Manager direct access	Virtual View Manager	Federation Server and Classic Federation
RDBMS (DB2, Oracle, SQL Server, Teradata, Sybase, Informix, and so on)	According to native client availability	Yes	Yes
Classic (VSAM, sequential files, DB2 for z/OS, and so on)	N/A	According to JDBC availability	Yes
Non-relational (OLAP, LDAP, XML, Web Services, and so on)	According to native client availability	Yes	Yes
ERP and other special sources	N/A	Yes	N/A

For a detailed and updated list of data sources that can be accessed by way of IBM Cognos Framework Manager direct access, refer to this address:

`http://www.ibm.com/support/docview.wss?rs=3442&uid=swg27014110`

For a detailed and updated list of data sources that can be accessed by way of IBM Cognos Virtual View Manager, refer to this address:

`http://www.ibm.com/support/docview.wss?rs=3442&uid=swg27014427`

For a detailed and updated list of data sources that can be accessed by way of IBM InfoSphere Federation Server, refer to this address:

`http://www.ibm.com/support/docview.wss?uid=swg27015299`

For a detailed and updated list of data sources that can be accessed by way of IBM InfoSphere Classic Federation Server, refer to this address:

`http://www.ibm.com/support/docview.wss?uid=swg27011950`

2.3.2 Deployment and maintenance

Ease of deployment and maintenance is also a meaningful factor when evaluating what consolidation strategy you should use. Even if some metadata definitions can be inherited, multiple mappings involve multiple steps for updates and maintenance. The benefits and costs of each solution should be considered before applying one of them.

If multiple metadata definitions exist, in order to choose a consolidation path, you should consider applying an ETL procedure to build a consistent warehouse. The delivery of a complete data warehouse requires a great deal of effort; an update procedure can be scheduled, but keep in mind that this activity could impact the time to get the most recent information from the BI platform.

Federating data sources is a big advantage because it allows you to avoid data redundancy. Federating data sources with direct access is a good option, because it reduces maintenance; the other options require multiple modeling and multiple forms of maintenance, and, as with an ETL procedure, different teams and resources are involved. However, this configuration provides information as soon as it is available in the original source and may improve performance.

2.3.3 Performance

Performance is obviously a key factor in evaluating the consolidation of Business Intelligence solutions. If you use fewer software layers, you usually get a better response time. But, even though all of the workload is managed inside System z, federation on different tools splits some activities into different environments.

In terms of systems performance management:

- Framework Manager direct access gives you a number of options for defining how volumes and resources will be managed.
- Virtual View Manager includes many options for caching and in-memory transformation.
- InfoSphere Federation Server enables more options in performance management, for example, providing embedded improvements in query execution. It also better addresses some extended enterprise needs that are not necessarily related to Business Intelligence purposes, with features such as pushing data updates on original sources.

3

Reporting and analysis

In this chapter, we describe the use of Cognos functions to solve business requirements. We provide an overview of the options offered to deliver content to the user and some considerations for their installation.

This chapter discusses the following topics:

- Cognos family of solutions
- Cognos Go! Mobile for Linux on System z
- Cognos Go! Search for Linux on System z
- Cognos Go! Office
- Cognos Go! Dashboard for Linux on System z
- Cognos portlets in WebSphere Portal Server
- Data lineage from data source to report

3.1 Cognos family of solutions

Chapter 2, "Scenario for deployment" on page 23 concentrated on consolidating business information in Cognos 8 BI. This information is delivered by way of a Web browser in the following Cognos standard formats:

- Hypertext document (HTML)
- Portable document format (PDF)
- MS Excel (XLS and CSV)
- XML

In this chapter, we discuss the Cognos family and the additional functionality that is available when Cognos 8 BI is combined with other IBM Information Management solutions. We discuss how this combination offers more output options to deliver content to the user, and how they are installed. For example:

- Cognos Go! Mobile adds various smart phones as clients for viewing Cognos content.
- Cognos Go! Office allows you to drag and drop Cognos content directly into Microsoft Office documents.
- Cognos Go! Search adds a professional search engine feature to Cognos for viewing Cognos content.
- Cognos 8 Go! Dashboard allows you to assemble a dashboard using multiple report sources.

We also discuss integrating Cognos with IBM WebSphere Portal Server using Cognos 8 BI portlets. This combination of technology allows you to add non-Cognos related content to your Cognos data (Gartner Group News, stock quotes, and so on).

Mixing all these technologies together opens even more opportunities. For example a business user could, from his BlackBerry device, connect to his company's private network, use an Internet type search, and discover that the information needed is contained in a Cognos report for which he is authorized. When the user gets back to the office, the user retrieves the report and drags it into a MS PowerPoint presentation. As MS PowerPoint is enabled as a client for Cognos by way of Go! Office, this user does not need to cut and paste the content from the Web browser to accomplish this task. In addition to having the presentation ready, the user can refresh the content by running another query in MS PowerPoint. All these options are focused on delivering the content or making it accessible to the business user in the way the user wants to access it or look for it.

Table 3-1 lists the products or functionalities described in this chapter as well as some general characteristics of the software, such as whether it is server or client based and whether it requires the installation of third-party tools.

Table 3-1 Cognos family of solutions

	Go! Mobile	**Go! Search**	**Go! Office**	**Go! Dashboard**	**BI Portlets**	**Data lineage**
Purpose	Provides Cognos Service to mobile devices (BlackBerry, Symbian devices, such as Nokia, and Windows Mobile devices).	Provides extended search capabilities in Cognos and integrates with a cooperative search engine.	Provides Cognos content inside Microsoft Office.	Provides extended portal functionality.	Integrates with existing cooperative portals.	Users can access and view major transformations to data as it moves through the system (both technical and business metadata).
Client installation	The client software is downloaded from the Go! Mobile enabled on Cognos 8 BI Server.	None. A Web browser is required.	Go! Office is a separate installation package.	None. A Web browser is required.	None. A Web is browser required.	None.
Server Installation	The installation extends Cognos 8 BI Server.	The installation extends Cognos 8 BI Server.	None. This is a standard functionality of Cognos 8 BI Server.	The installation extends Cognos 8 BI Server.	None. This is a standard functionality of Cognos 8 BI Server.	None. This is a Cognos 8 BI V8.4 feature.
Non-Cognos components	The BlackBerry requires the BlackBerry Enterprise Server.	None.	Microsoft Office.	None.	Enterprise Portal (such as WebSphere Portal Server).	None.

In the following sections, we discuss the purpose of each package and then discuss the installation and configuration.

At the time of writing, the available level for IBM Cognos 8 Business Intelligence 8.4 is Fix Pack 2, which is described at the following address:

`http://www.ibm.com/support/docview.wss?rs=3442&context=SS9RTN&dc=D400&uid=swg24023803&loc=en_US&cs=UTF-8&lang=en&rss=ct3442db2`

By default, IBM Cognos 8 uses Tomcat as an application server. You can configure IBM Cognos 8 products to run on supported application servers that you currently use in your environment.

3.2 Cognos Go! Mobile for Linux on System z

The Cognos Go! Mobile component can add smart phones (Symbian based, such as Nokia, Windows Mobile based, such as HTC, and BlackBerry) as potential clients.

For the BlackBerry, you need to add the BlackBerry Enterprise Server (BES) to the Cognos Infrastructure, and the MDS Services must be enabled. In large companies, there might be a cluster of BlackBerry Enterprise Servers. In this case, the Cognos Go! Mobile gateway needs to be configured to talk to the primary BlackBerry Enterprise Server.

The overview diagram shown in Figure 3-1 depicts the relationship of all these components. Note that, except for the BlackBerry, all smartphones can communicate directly with Cognos.

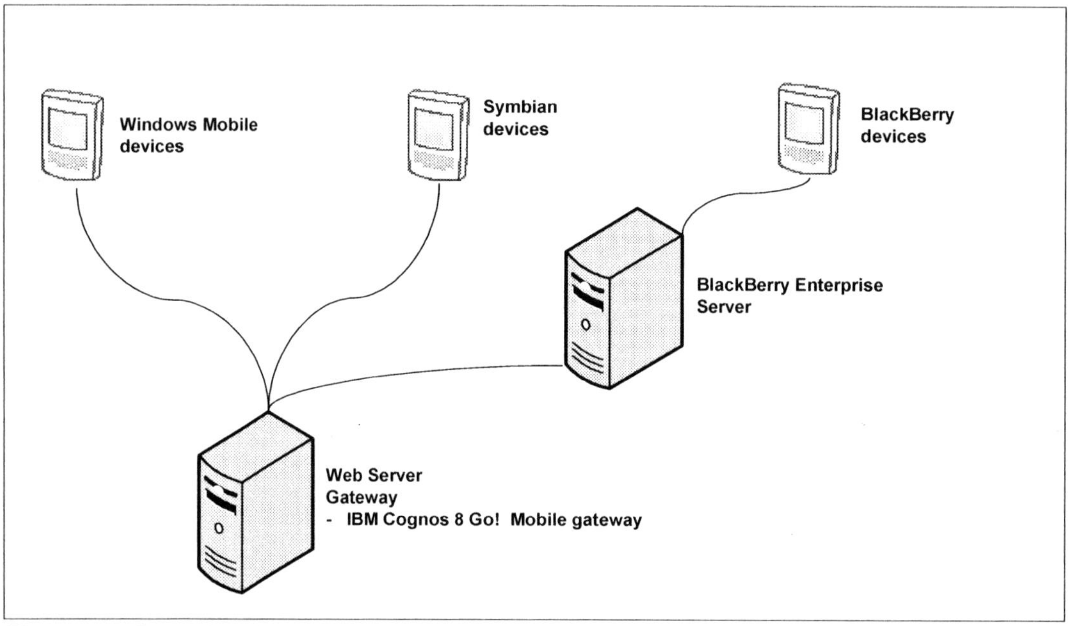

Figure 3-1 General architecture for the mobile components of Cognos

3.2.1 Special considerations for providing content to mobile devices

Mobile devices are not an efficient replacement for a desktop or mobile computer. The screen's size allows only a limited amount of information to be displayed. Also, prompting should be minimized because of the form factor of the device.

The target user community for mobile devices are traveling business people that need to access information at a moment's notice. They might be high level management, which get key performance indicators of the business unit, or sales people, who get a refresh of their key customer data.

The typical information delivery formats are small tables or charts. For example, traffic light charts are very useful because they provide the option of general current status information (for example, all green).

Figure 3-2 on page 79 shows an example of such as report, a Research in Motion (RIM) simulator report that can be displayed on a BlackBerry Storm or the Symbian or Windows Mobile operating systems. We tested all of our examples on the BlackBerry.

Note: Cognos Go! also works with the Symbian and Windows Mobile operating systems. We will only be showing BlackBerry in our examples, but be aware it works in a similar way for other smartphones.

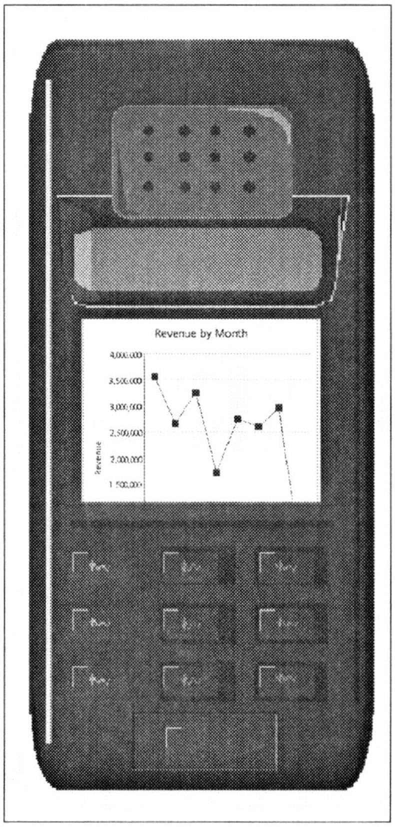

Figure 3-2 Sample mobile phone

3.2.2 Installation of the necessary components on a BlackBerry

Table 3-2 lists the software that needs be installed or enabled prior to starting the installation process.

Table 3-2 Cognos Go! Mobile client prerequisites

Client	Software
BlackBerry	The BlackBerry MDS Services must be enabled.
Symbian	N/A.
Windows Mobile Client	Microsoft .NET Compact Framework Version 2.0 SP1 (Windows Mobile 6 already includes this software).

The Web server MIME types are required by each mobile vendor (BlackBerry, Symbian, and Windows Mobile). The extensions shown in Table 3-3 need to be added to the mime.types file on the Web server.

Table 3-3 MIME types

MIME type	Extension
application/vnd.rim.cod	.cod
application/vnd.ms-cab-compressed	.cab
text/vnd.sun.j2me.app-descriptor	.jad

Once you have installed the product, the client is available for download at the address http://<Server>/cognos8/mobile/index.html, where "Server" is your installation location. Open the Web browser on your mobile device and download the client for your mobile device.

Figure 3-3 shows the download page on the mobile phone.

Figure 3-3 Download software for the mobile phone

Once the client is downloaded, start it and enter the URL of the Cognos instance you want to access (<Cognos Server>/cognos8). If security is enabled on the Cognos server, the login window appears; otherwise, you will go directly to the folder structure and will be able to run reports.

There are additional options on the BlackBerry to integrate the Cognos client into the platform so that it is either already there or pushed wirelessly. If it is already downloaded, it can be preconfigured to access the right server.

3.2.3 Components to be added to the Cognos 8 BI Server

A prerequisite for installing Cognos Go! Mobile is an existing Cognos 8 BI Server installation. Even with a distributed approach, Cognos Go! Mobile can only run on a server where there is at least a report service deployed.

Start the installation by running the **./issetup** command. In the course of the installation, you must enter the installation directory (/opt/cognos/c8) of Cognos 8 BI Server.

After the installation has finished, no tables need to be created, because they have already been created by default by Cognos during the startup in the already existing Cognos 8 content store.

Note: Cognos 8 Mobile content cannot be kept in a DB2 z/OS Content Store.

Start the Cognos configuration on the server by running the cogconfig.sh script. The Cognos Go! Mobile package adds the following new items to the Cognos configuration:

- The mobile service in IBM Cognos 8 Service
- The Mobile section in the data access area
- The BlackBerry settings in the Environment area

The circle in the right pane of the window shown in Figure 3-4 shows the new mobile service. The circle in the left pane shows the new mobile data access. This new data access needs to be configured.

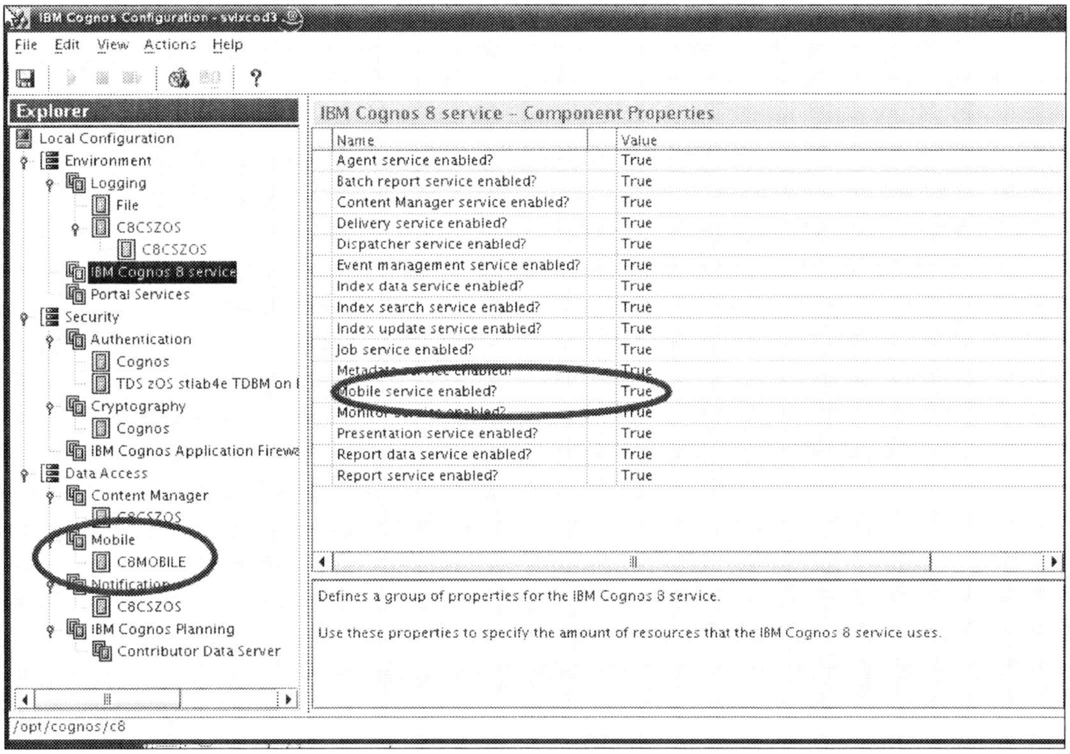

Figure 3-4 Cognos mobile service

Right-click **Mobile** and add a new database resource of type DB2. You need to configure it to access the database just created by using a type-4 driver.

Configuring a type-4 DB2 JDBC driver under Cognos

The driver consists of three files.

- `java/db2jcc.jar`: Actual class file.
- `java/db2jcc_license_cu.jar`: The type-4 LUW license, which included in DB2 for LUW Server packages.

The files are typically found in `/opt/ibm/db2/V9.5/java/` (V9.5 is the version). Cognos needs theses files to be accessible in the following directories:

- `/opt/cognos/c8/bin`
- `/opt/cognos/c8/webapps/p2pd/WEB-INF/lib`

It is sufficient to link the files to these directories (run the **`ln -s`** command to perform this task). The files in `/opt/cognos/c8/bin` are used by cogconfig.sh to perform the configuration test. The files in `/opt/cognos/c8/webapps/p2pd/WEB-INF/lib` are used to create the EAR files for WebSphere Application Server.

> **Note:** If you added any of the JDBC type-4 files to your Cognos environment, you need to regenerate the P2PD.EAR file and re-deploy it to the WebSphere Application Server.

The differentiation between type-2 and type-4 access in Cognos is made by the highlighted column "Database Server and Port" shown in Figure 3-5. If you enter "ip:port", type-4 is used; otherwise type-2 is used.

Note: Do not change the database server and port if you do not plan to use type-4!

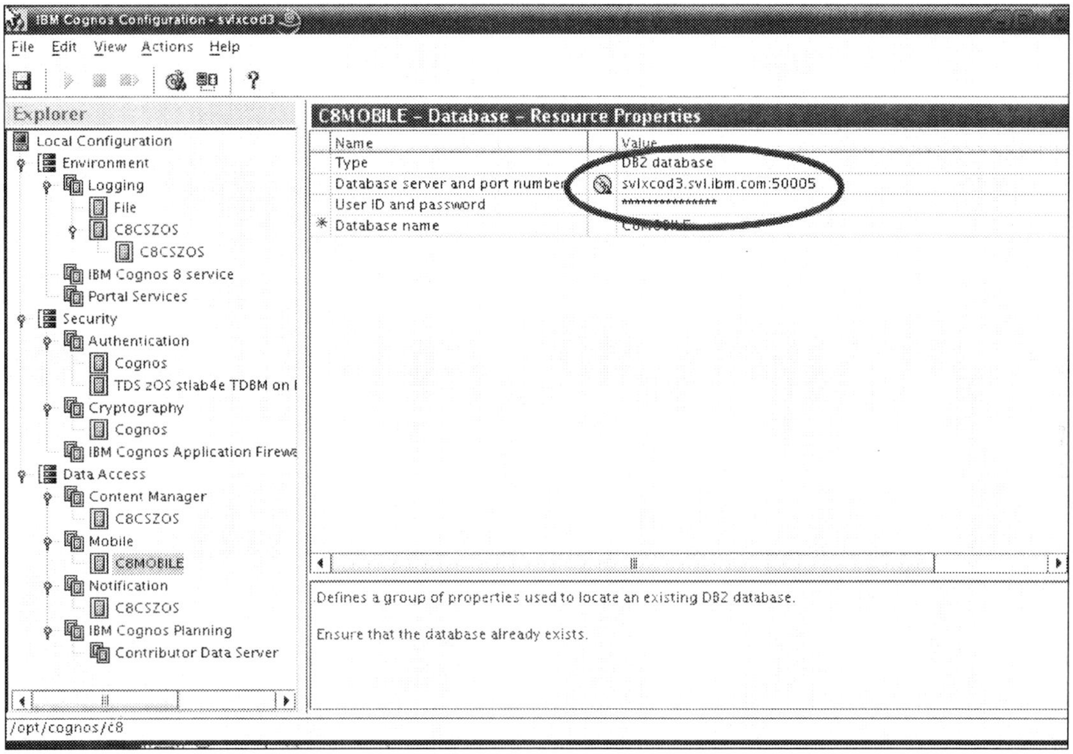

Figure 3-5 Sample configuration of Cognos Go! Mobile content store database

Configuring the BlackBerry Enterprise Server

If you plan to enable BlackBerry as an access device, you need to configure the BlackBerry Enterprise Server in the Cognos Environment settings (see Figure 3-6).

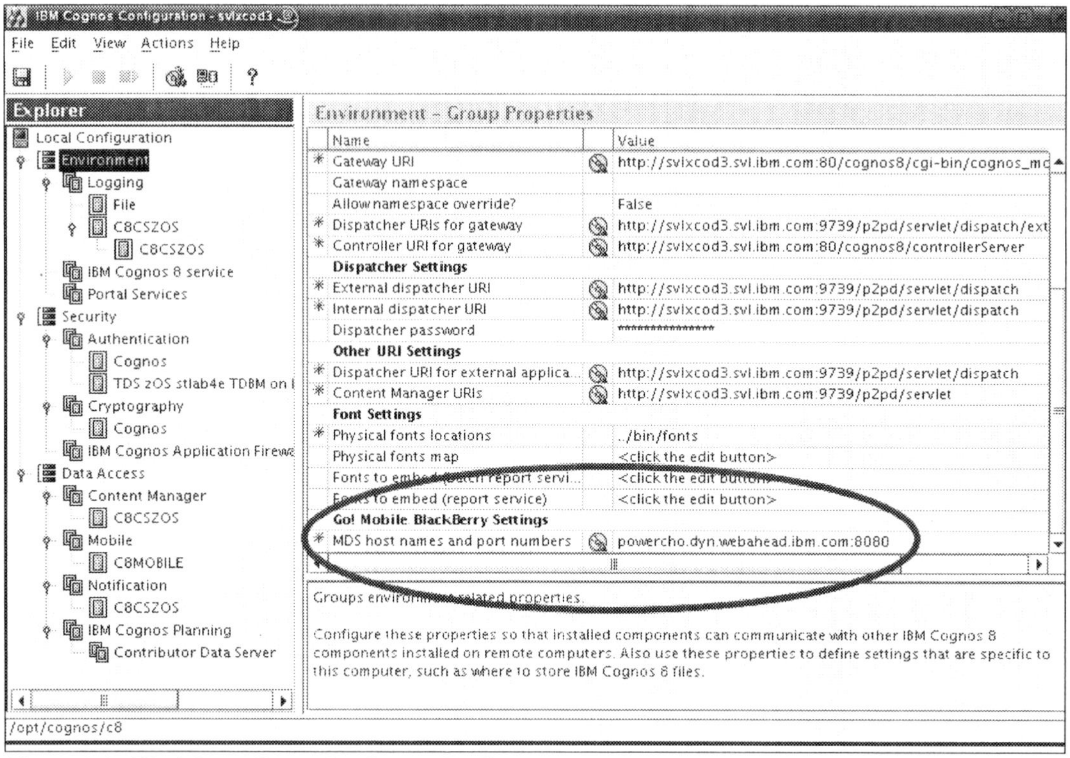

Figure 3-6 BlackBerry Enterprise Server (BES) setting in Cognos configuration

3.2.4 Scaling and distribution

Cognos Go! Mobile needs to be installed in a location together with a report service, because Cognos Go! Mobile transforms the output of the report service so that it can be used on the mobile device.

As the number of mobile users are usually far less than other users, you might want to add mobile services only to a few report services. In this case, set the service affinity correctly so that PC users are the primary users of the report services.

3.3 Cognos Go! Search for Linux on System z

IBM Cognos Go! Search is primarily an enhancement of the built-in search function of Cognos. The built-in function only searches for names and descriptions of Cognos objects (report, queries, dashboard, and so on). IBM Cognos Go! Search goes deeper. It also indexes content within the Cognos object (Label, Prompts, and so on). If set up properly, it even goes one level deeper and indexes the contents of report runs. Therefore, queries about what information exists for a certain customer are possible, and all the results are listed, where the customer (the string expression) is either in the Cognos object name or in the content.

From a "look and feel" perspective, Cognos 8 BI Server enabled with IBM Cognos Go! Search is not much different from an installation without it, as shown in Figure 3-7. Just the result page looks different and the identified Cognos Objects in the results set are different.

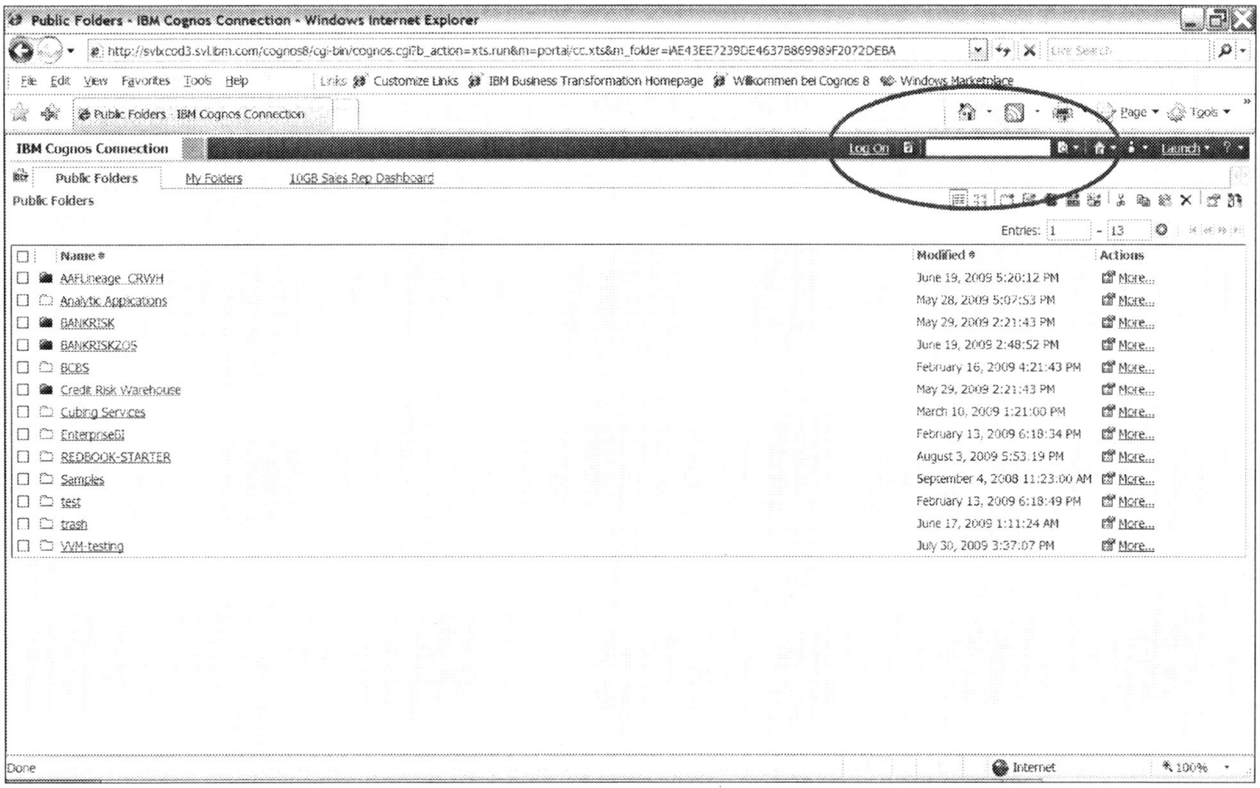

Figure 3-7 Location of Cognos Search facility

Figure 3-8 show the result page of a search without Cognos Go! Search installed. The search options are similar to SQL:

- The method option offers certain search predicates for the name and description field inside the content store (much like a “like” clause).
- The modified option allows you to limit your search to a certain time range (for example, between time a and time b).
- The type option is list of dedicated values (report, package, and so on).
- You are able to limit the search range by defining a folder to search.

In general, this is a form that allows you to generate an SQL type query on the Cognos content store.

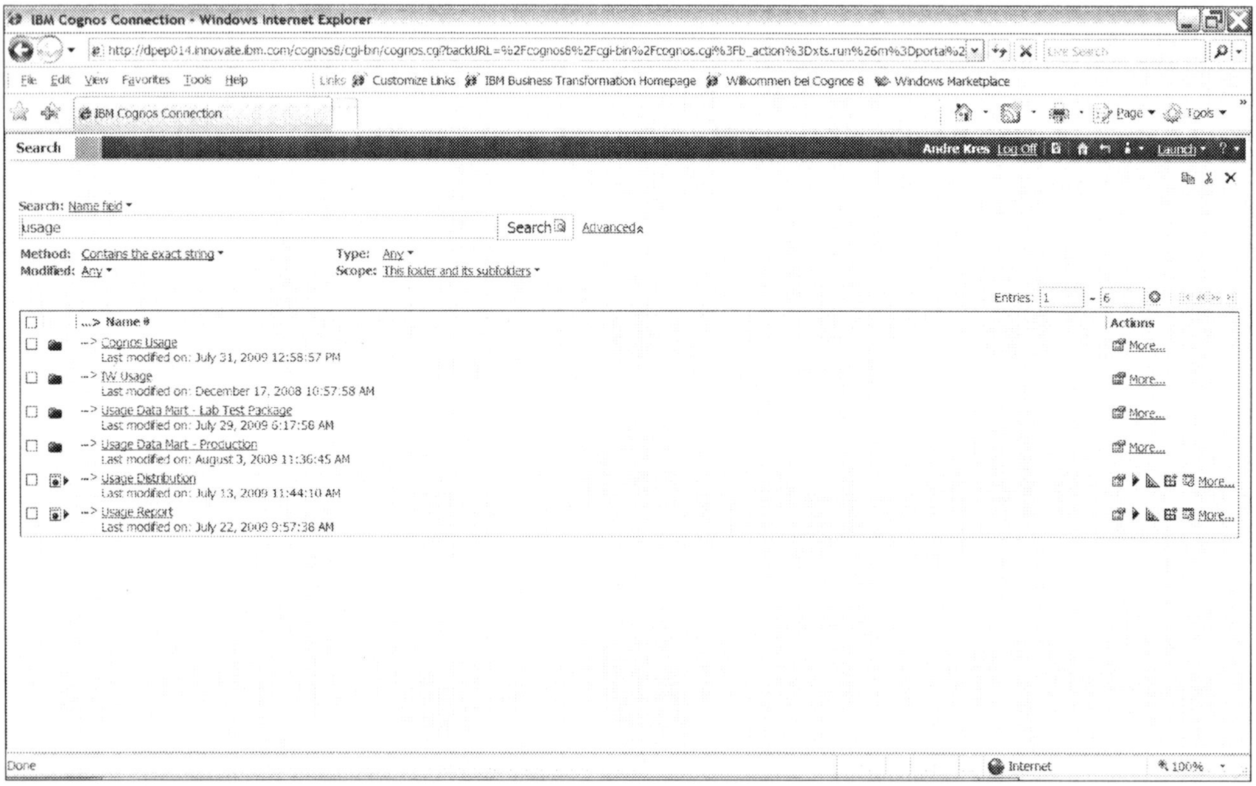

Figure 3-8 Cognos standard search results

Figure 3-9 shows some search results when using IBM Cognos Go! Search. The general handling is more like a search engine, such as Yahoo, Google, and so on. The result is rated by Cognos Go! Search according to the relevance of the search term and presented as sorted by this rating. In the left pane is a list of check boxes with the found object types and packages these objects contain.

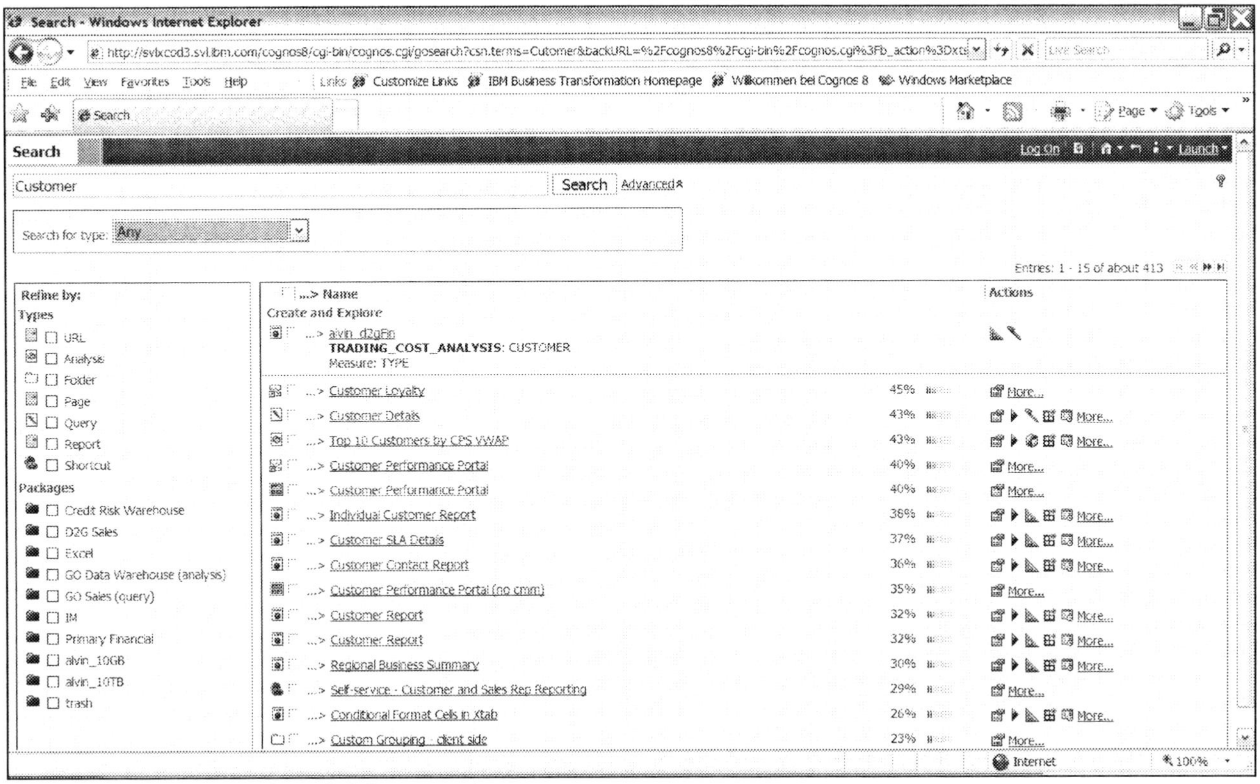

Figure 3-9 Cognos Go! Search full text result page

Checking and unchecking these boxes immediately updates the search result. If the returned result is too big and the type of object is known, it is possible to limit the search to a certain type. Click the **Advanced** link (beside the Search button), which will reveal a drop-down menu that allows you to select Cognos object types (Report, Query, and so on). Executing another search after choosing that object will limit the search to that object. Note that after we select the Cognos object types to search, there is a new search option named "Full text and all fields", which is selected by default (Figure 3-10). This sets the parameters for our new search.

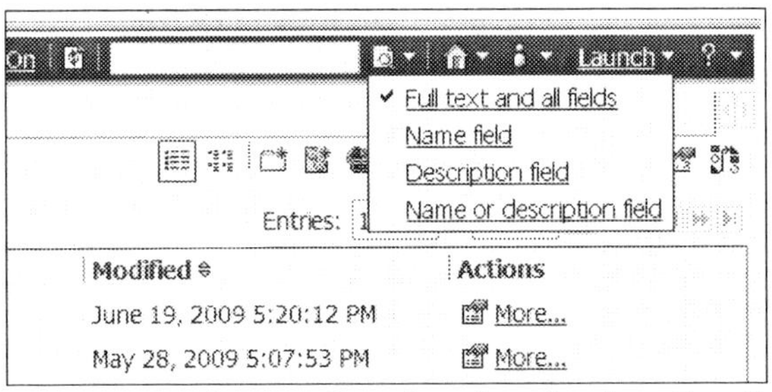

Figure 3-10 Cognos Search option after installing Cognos Go! Search

If you choose one of the other options, the search function reverts back to the "standard" search.

3.3.1 Installation and setup of Cognos Go! Search

As with Cognos Go! Mobile, Go! Search needs to be installed on an existing Cognos 8 BI Server or report service instance. The content store needs to have some reports inside it in order to run the index service.

To install this feature, perform the following steps:

1. Start the installation by running the ./issetup installation script.
2. During the installation, you will be prompted for the Cognos installation directory. Enter the directory to finish the installation.
3. Review the Cognos configuration by running the ./cogconfig.sh script.

Installing the package adds additional services to the Cognos 8 BI Server, as shown in Figure 3-9 on page 87. This additional services are:

- Index data service
- Index update service
- Index search service

All the services need to know the URL of the content store set in the Cognos configuration Run ./cogconfig.sh, and, in the Explorer, expand **Environment**, as shown in Figure 3-11. If the services are distributed for performance reasons, it is a best practice to have this setting initially set. If Cognos scales horizontally (across multiple computers), then the setting needs to be available on all systems (the same situation applies to the notification store settings).

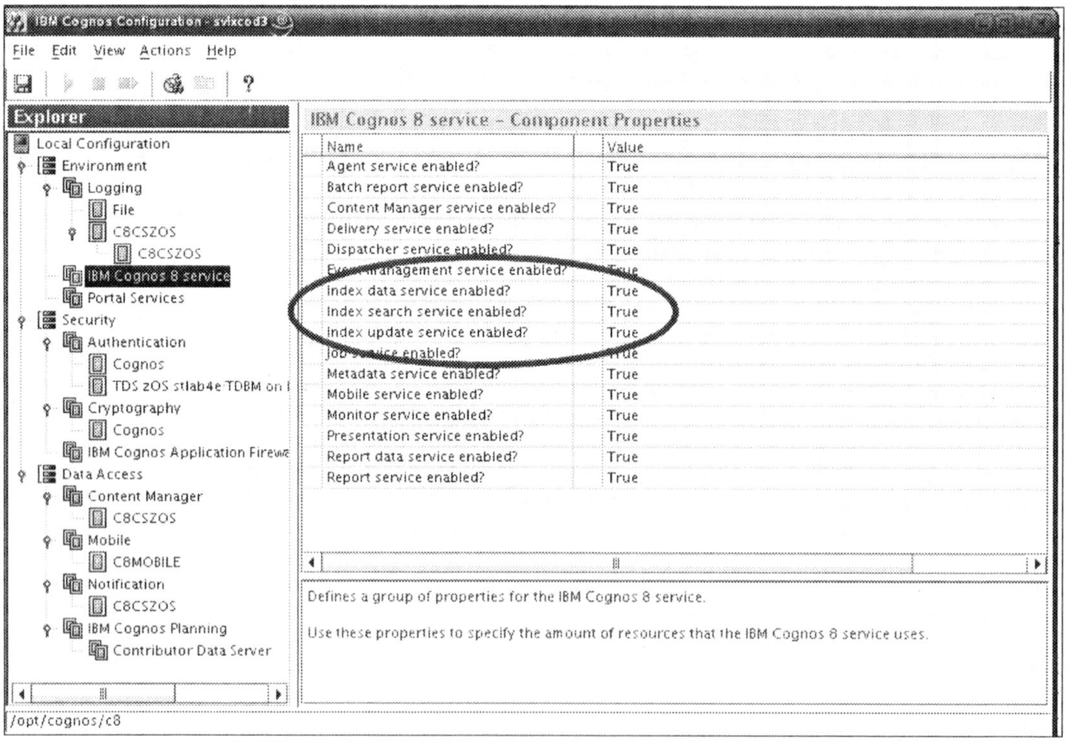

Figure 3-11 Cognos Go! Search index service

The index data service manages the index files. Depending upon the setup, there are scenarios to scale either the index data services or index files. According to the relevant documentation, there should be at least as many data services as there are index files.

The index update service uses the batch reporting service as a source and the index data service as a destination. As with the reporting batch service, it is possible to scale the service by the amount of threads to be configured. The advised ratio between batch report service threads and index update service threads is 2:1. This means there should be only half as many index update service threads as batch report service threads. The expected load pattern is large data movements. I/O should be watched, as the index data service can be a potential bottleneck.

The index search service is the service triggered by the user by way of the dispatcher service. This service accesses the index data service to get search results. If the user experiences delays while searching for content, then adding more search services helps. Be aware that you need scale the index data services appropriately.

3.3.2 Configuring Cognos Go! Search

Cognos Go! Search is configured using the Cognos Administration front end, which is part of Cognos Connections.

Index files

Cognos Go! Search needs a file system on which to store the index files. If you go to the Cognos Administration window inside Cognos Connection, you find a tab named Go! Search. This contains the storage settings (see Figure 3-12). Click **Advanced** to get the file settings. If you plan to set up multiple files, this would be the place to do so. As Linux on System z runs in a virtual environment, you will not have a significant benefit from using this function. For our scenario, the index files are as large as the content store itself.

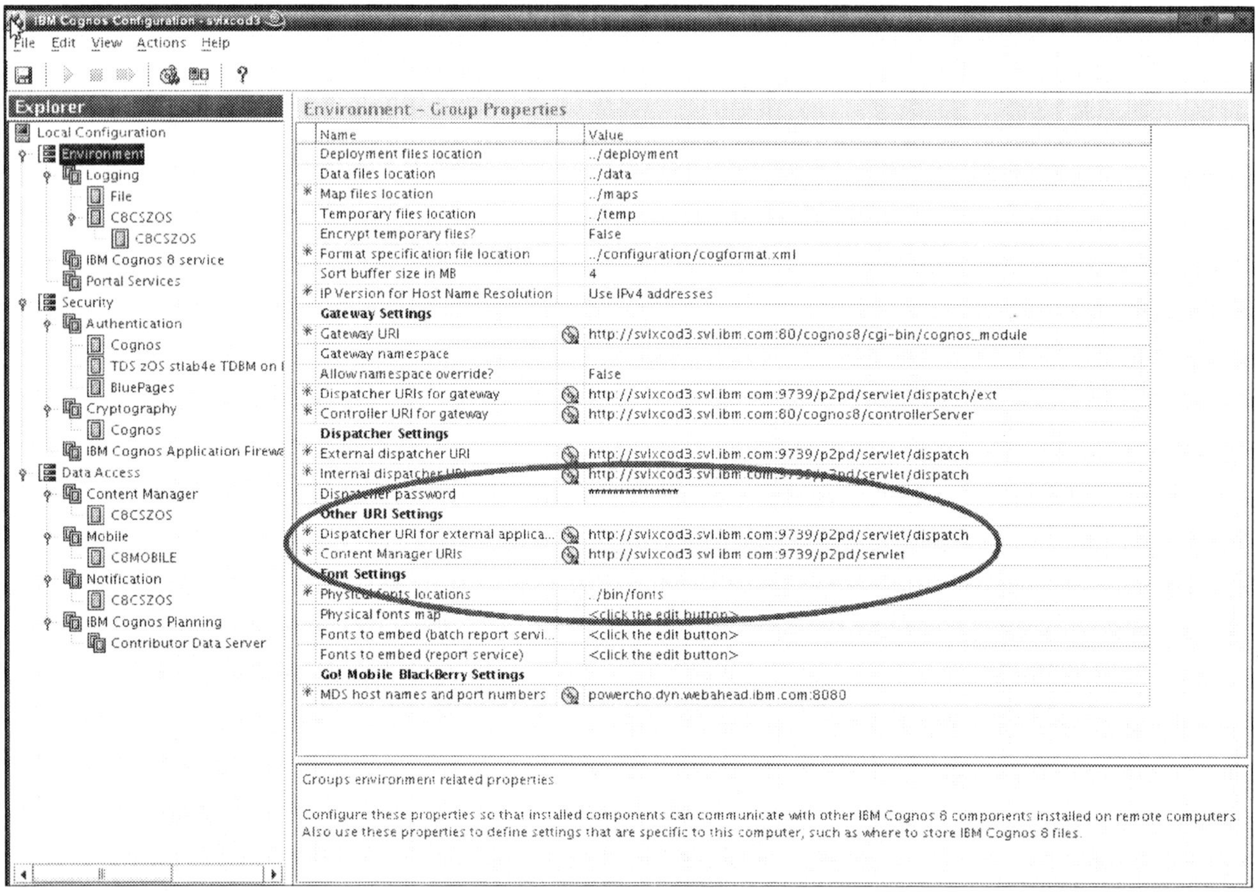

Figure 3-12 Content manager URI settings

Set the parameter "CSN.IndexLocation" to the value of your file system (index root directory).

Update index

Cognos Go! Search can only find objects that have been indexed. Configuring the index limits the list of objects to be found. Table 3-4 lists all the object that can be indexed. Note that Cognos Go! Office objects are not listed; this means you will never find content that is inside a PowerPoint presentation or Excel file in this search.

Consider the impact on the size of the index files. For example, if you decided to index all the files, you have to include all the prompts for the reports that you run, so the index might be even bigger than your information warehouse.

Table 3-4 Cognos object being indexed with Cognos Go! Search

Entry	Indexed
Agent	X

Entry	Indexed
Agent view	X
Analysis	X
Cognos planning task	
Data Manager catalog	
Documents, such as a Microsoft Word document or Excel spreadsheet	
Folder	X
Job	
Metric	X
Metric export	
Metric import	
Metric maintenance	
Metric package	X
Metric studio group	
Metric studio group type	
Metric studio project	
Metric type	X
Metric comment	X
Package	X
Page	X
Planning package	X
PowerCube (appears as a package)	X
PowerPlay® report	X
PowerPlay report view	X
Query	X
Report	X
Report template	X
Report view	X
Saved report output	X
Scorecard	X
Series 7 PowerCube	X
Series 7 PowerPlay report	X
Shortcut	X
URL	X

To actually configure the index update, select **Cognos Connection → Cognos Administration → Go! Search → Index → General** (see Figure 3-13).

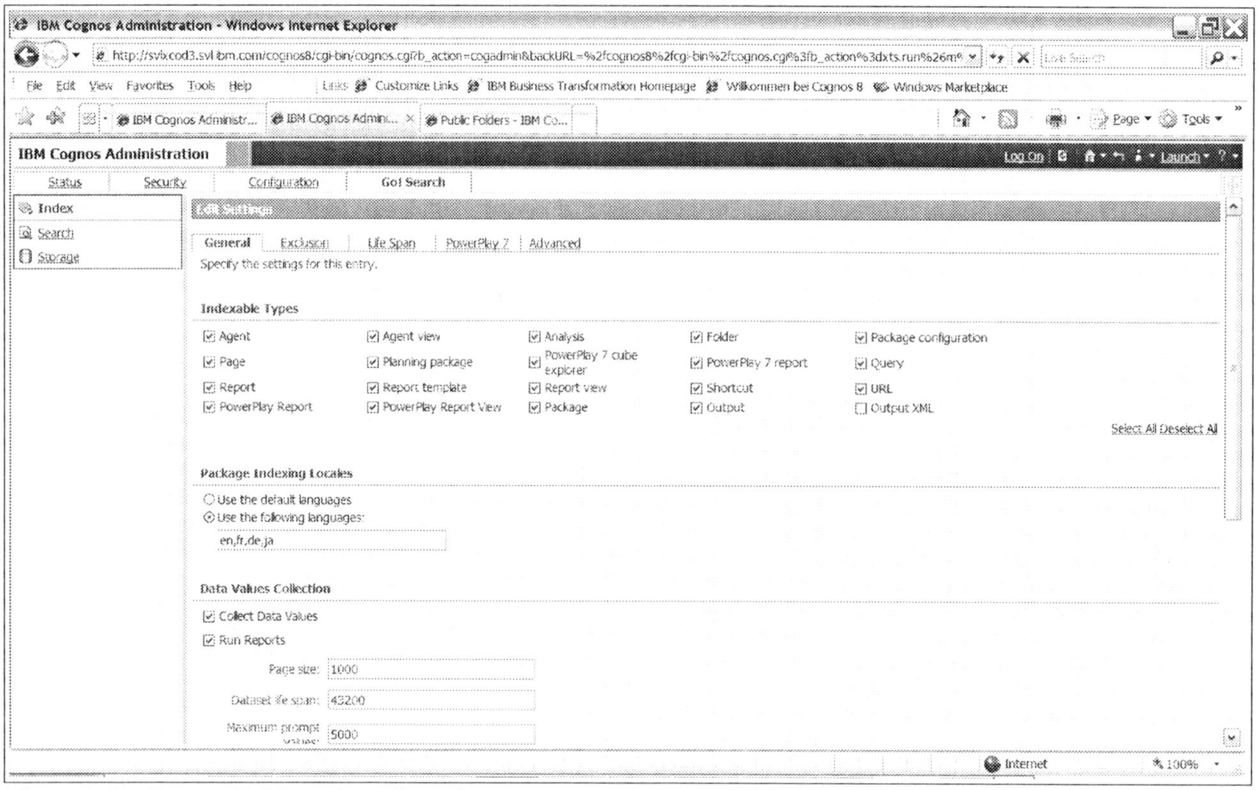

Figure 3-13 Cognos Go! Search configuration

Note the following tabs, which are shown in this window:

- The General tab shows the object to be included in the index. You can define the local language as well. The reports that can be run are the ones where the report content can be indexed. All the items (report, query, report results, and so on) you select make the index larger and make the update take longer to complete.
- The Exclusion tab allows you to exclude certain dimensions from being indexed (such as time) or change the life span of certain volatile content. (Life span means the content is considered valid for a specified amount of time, which might vary for the various content.)
- The PowerPlay 7 tab allows you to set special settings, which are relevant to PowerPlay, to enable data compression.
- The Advanced tab has settings for the update indexing service. By default, there is only one setting (CSN.Indexing.Threads) and it is set to 5. This represents the number of threads running parallel.

  There is only one instance of Cognos running, so all instances are equal to one. If you have installed multiple instances of Cognos for scaling, you can specify a different number of threads for each instance using the instance drop-down menu. The default value is All, and clicking the down arrow displays all the known instances.

The updating of the index does not happen automatically; it needs to be scheduled. This is done by using the general task scheduler, which can accessed by selecting **Cognos Connections** → **Cognos Administration** → **Status** → **Schedules** (see Figure 3-14).

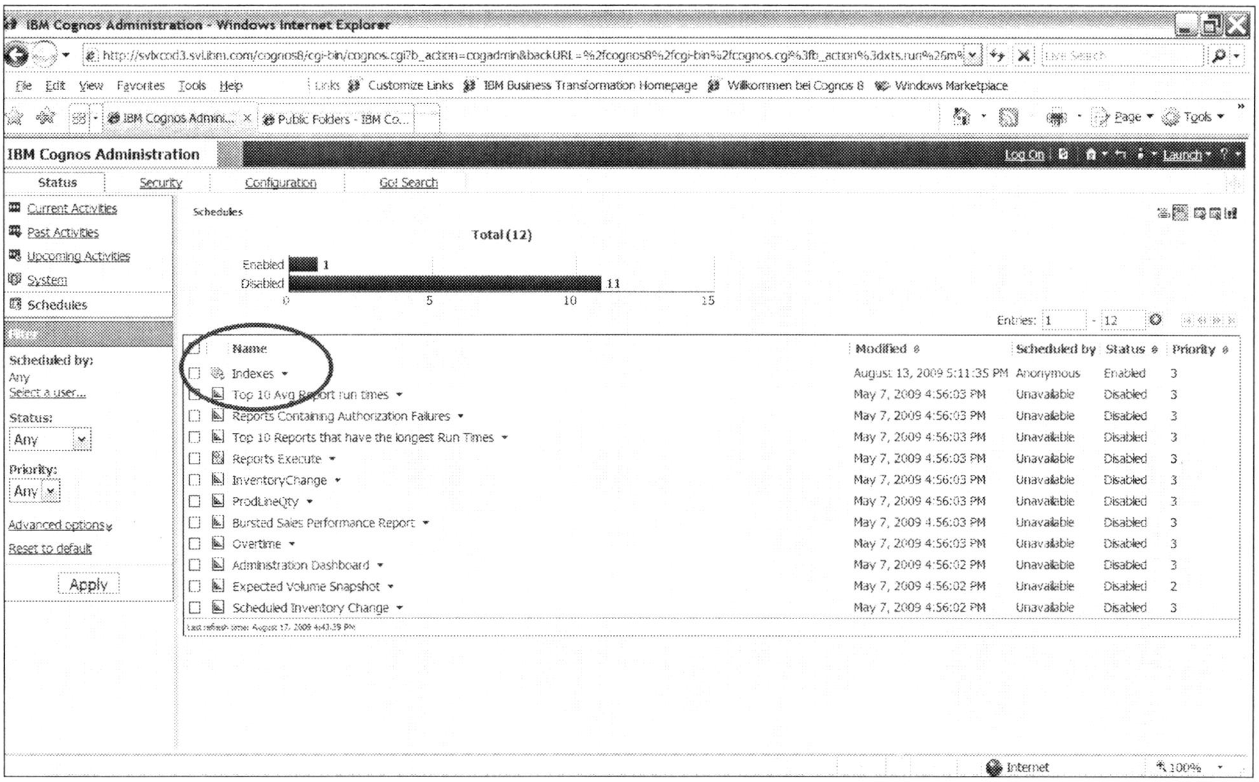

Figure 3-14 Cognos Go! Search index update schedule

In order to create a new schedule, select **Cognos Connections** → **IBM Cognos Administration** → **Configuration** and click the little icon in the right upper corner (see Figure 3-15). This action executes the index update wizard.

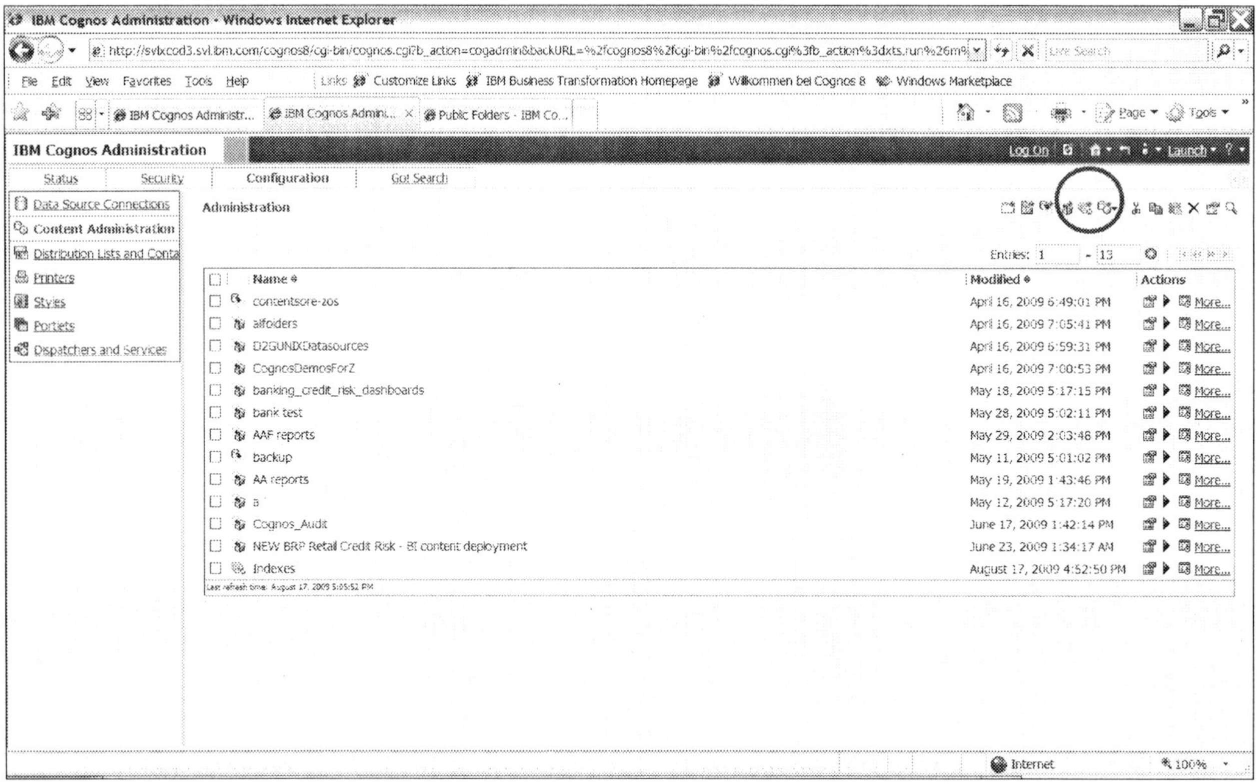

Figure 3-15 Cognos content administration for creating new index jobs

In the window shown in Figure 3-16, you can define inclusions and exclusions for packages and folders. This action makes it possible to limit the scope of the update job. For example, if certain packages are only updated monthly, then it is not efficient to re-index them on a daily schedule; you would create a second index update schedule to update those monthly packages. If you have multiple schedules, you would create multiple index update jobs and schedule them accordingly.

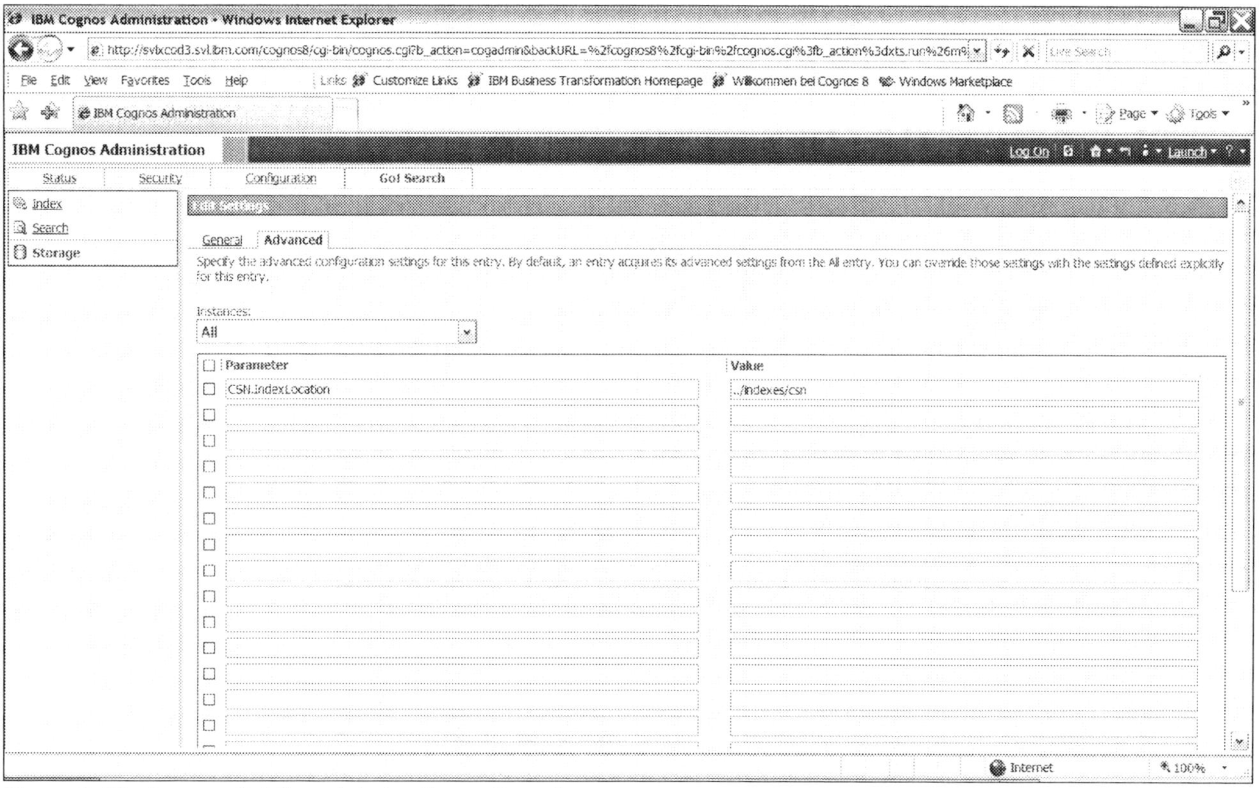

Figure 3-16 Cognos Go! Search index file configuration

3.3.3 Summary

It is generally a best practice to have a search capability that can discover Cognos content within the normal enterprise. However, the index itself takes up space and the workload from the update service itself could be considered as an additional user with the task of searching through all your folders and running reports a few thousand times, possibly on a daily basis.

This activity puts extra load on your system and increases costs. You need to make sure that the actual effort to create this index is balanced against the value that the cooperation search function provides.

You can optimize this cost / value relationship by tailoring the update cycles of the index to match the update cycles of the content. You can also reduce the scope of the index to the cooperative content and leave "private" content alone.

3.4 Cognos Go! Office

Cognos Go! Office allows you to view and consume Cognos content within MS Office products. Unlike Cognos Go! Mobile, each client must install the Cognos Go! Office product separately in their workstation. In addition, you must configure Cognos Go! Office separately for each client. An advantage over other client packages of Cognos is that Go! Office allows you to configure multiple Cognos instances (for example, you may want to consume content from both a production and a training instance of Cognos 8 BI), which can also be used in combination within one document.

For simplicity, in the context Cognos Go! Office, we refer to Word documents, Excel workbooks, and PowerPoint presentations as *documents*.

3.4.1 Setup and installation

The software prerequisites on the client side require certain versions of MS Office. Go to the following address for an up-to-date list:

http://www.ibm.com/support/docview.wss?rs=3639&uid=swg27015630

In addition, Microsoft .NET Framework Version 2.0 must be installed.

Running `setup.exe` will check for the software prerequisites and install a new toolbar in the Office products. Cognos Go! Office is controlled in Office products by this toolbar.

Refer to Figure 3-17 for an example of this toolbar.

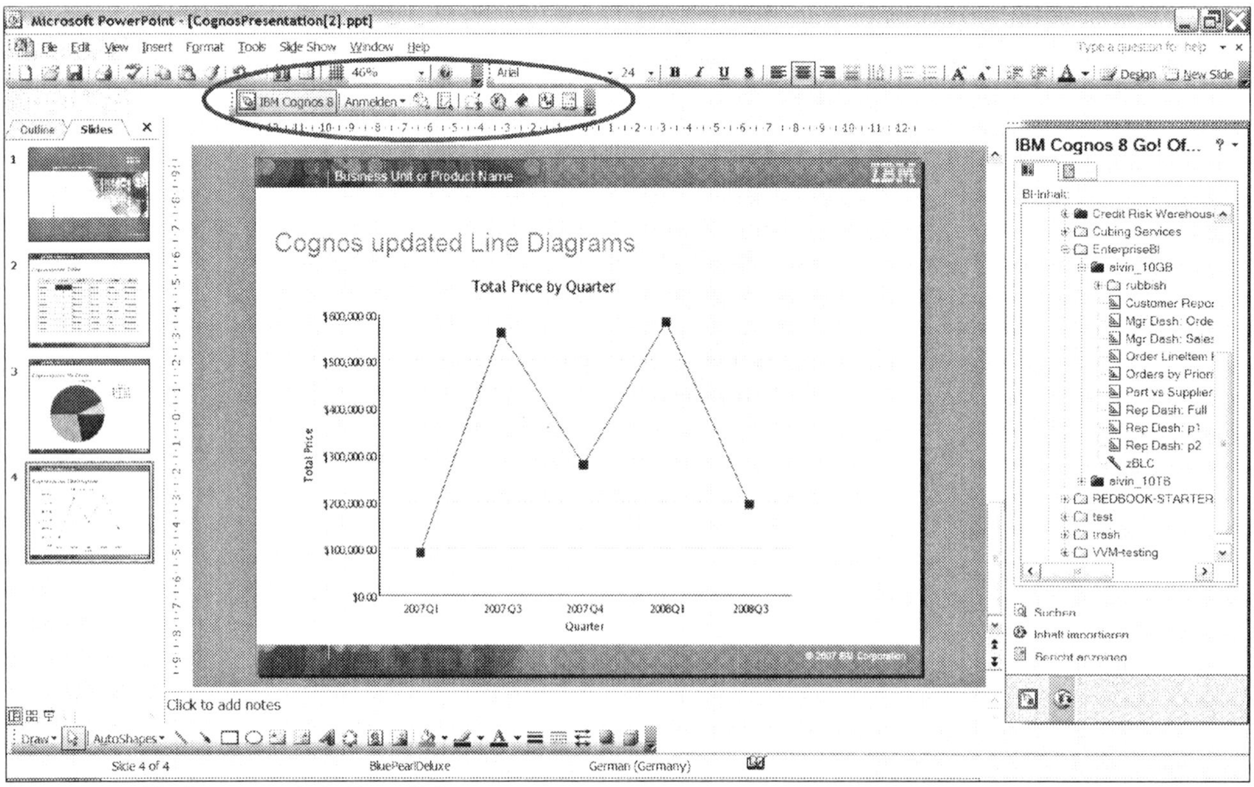

Figure 3-17 Toolbar example in PowerPoint

Because Cognos Go! Office needs to access the Cognos gateway, you need to configure the URL that leads to the gateway. In a standard installation, the URL is:

```
http://<server>/cognos8/cgi-bin/cognos.cgi
```

It is possible to configure multiple Cognos servers. Use the option button to accomplish this task (refer to Figure 3-18).

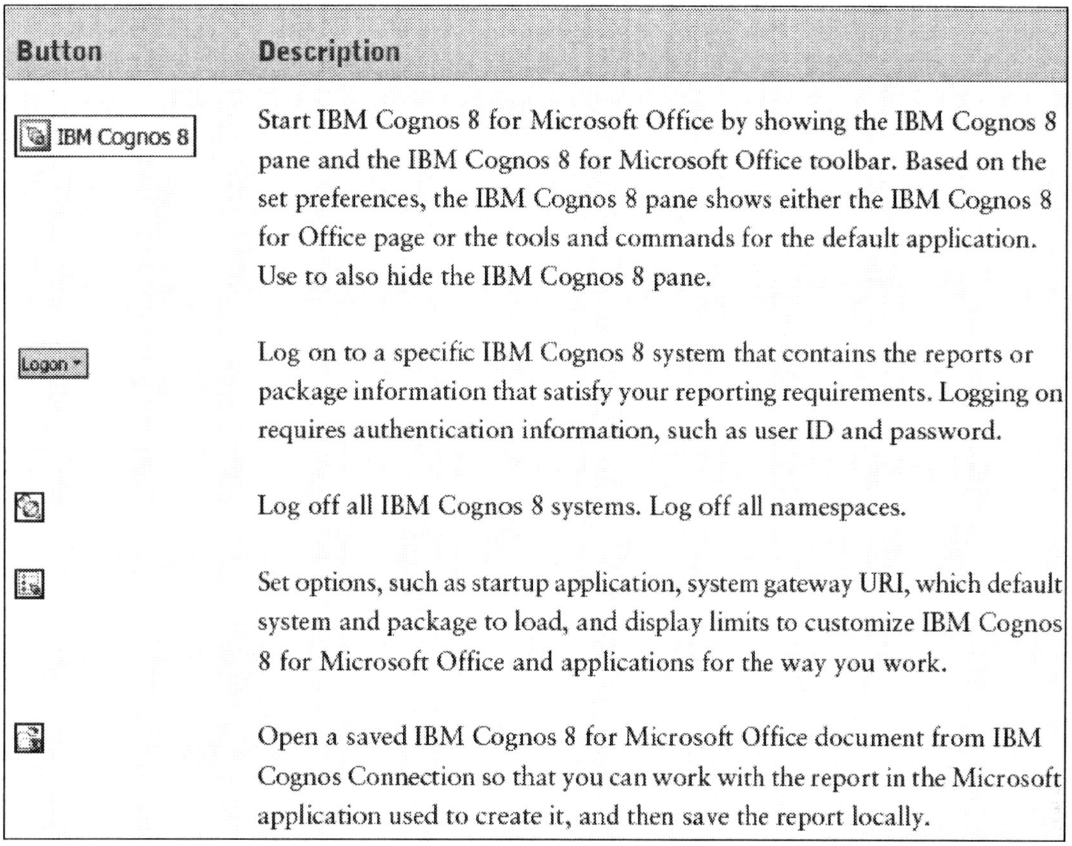

Button	Description
IBM Cognos 8	Start IBM Cognos 8 for Microsoft Office by showing the IBM Cognos 8 pane and the IBM Cognos 8 for Microsoft Office toolbar. Based on the set preferences, the IBM Cognos 8 pane shows either the IBM Cognos 8 for Office page or the tools and commands for the default application. Use to also hide the IBM Cognos 8 pane.
Logon	Log on to a specific IBM Cognos 8 system that contains the reports or package information that satisfy your reporting requirements. Logging on requires authentication information, such as user ID and password.
	Log off all IBM Cognos 8 systems. Log off all namespaces.
	Set options, such as startup application, system gateway URI, which default system and package to load, and display limits to customize IBM Cognos 8 for Microsoft Office and applications for the way you work.
	Open a saved IBM Cognos 8 for Microsoft Office document from IBM Cognos Connection so that you can work with the report in the Microsoft application used to create it, and then save the report locally.

Figure 3-18 Cognos Go! Office buttons

Clicking this button opens the Options window, shown in Figure 3-19. You can configure multiple IBM Cognos 8 servers in the IBM Cognos 8 Systems pane. Enter the gateway URL in the first field (System gateway URI) and type a name for it in the second field (Friendly name). Then click **Add**. This adds the URL of the gateway to a list of gateways that are available for use with MS documents. Click **OK**.

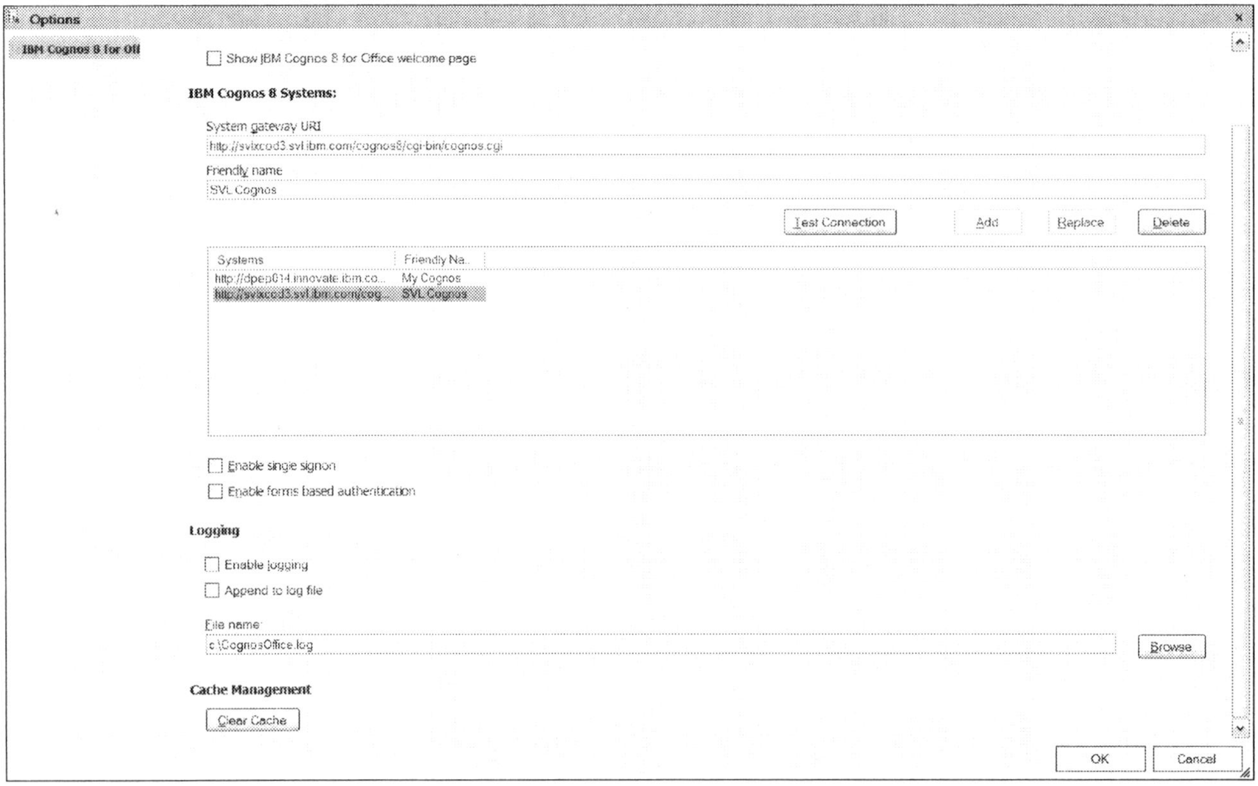

Figure 3-19 Cognos Go! Office settings page

Our scenario only contains “IBM Cognos Go! Office”. If IBM Cognos Business Intelligence Analysis is also installed, it would appear in the list as well. The same applies to the IBM Cognos 8 for Office Welcome Page, shown in Figure 3-20. Clearing the **Show IBM Cognos 8 for Office Welcome Page** check box opens the Cognos Content folder structure. The same check box exists on the Welcome window itself, right over the navigation button at the bottom of the pane, and is labeled “Show this page in Future”.

Figure 3-20 Cognos Go! Office welcome window

The two check boxes under the list of configured Cognos 8 Systems are related to the single sign-on function. If the Cognos administrator did not set up this feature on the Cognos server, then checking these boxes will lead to empty reports.

This feature is useful if you use multiple Cognos applications during the day and do not want to constantly re-authenticate. On the other hand, Cognos uses session management, which means if you are not continuously working with it, then your session times out and you need to re-authenticate.

The last section contains logging settings. This generates a log file that grows rapidly, which is, compared to the Cognos server logs, hard to read. Use this setting only if you are advised to do so by Cognos support.

Note: Do not change the Cognos Go! Office settings while an MS Office application is open and Cognos Go! is enabled. Cognos will not save the settings in this case.

3.4.2 Using Cognos Go! Office

Clicking the Cognos 8 button in the Cognos 8 toolbar (see Figure 3-7 on page 85) opens the Cognos Go! Office side bar (see Figure 3-20 on page 99). The initial view depends on your settings regarding the welcome window.

Clicking the IBM Cognos Go! Office icon opens the Cognos Content Store folder structure, as shown in Figure 3-21. Navigate through the folder structure until you find the desired object (report, query, and so on). Then drag and drop it on to the relevant MS document. Cognos enters charts and other graphics as pictures and any kind of table as tables. After Cognos inserts these objects, it is possible to rearrange them or even distribute them across slides or spreadsheets within the same document.

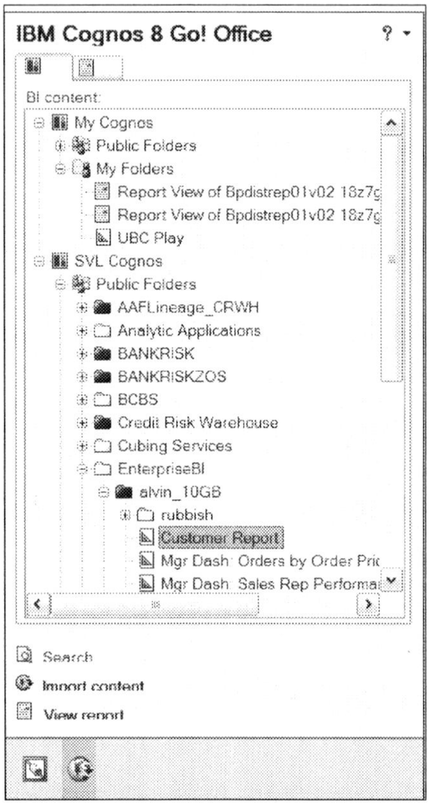

Figure 3-21 Cognos Go! Office view on Cognos content

Just as it is possible to drag and drop a Cognos object to any place in the document, it is easy to put some supportive text, picture, graphs or other objects around it. It is also possible to have the contents of multiple reports or other Cognos objects inserted into the same document.

By performing these functions, it is possible to create Cognos reports in MS Office products.

Note: There are certain design elements in Cognos objects that are not supported by Cognos Go! Office. Please refer to the section "Unsupported Report Objects and Formatting Properties", found in *IBM Cognos 8 Business Intelligence IBM Cognos 8 Go! Office User Guide.*

3.4.3 Dedicated import from parts of the Cognos report into MS documents

At the bottom of the Cognos side bar is the import button. This feature allows you to import a dedicated object from a report, define import ranges (for example, Excel A1), link prompts to Excel documents, and so on.

3.4.4 The Cognos side bar

If you select a certain report or other Cognos element, you can flip to the Imported report elements tab and inspect the properties of this object, as shown in Figure 3-22. You can see:

- What type of object it is
- Where it resides on the content store
- When it last ran
- The properties of sub items

This view makes the data very transparent, even if it is stored in MS documents.

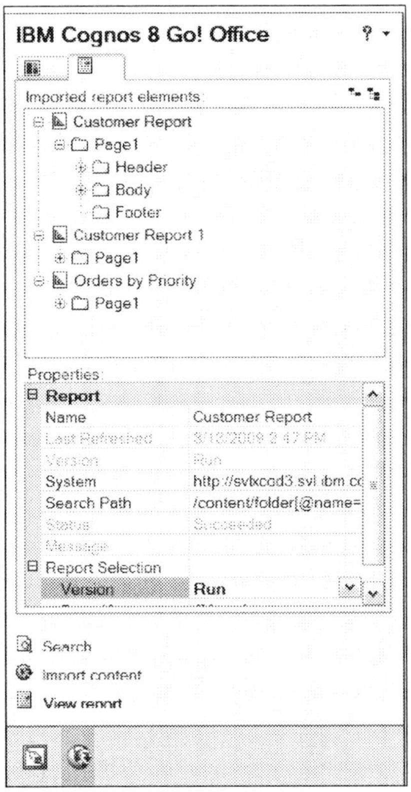

Figure 3-22 Properties of an Cognos report viewed in Cognos Go! Office

Further down on the Cognos side bar is the Search button. Clicking it opens the IBM Cognos Go! Office search window, shown in Figure 3-23.

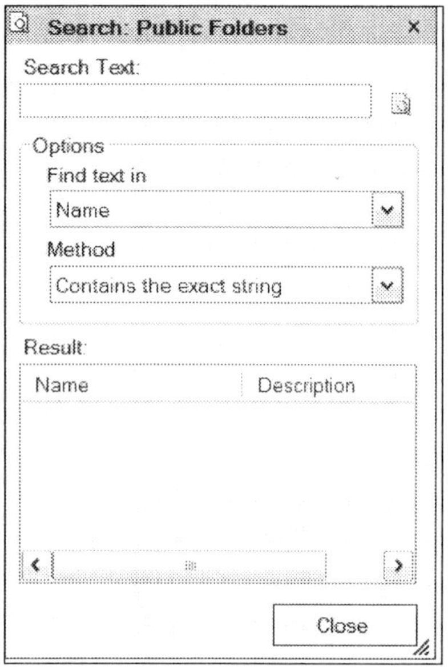

Figure 3-23 Cognos Go! Office search window

This feature is useful if you are looking for certain content in a folder or package. The Options drop-down menu allows you to select Name, Description, or Both. The Method drop-down menu allows you to select “Contains the exact string:” (equivalent to ...like “%text%”), “Begin with exact string” (equivalent to ...like “text%”), and Exact match. If IBM Cognos Go! Search is installed, then the search includes parts from the report as well. For details about this function, refer to 3.3, “Cognos Go! Search for Linux on System z” on page 84.

There is also View Report button, which runs the report in the Web browser (Cognos View) and give a preview of the content imported in Cognos.

3.4.5 The other buttons

In addition to the features of the side bar, there other buttons on the toolbar. The first three have already been discussed (the Cognos 8 button to toggle the sidebar, logon, logoff, and options).

The next two buttons must be discussed in combination. The first one is “Open documents stored in the content store” and the other one is “Publish documents to the content store (save to Cognos)”. These functions allow to you use Cognos as a sort of file server with enterprise backup capabilities and also provides versioning. Depending on your settings, endless prior versions can be kept and accessed.

The next button is “Clear data”. When this button is clicked, all table content and charts are erased. The metadata stays in the document, which means if you use the “Refresh all data” button, all the metadata reappears. Such an empty document could be used as a template or in a query.

The last button converts a Cognos enabled document to an ordinary static document, which means updates are no longer possible. You could use this function to create a document that acts as a scorecard of information that should not be updated.

3.4.6 Other features

Apart from the GUI, there is also a complete description of the API of IBM Cognos Go! Office in the *IBM Cognos 8 Business Intelligence IBM Cognos 8 Go! Office User Guide*. This allows you to use Visual Basic to script any type of desired update access behavior.

3.5 Dashboard solutions in Cognos

A dashboard in a business sense is a set interface with all the information you need to run the business or at least the business health indicators organized and presented in an easy to read format. As an analogy, if, on a car dashboard, the oil pressure decreases, then you know that there is problem and you need to fix it, but you do not necessarily know what the problem is or why it happens. In the same way, dashboards in software only display key performance indicators (KPIs), which are the gauges of business health.

Understanding the meaning of KPIs often requires other business data to measure them against. A possible example may be that if a certain KPI goes down, it is a greater concern if it just happens to the company rather than as a side effect of a general economic downturn. So the business dashboard needs gauges that indicate the general situation of business in our area.

There are multiple solutions for displaying Cognos content in a dashboard format. The simplest one is writing Cognos reports as a dashboard and use HTML items to generate interactivity. If the KPIs are separated among individual reports, you could use Cognos Connection portal pages to integrate the report and form a single interactive dashboard portal page. The IBM Cognos Family also contains a separate product called IBM Cognos Go! Dashboard to create dashboards. The same portlets displaying the content in Cognos Connection are available as installation packages for portal servers in general and WebSphere Portal Server in particular. So you could also use a portal server to generate a dashboard.

Table 3-5 provides an overview of the various dashboard options.

Table 3-5 Compare various options creating a dashboard with Cognos

	Cognos Report	**Cognos Connection page**	**Cognos Go! Dashboard**	**WebSphere Portal Server (portal server example)**
Client Installation	None.	None.	Adobe® Flash9 and Microsoft Core XML Services (MSXML) 6.0 Service Pack.	None.
Server Installation	Part of Cognos 8 BI Server.	Part of Cognos 8 BI Server.	Requires Cognos 8 BI Server and Cognos Go! Dashboard.	Requires Cognos 8 BI Server and WebSphere Portal Server.
Application Server	Cognos standard (Tomcat 4, WebSphere Application Server, and so on).	Cognos standard (Tomcat 4, WebSphere Application Server, and so on).	Cognos standard (Tomcat 4, WebSphere Application Server, and so on) and Tomcat 6, which is not supported by Cognos 8 BI Server.	WebSphere Application Server, which can run Cognos 8 BI Server and WebSphere Portal Server.
Tailoring to individual users	Requires code changes.	Change content of viewers or add / remove other portlets by changing the page layout.	The dashboard design needs to be edited.	Portlets can simply be dragged by the user out of portlet palette on the right hand side.
Cognos Content	Elements to create reports.	Reports, queries, dashboards, and so on.	Reports, queries, and parts of reports (charts and tables).	Reports, queries, dashboards, and so on.
No Cognos Content	Is generally possible using HTML items.	There is a special portlet called HTML viewer, which is the same as the RTF viewer.	There is a special portlet called HTML viewer, which is the same as the RTF viewer.	There are WebSphere Portal standard options allowing this function.

Figure 3-24 shows an example of the Cognos 8 BI Server portal page dashboard.

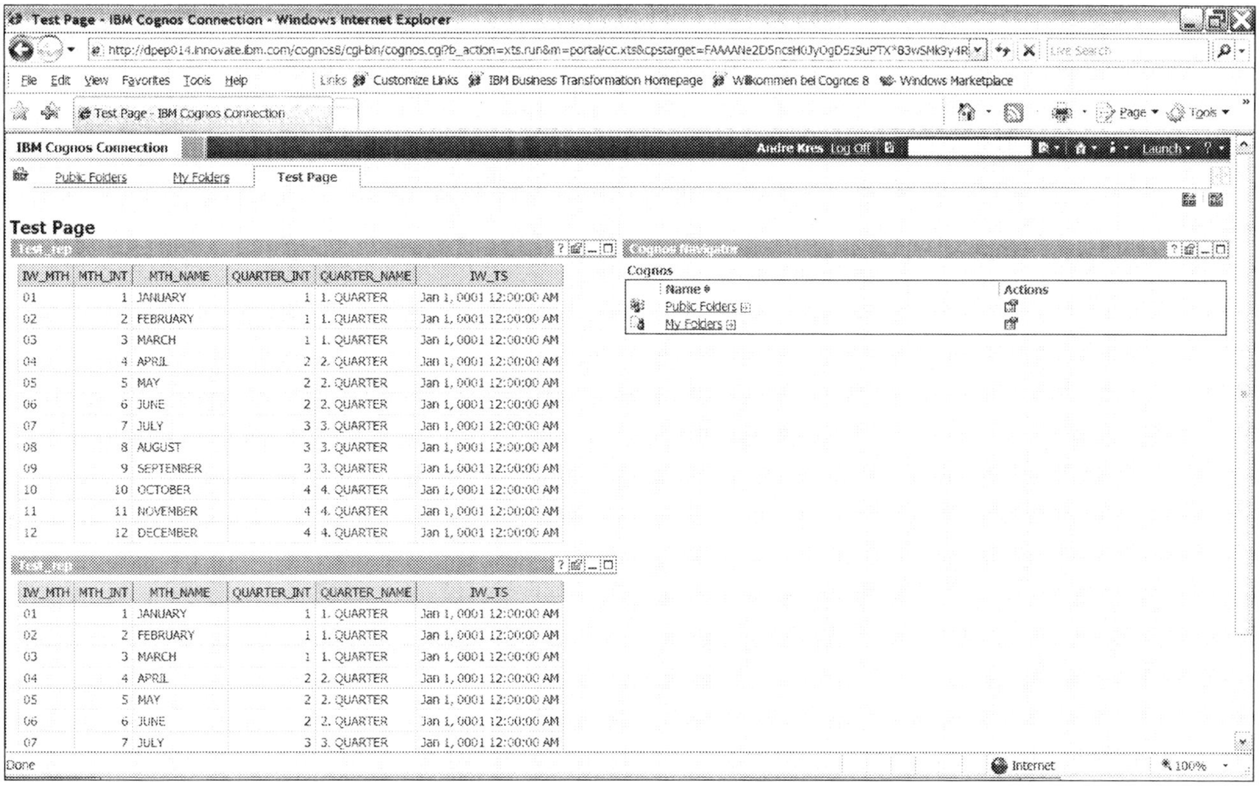

Figure 3-24 Cognos Connection portal page example for a dashboard

Figure 3-25 shows an example of a dashboard using Cognos Go! Dashboard.

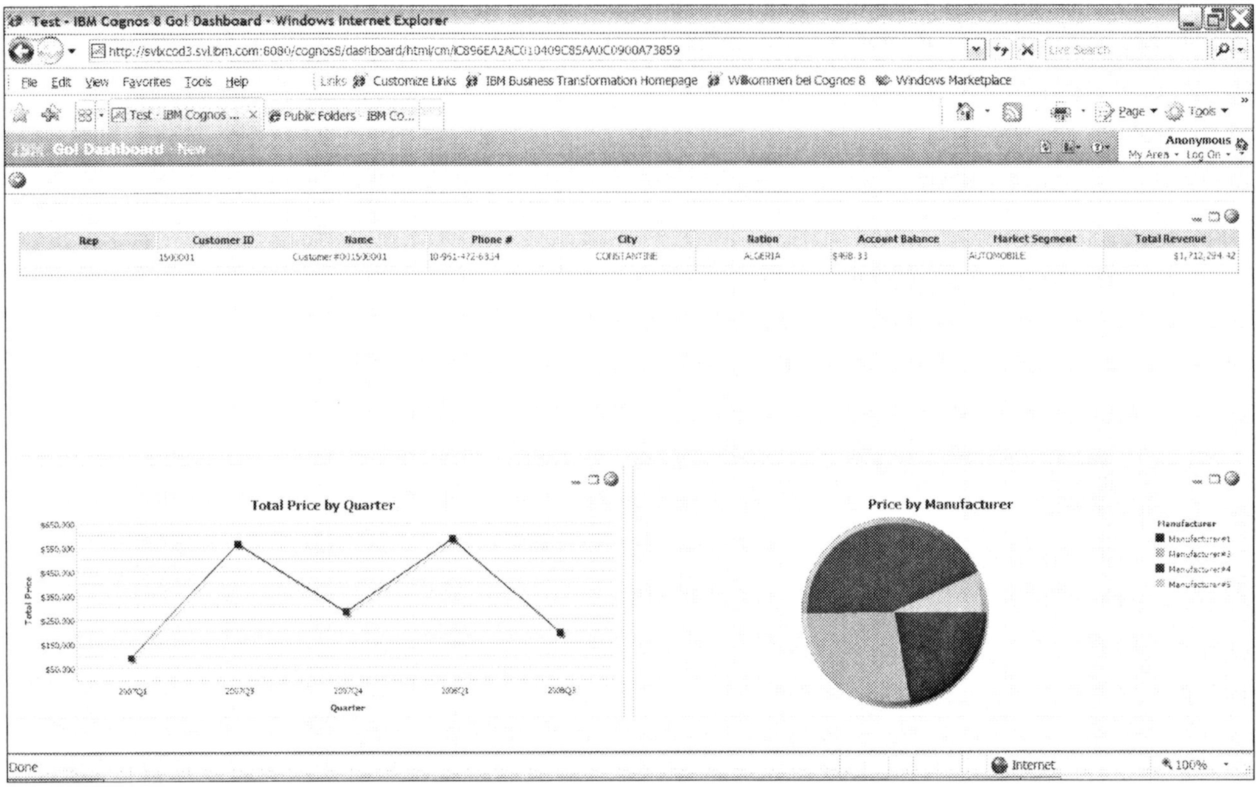

Figure 3-25 Cognos Go! Dashboard example for a dashboard

Figure 3-26 shows the WebSphere Portal Server example.

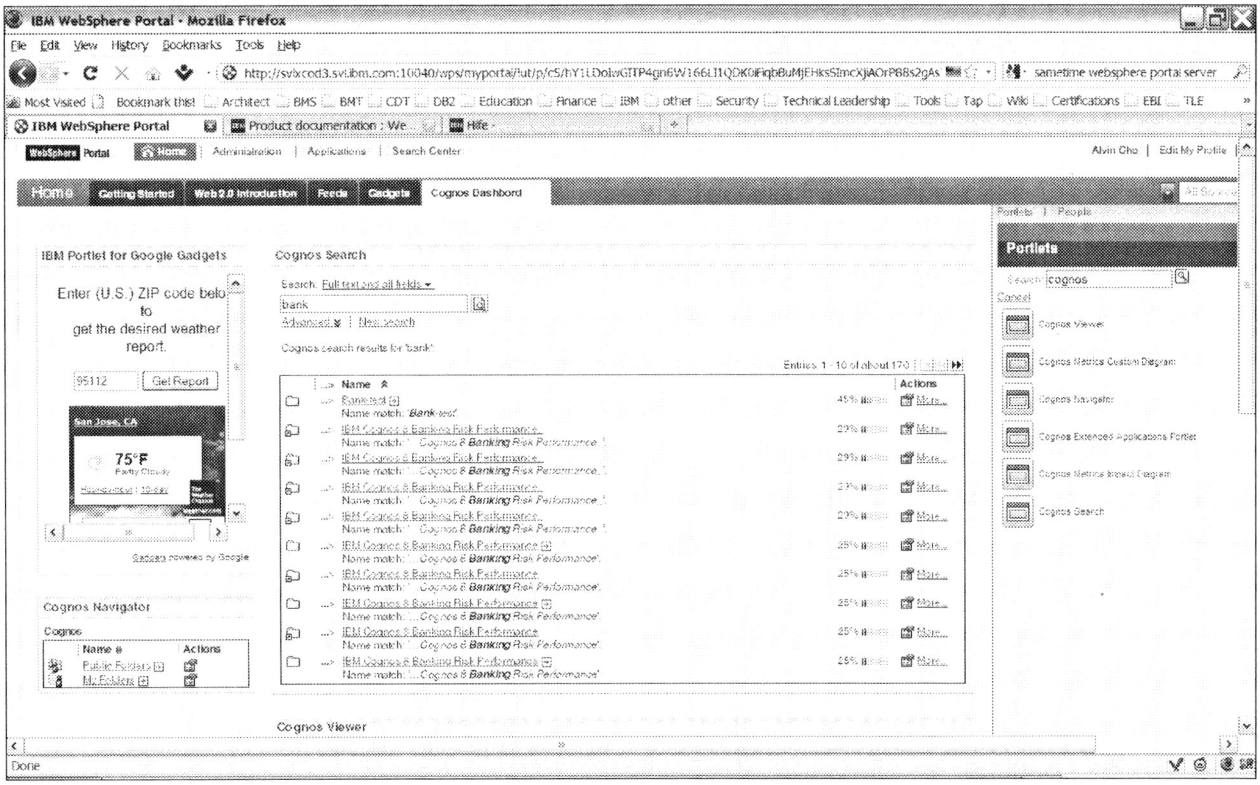

Figure 3-26 WebSphere Portal Server example of a dashboard

The weather chart is actually a Google Gadget and the integration with Sametime® mail and so on is also already preconfigured on WebSphere Portal Server. Cognos Content is added to complete the picture.

In the next section, we describe the Cognos Go! Dashboard and WebSphere Portal in a little more detail.

3.6 Cognos Go! Dashboard for Linux on System z

Cognos Go! Dashboard is a portal solution. It requires MS XML support and Adobe Flash Player on the client side. We use the most recent MS Windows versions.

Cognos Go! Dashboard generally supports the functionality of the portlets used for Cognos. The tailoring of existing dashboards in Go! Dashboard is not as easy as it is in, for example, the WebSphere Portal, where you just drag and drop content onto your page. In Cognos Go! Dashboard you need to edit the content, change the layout, and add, remove, and configure portlets to change the layout. It works well, but is not as intuitive as WebSphere Portal.

3.6.1 Prerequisites for Cognos Go! Dashboard

Any client accessing Cognos Go! Dashboard needs to have the following components installed:

- Adobe Flash 9
- Microsoft Core XML Services (MSXML) 6.0 Service Pack 1
- Microsoft Internet Explorer 6.0 or higher or Mozilla Firefox 2.x or higher

Most MS Windows clients should have these components installed, but sometimes you may need to update to the latest version of the software.

Cognos Go! Dashboard requires a completely different set of software to run on the server, which are:

- Java 1.5
- Apache Tomcat 6

Even if you already have Apache Tomcat running, you must make sure you have Version 6, because IBM Cognos Go! Dashboard will not function without it.

3.6.2 Installation

The installation itself is quite straightforward. Running the installation script installs the Web application on the application server. This application server is different from the rest of the environment, so the Cognos Application Firewall in Cognos Configuration (`/opt/cognos/c8/bin/cogconfig.sh`) needs to configured to accept requests from this external application server. Also, all instances of the dispatcher service need to be informed about this new presentation layer (you can accomplish this task by selecting **Cognos Connections** → **IBM Cognos Administration** → **Dispatcher** → **Services**). From here, add the Cognos Go! Dashboard URL to the properties of the presentation service inside the dispatcher:

- Add parameter: `WEB.GATEWAY_URI`
- Value: `http://machinename:port/context_root/dashboard/html/`

> **Note:** If you have applied V8.4 Fix Pack 1 and Fix Pack 2, instead of the `WEB.GATEWAY_URI`, you need to specify the Gateway Proxy.

To apply the configuration changes immediately, stop and then restart the dispatcher.

3.7 Cognos portlets in WebSphere Portal Server

An alternative to Cognos Go! Dashboard is deploying Cognos 8 BI Portlets on WebSphere Portal Server.

Cognos 8 BI Server provides a set of portlets ready for the deployment. These six portlets are listed in Table 3-6 on page 109.

Table 3-6 Cognos 8 BI Server portlets

Portlet	Description
Cognos Viewer	Allows you to view a report.
Cognos Navigator	Lists Cognos content.
Cognos Search	Enables Content Search on Cognos (see Go! Search).
Cognos Extended Application Portlet	Access a customer created Cognos SDK application.
Cognos Metrics Custom Diagram	Displays custom diagrams associated with a scorecard.
Cognos Impact Diagram	Displays impact diagrams associated with a metric.

All of these portlets are in a single WAR file named `/opt/cognos/c8/cps/ibm/portlets/CognosBIPortlets.war`.

Installing and configuring these portlets is just a matter of dragging and dropping them onto the portal page, just as we would for any other portlet developed for WebSphere Portal Server (see Figure 3-27). In this figure, we show a Google Gadget portlet, which shows the weather forecast of San Jose. Compared to IBM Cognos Go! Dashboard, the WebSphere Portal Server solution allows you to integrate all kinds of content.

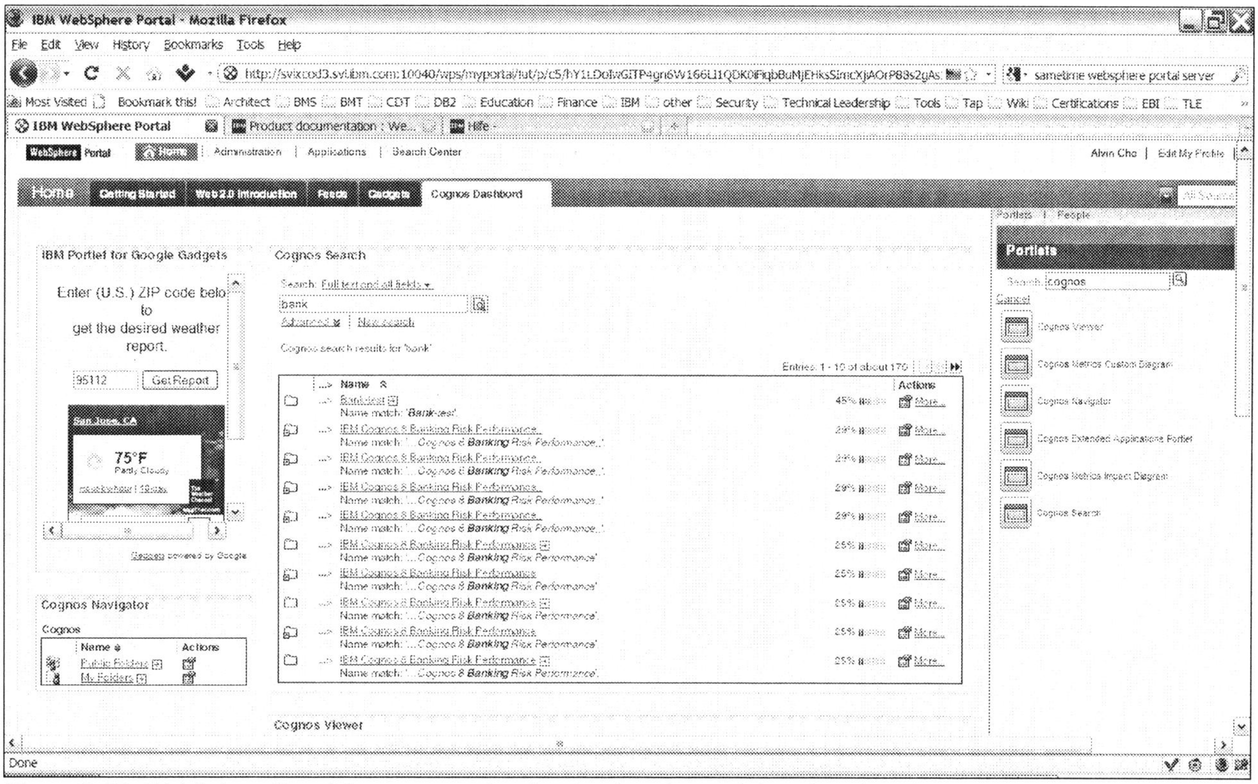

Figure 3-27 WebSphere Portal Server page showing the dragging and dropping of portlets

3.7.1 Installation

Download `<Cognos Server>/opt/cognos/c8/cps/ibm/portlets/CognosBIPortlets.war` from the Cognos server and install it on the portal. If the portal server is on the same machine as Cognos and has no security turned on, no additional configuration is necessary.

To make this setup work on a different machine, change the properties for the gateway to point to your Cognos server. Enabling security requires setting up single sign-on, which was not done in our scenario. Refer to the *Cognos Administration and Security Guide* for details about setting up single sign-on.

3.8 Data lineage from data source to report

A remarkable feature of IBM Cognos 8 BI Server from Version 8.4 onwards is data lineage. It is generally available for all packages, reports, and other content that has been developed and deployed with IBM Cognos 8 BI. You can view lineage information of a data item to see what the item represents before you add it to a report. A data item's lineage information traces the item's metadata back through the package and the package's data sources. Viewing lineage information ensures that you add the correct data items to a report. For example, you can view the lineage information of a model calculation to see how it was created.

To invoke this function, right-click any figure in a report table or chart and then click **Lineage** (see Figure 3-28).

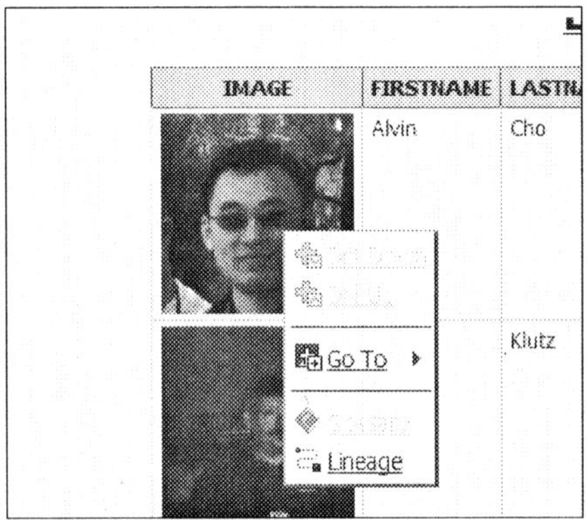

Figure 3-28 Sample for executing lineage on a Cognos report

This action opens the business view of the lineage.

The business view contains a summary of all available metadata (see Figure 3-29). It contains the owner of the report item, the package, and the database. If this information was already entered during the development of the package and report, then this could be a useful resource for the user.

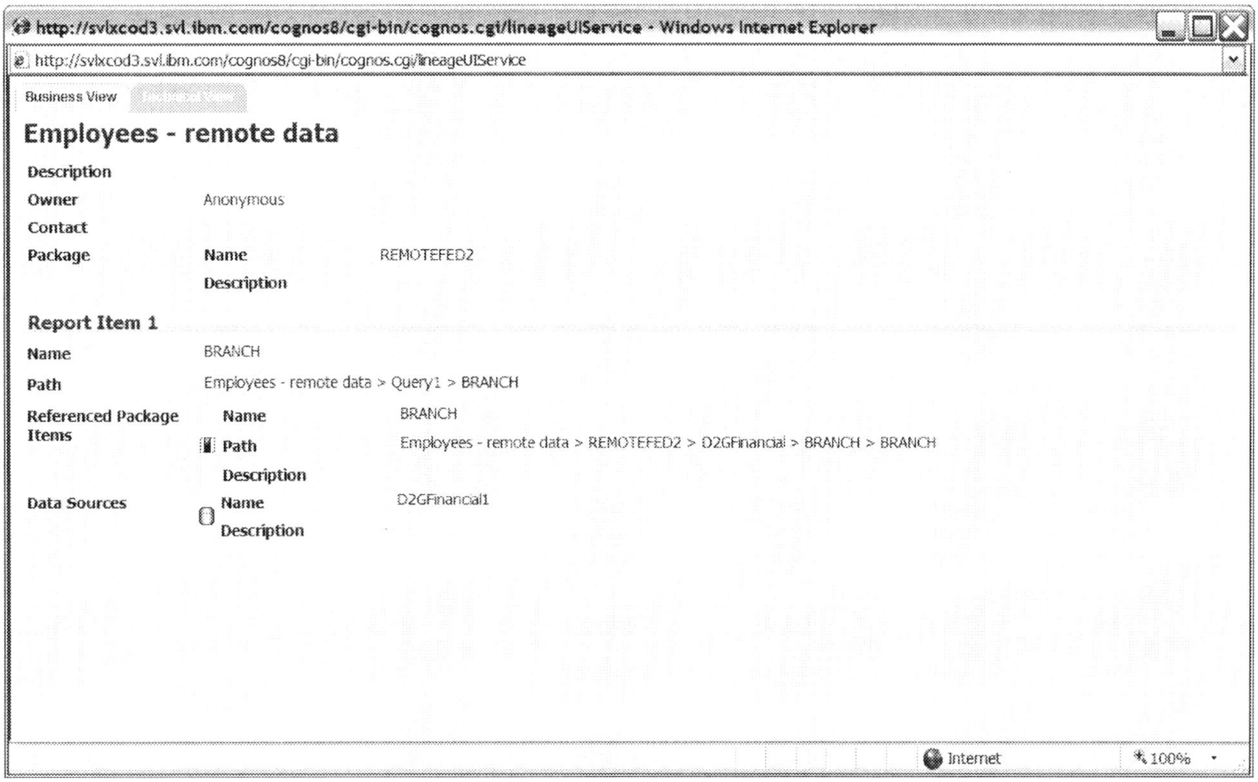

Figure 3-29 Business View of lineage data

The Technical View tab of the lineage view shows the technical details (see Figure 3-30).

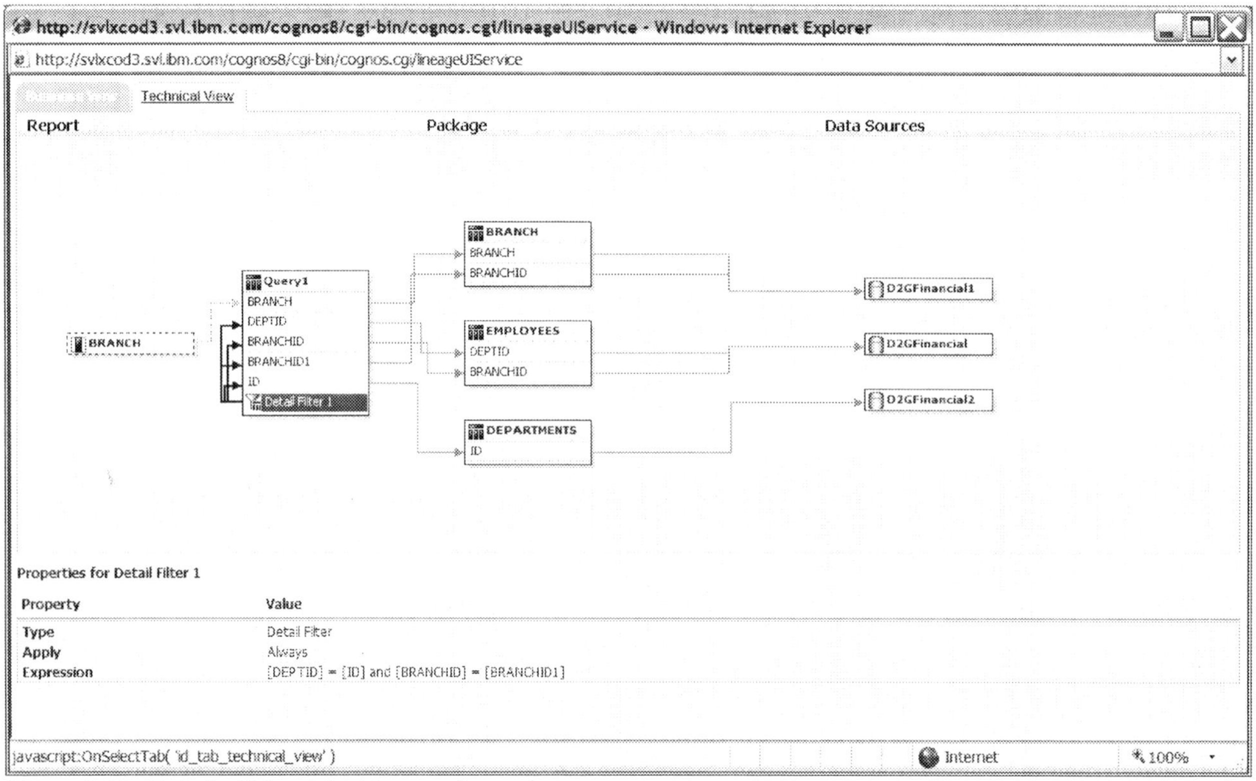

Figure 3-30 Technical View tab of lineage data

This tab gives you get an idea about the formula and source of the report item without disassembling the report.

4 Information on Demand integration

Information On Demand (IOD) is a comprehensive vision for unlocking the business value of information for competitive advantage by enabling organizations to establish and leverage trusted information to optimize business performance. Combining this vision with the IBM premier architecture and software portfolio enables the enterprise to access timely accurate information where and when the enterprise needs it. This chapter describes the value of Cognos 8 BI on Linux on System z and its relationship, synergy, and main integration points in the IBM IOD software portfolio.

IBM is committed to the IOD architecture and continues to improve the integration between IOD components.

In this chapter, we discuss the following:

- WebSphere Portal consuming Cognos content on Linux on System z.
- InfoSphere Cubing Services on Linux on System z.
- InfoSphere Information Server on Linux on System z and InfoSphere Business Glossary on Linux on System z.

4.1 Synergies between Cognos and InfoSphere components

You can gain a lot of synergy by incorporating InfoSphere components with Cognos 8 BI for Linux on System z.

For example, you can define your business terms in InfoSphere Information Server Business Glossary on Linux on System z, so that you can provide common terminology for both business users and Cognos report developers. Once the terminology is defined, it is extremely easy for any Cognos user to discover the definition of the term. The big benefit for organizations is that it leads to trusted information by providing a means for everyone to use common terminology when accessing or displaying the same piece of information. This reduces complexity and misunderstanding.

If you use the InfoSphere Business Glossary from within Cognos 8 BI, you can access the glossary from any of the following data objects in Report Studio:

- Query subject
- Query item
- Measure
- Dimension
- Hierarchy
- Level
- Property/attribute
- Top node member
- Member
- Level item

There is also synergy between the InfoSphere Warehouse on System z and Cognos 8 BI for Linux on System z because you can have your Cognos reporting functions in close proximity to the data that is being reported. This is really apparent when a report needs a large amount of data because of the ability to use HiperSockets on the System z machine. HiperSockets allows a 6 MBps connection between Cognos 8 BI for Linux on System z and the InfoSphere Warehouse on System z.

In addition, by combining Cognos with WebSphere Portal, you can easily provide trusted information through easy to create Web pages.

Other synergies between Cognos and InfoSphere include:

- The IBM Smart Analytics System is a preconfigured and optimized system that provides Business Intelligence Capabilities with Cognos 8 BI, Advanced Analytics with InfoSphere Data Mining, and a scalable Data Warehouse platform with InfoSphere Warehouse.
- InfoSphere Information Server can generate data lineage data based on DataStage jobs that allow the analysis of data lineage using Metadata Workbench from source to target. Cognos 8 BI has data lineage capabilities from report to data warehouse table/views. With the integration, Cognos data lineage data can be imported into Information Server, which allows data lineage from source to report.
- InfoSphere Warehouse Cubing Services provides large scale OLAP capabilities inside the data warehouse. Cognos can provide powerful analysis capabilities.

4.2 WebSphere portal consuming Cognos content

Cognos 8 BI for Linux on System z is easily integrated with WebSphere Portal. By integrating Cognos into your WebSphere Portal, you can easily extend the reach of IOD in your enterprise. This makes it easy to give divisions, departments, or job functions customized, easy to access, and critical business data housed inside the Cognos 8 BI system.

Before we set up Cognos within WebSphere Portal, it is necessary to deploy the Cognos portlets. Refer to 3.7, "Cognos portlets in WebSphere Portal Server" on page 108 for information about deploying these portlets.

Perform these steps:

1. The first step in adding Cognos 8 BI for Linux on System z is to decide whether to add a Cognos portlet to an existing portal page or create a totally new page. Figure 4-1 shows creating a new page. If you hover the cursor over the end of the Manage Pages menu item, you can select **New Page** from the drop-down menu.

Figure 4-1 Creating a new WebSphere Portal page

2. Figure 4-2 shows the first window for creating a new portal page. All you need to do is give the details for the creation of the new page, such as the name of the page, and then click **OK**.

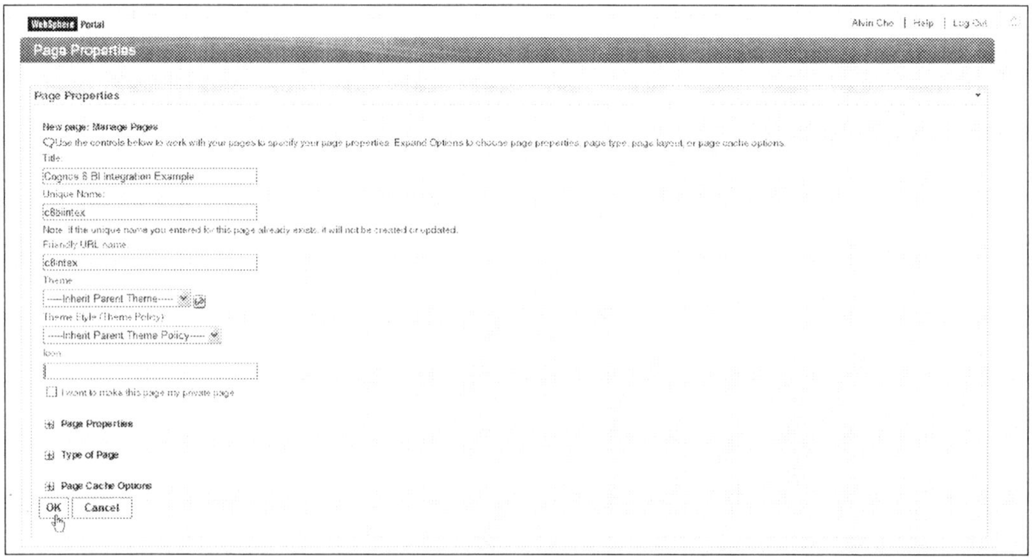

Figure 4-2 New page setup

3. Figure 4-3 shows the basic layout for the page. You can select from one of six basic layouts: either a single column on a page to a page layout with multiple columns and rows. Once you have the basic layout, you can always modify it. In this case, we choose the default, the one that looks like a whole page, then click the **Add portlets** button.

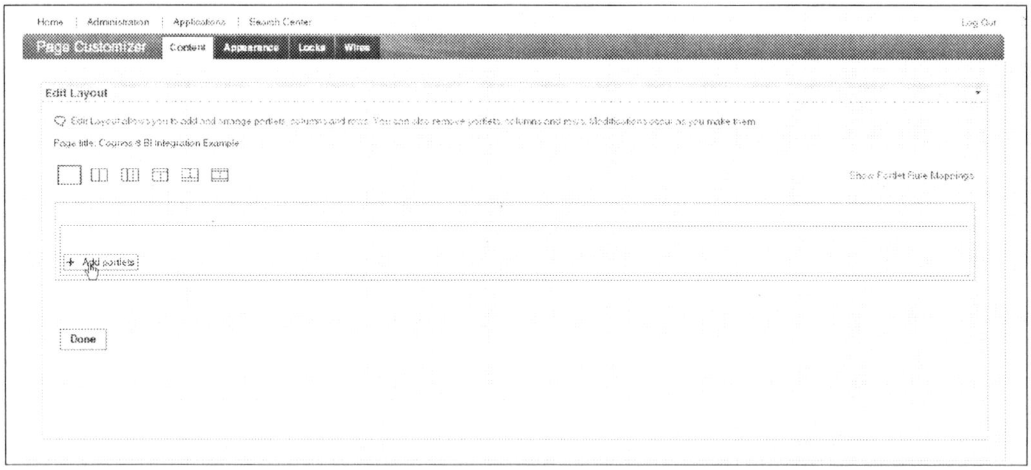

Figure 4-3 Portal page layout

4. Now it is time to add the portlets to this page. Because we chose the portal layout that has a single column, all portlets added will be the page width. In Figure 4-4, you can see the portlets that you can choose. Because there are no Cognos portlets displayed, you need to search for them. The best way to do this is to type "Cognos" in the search box and let the Search by box default to "Title starts with". Press **Search**.

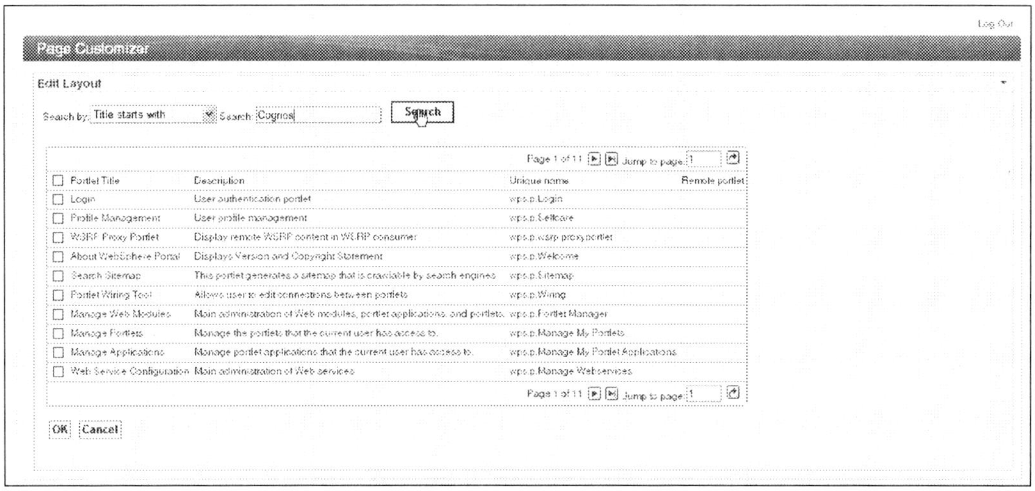

Figure 4-4 Add portlets page

5. Now that you have the search results, which are displayed in Figure 4-5, you can select the Cognos portlets you want displayed on your page. In this case, we select two portlets: Cognos Viewer and Cognos Search. Cognos Viewer allows you to view Cognos reports that have already been created. Cognos Search allows you to search through folders looking for Cognos reports and applications. Once you have selected the portlets, click **OK**.

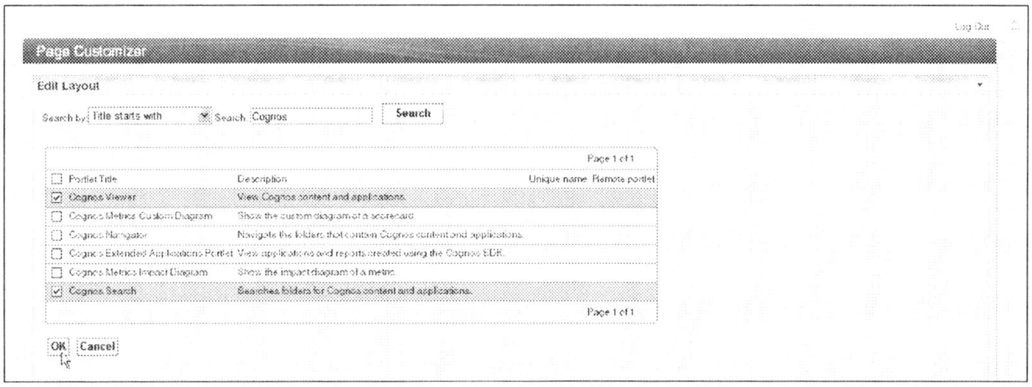

Figure 4-5 Selecting the Cognos Portlets

6. Now you can see the layout of the portlets on the page shown in Figure 4-6. This layout is based upon the layout you chose. Refer to Figure 4-3 on page 116 if you want a different layout.

Figure 4-6 Viewing the portlet layout

7. We need to configure the Cognos View portlet so that the initial report you want to view is displayed. Figure 4-7 shows how to edit the portal settings. Click the down arrow at the right most end of the portal name (in this case, it is Cognos Viewer). Then click **Edit shared settings**.

Figure 4-7 Editing portal settings

8. The next window is titled Cognos Viewer, as shown in Figure 4-8.

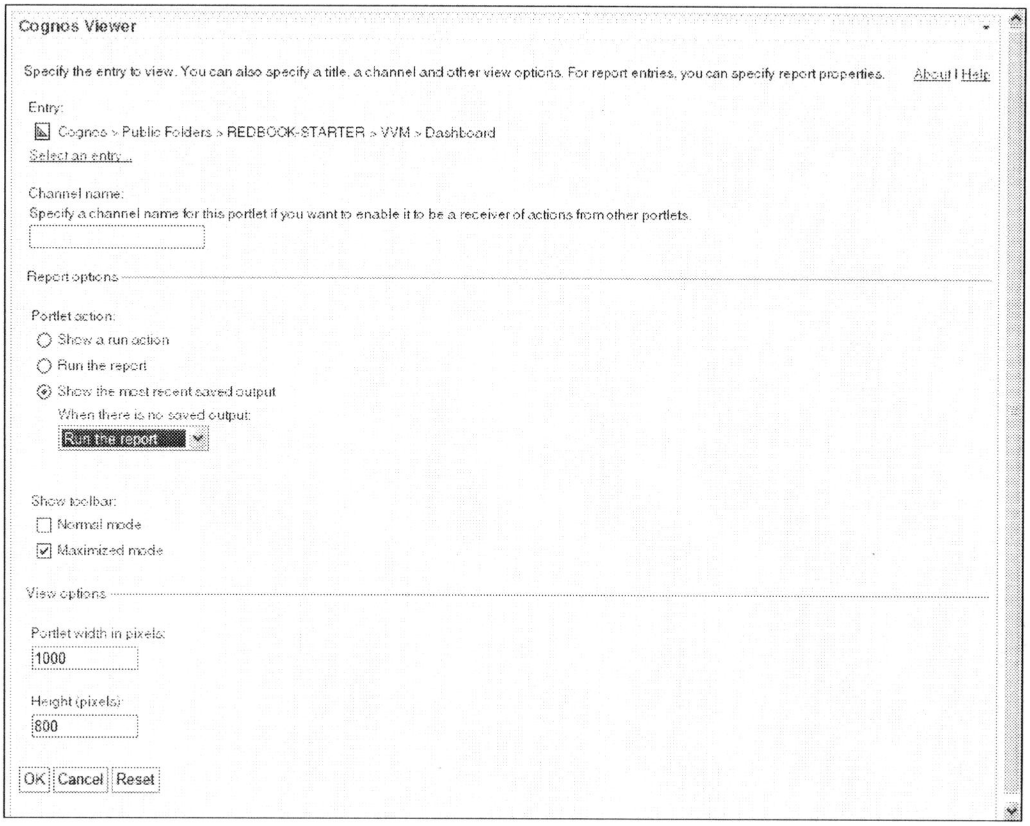

Figure 4-8 Edit portlet shared settings

In this window, you select the Cognos Report that you want to show and the action you want to take. You can choose one of three options:

a. Show a run action.

b. Run the report.

c. Show the most recent report and choose what to do if there is no saved output for the report. In this case, we select **Run the report**.

Also, you can choose the size of the portlet window. Click **OK** to continue.

9. The portal page appears. In this case, we see the Cognos report, as shown in Figure 4-9.

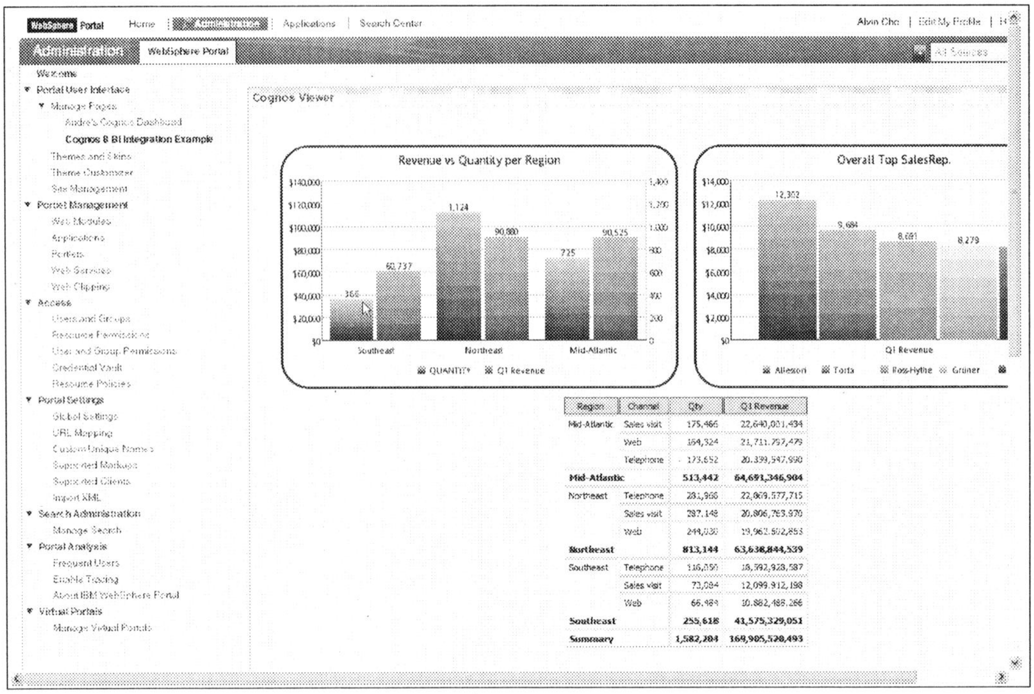

Figure 4-9 Display of Cognos report in portal page

At this point, the portal page is complete and functional.

10. Now let us discuss some advanced functions of the portal page. To maximize the Cognos Viewer portlet, click the drop-down arrow in the upper right portion of the portlet.

Refer to Figure 4-10. By selecting **Maximize**, you are able to access other Cognos functions located on the Cognos report toolbar.

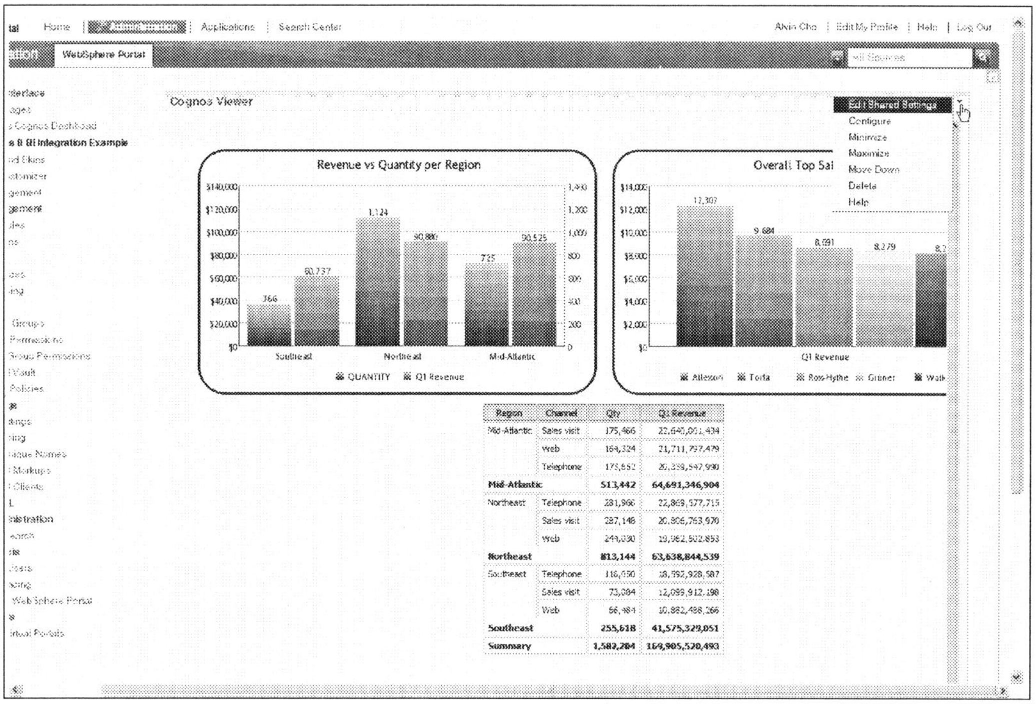

Figure 4-10 Accessing additional Cognos functions

11. Figure 4-11 shows the Cognos report toolbar. From here you can run the report and, if you so choose, you can export the report to Excel, to a PDF, or to an HTML file. Other Cognos functions are also available.

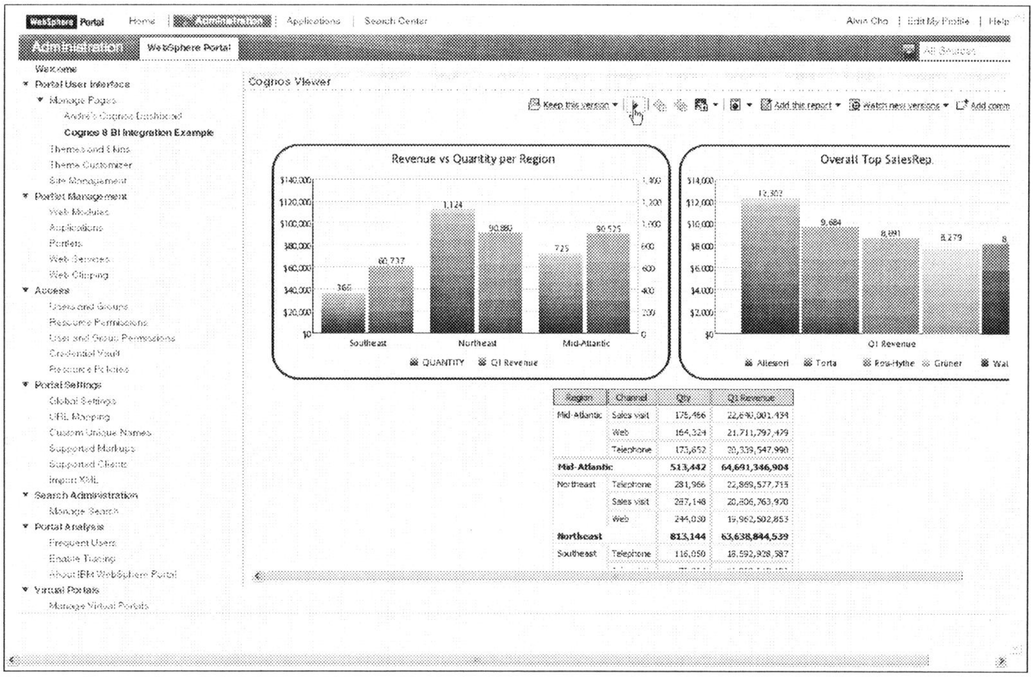

Figure 4-11 Cognos report toolbar

4.3 Using InfoSphere Cubing Services OLAP with Cognos

The InfoSphere Warehouse on System z is a prime example of IBM's dedication to delivering on the IOD architecture. For most large enterprises, a vast amount of the operational data resides on System z in databases such as IMS, DB2, VSAM, and third-party databases like IDMS, ADABAS, or CA Datacom. IBM recognizes that an enterprise can obtain significant value by co-locating a data warehouse in close proximity to the operational data.

InfoSphere Warehouse on System z was designed to move the enterprise towards dynamic data warehousing capabilities and enable the enterprise to leverage trusted accurate information through Cognos 8 BI in order to make better business decisions and gain a competitive advantage.

IBM is continuing to enhance the InfoSphere Warehouse on System z and now offers InfoSphere Cubing Services. This gives you the ability to create OLAP cubes for use in Cognos. Now there is a cubing engine co-located within close proximity to your System z data.

For instructions about how to set up an InfoSphere Cubing Services cube in Cognos, refer to 6.3, "Cubing Services overview" on page 159 and 6.4, "Cubing Services for large cubes" on page 171.

Once the cube is set up in Cognos, it is just like any other cube. In Figure 4-12, you can see the results of opening up the cube. This is extremely easy to do (just like adding any other cube to Cognos) and gives you increased functionality for your InfoSphere Warehouse on System z.

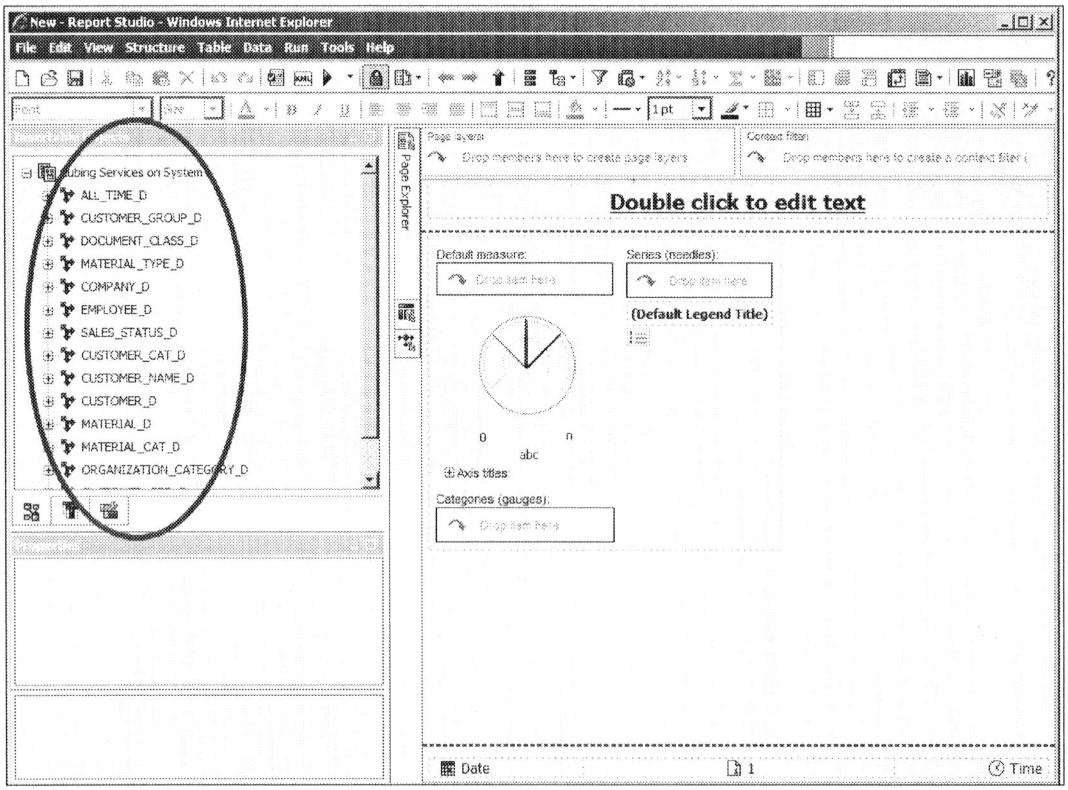

Figure 4-12 InfoSphere Cubing Services Cube displayed in Cognos

4.4 InfoSphere Business Glossary

IBM InfoSphere Business Glossary enables an enterprise to create, manage, and share a vocabulary and classification system across the organization. The Business Glossary is integrated into InfoSphere Information Server. The Metadata Workbench and Business Glossary share the same metadata repository. Cognos 8 BI integrates with the metadata repository through the Business Glossary to make it easy for a Cognos 8 BI user to access business definitions. The following figures show how easy it is to access Business Glossary from Cognos 8 BI reports.

Figure 4-13 shows the integration point. With your mouse pointer, point to a heading in a Cognos Report, right-click it, and select **Glossary**. If a matching word is found in the Business Glossary, a window will open and show the definition of the word or term.

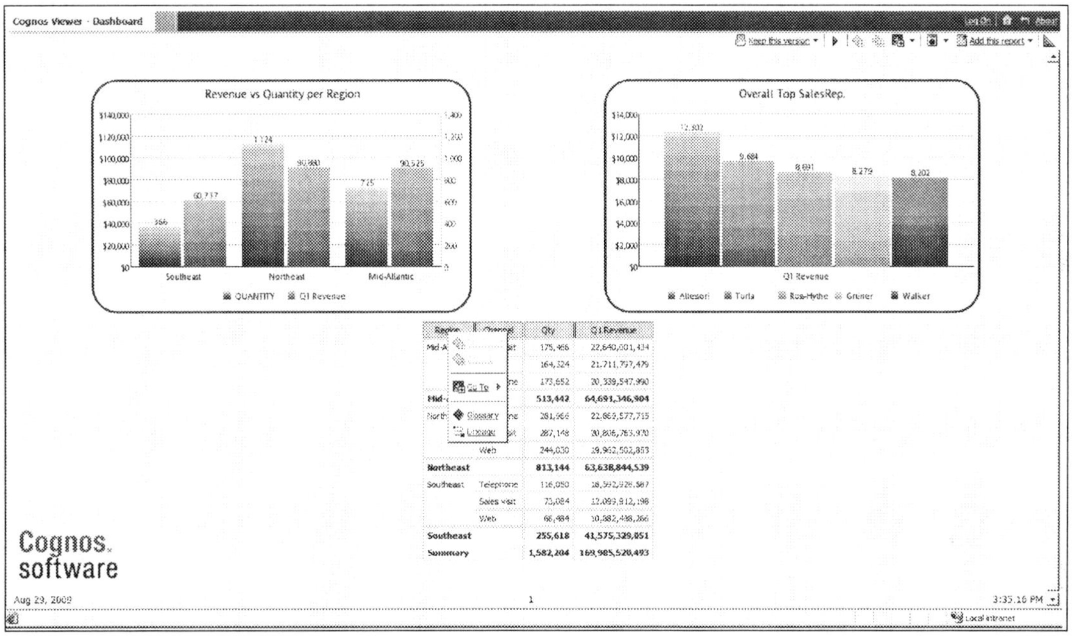

Figure 4-13 Clicking a report heading

Refer to Figure 4-14 to see an example of the window with the term definition.

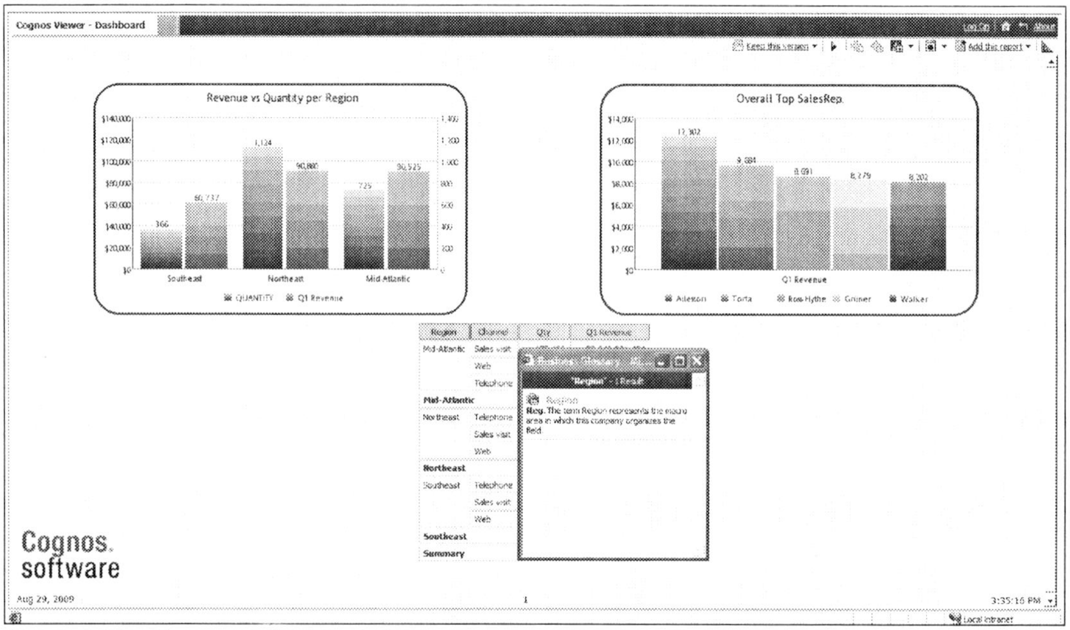

Figure 4-14 Glossary definition window

If the glossary window does not give you enough information, it is also possible to drill further down into the Business Glossary. Double-click the word or term in the dialog box. Figure 4-15 shows the window with more detailed information that opens.

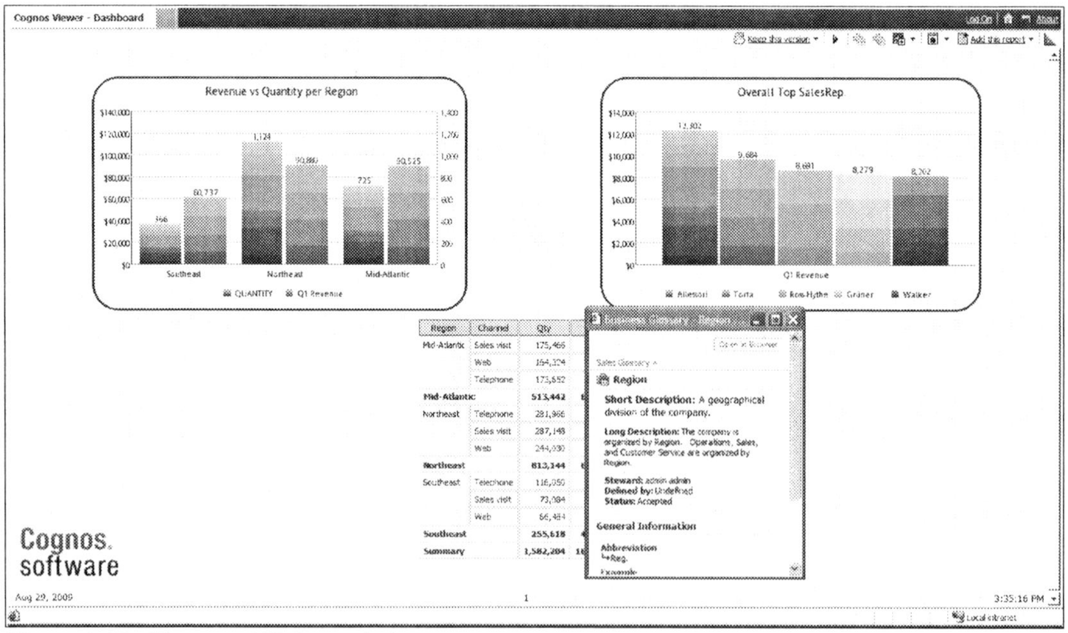

Figure 4-15 Glossary drill-down window

Sometimes, it may be necessary to discover even more information. If that is the case, then it is possible to open a Web browser in the Business Glossary. If you look closely at the top of the dialog box Figure 4-15 on page 124, you see a button that says "Open Web Browser". By clicking this link, a Web browser will open. Figure 4-16 shows the results.

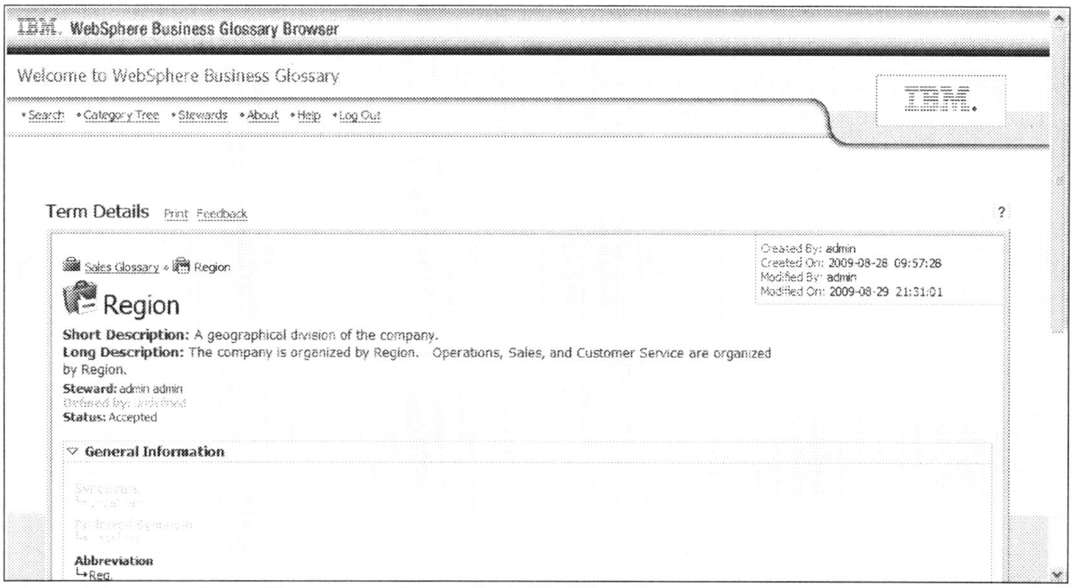

Figure 4-16 Opening a Web browser in the Business Glossary

Once the Web browser is open, there are many more functions available. It is possible to search the glossary, discover information about stewards, and discover information about categories and the ability to print the information.

The Cognos 8 integration with the InfoSphere Business Glossary is a powerful tool for employees of the enterprise to use in order to eliminate any misunderstanding about business terms. The Business Glossary and Cognos integration helps attain the IOD objective of trusted information.

For more information about Business Glossary and Cognos, go to the following address:

http://www.ibm.com/developerworks/data/library/techarticle/dm-0907metadataintegration/index.html

5

Best practices for scalability and availability

In the previous chapters, we described the component functions of Cognos 8 BI and their capabilities on Linux on System z.

In this chapter, we concentrate on how to properly package the components when building a fully scalable system with Cognos on Linux on z. We also provide recommendations about operational aspects.

For Cognos Proven Practices documentation, created by Cognos experts from real-life customer experiences in specific technology environment, refer to the following address:

http://www.ibm.com/developerworks/data/library/cognos/cognosprovenpractices.html

This chapter contains the following sections:

- General considerations
- Architectural blueprint
- Scaling of the architecture

5.1 General considerations

Before we can talk about best practises for Cognos on Linux on System z, it is important to mention again what makes System z special in comparison to other platforms.

System z is designed for business areas that require high availability and have huge workloads (for example, banks typically use System z). High availability is achieved by hardware virtualization. Linux on System z is transparent to the hard disks on which it is running. The Linux system itself just sees the size of the logical volumes.

In terms of processors and memory, it is possible to run Linux on System z on a logical partition (LPAR) with specialized Linux processors known as the Integrated Facility for Linux (IFL), a central processor (CP) dedicated to Linux workloads, either natively or as a virtual machine (VM) under z/VM. z/VM is the current virtualization technology that is designed to provide the capability for clients to run hundreds to thousands of Linux virtual servers on a single mainframe coexisting with other LPARs running System z operating systems, such as z/OS, or as a large-scale Linux-only enterprise server solution.

Running an LPAR requires you to dedicate physical memory to this particular machine. As a consequence, if the LPAR is idle, then the memory is idle too. Processors do not need to, and are usually not, dedicated.

In a z/VM environment, just the size of the virtual machine is defined, and may be easily changed. This means that a Linux on z/VM guest server can utilize up to *n* processors and up to *m* GB of memory. The total of all defined resources among all virtual machines can be higher then the total of real existing resources (memory and processors). This is called *overcommitting resources*. This is useful if not all the defined virtual Linux machines are expected to run at the same time at 100% resource utilization. In this case, the overall utilization of the System z can be increased to reduce the overall cost.

Whether you use z/VM or an LPAR to run the Linux, a single instance of Linux cannot be larger then the available resources. The resources on the IBM System z10 Enterprise Class (z10 EC) scale up to 64 processors (E64 model), 4.4 GHz CP, and from 16 GB to 1.5 TB of real memory.

In the following sections, we concentrate on vertical scaling (scale over multiple application server profiles in a single LPAR) and component distribution. If you have decided to install Linux natively (no z/VM) on a System z LPAR, the comments regarding overcommitting resources do not apply.

For more information about why and how you might want to migrate to Linux on System z, refer to *Practical Migration to Linux on System z*, SG24-7727.

5.2 Architectural blueprint

An overview of the architecture with all the main components that we have mentioned in this book is represented in Figure 5-1 on page 129. The main components are:

- DB2 Federation Server
- InfoSphere Information Server
- Virtual View Manager
- Cognos 8 BI Server

- The Cognos Family of products:
  - Go! Mobile
  - Go! Office[1]
  - Go! Search
  - Go! Dashboard

IBM WebSphere Application Server and Portal Server are considered to be middleware components and therefore included in the chart. Our general objective in this book has been leveraging the advantages of the System z platform for Cognos 8 BI. This implies that we first outline what is generally available from the Cognos 8 BI family of products as features for Linux on System z. Now this best practice architecture concentrates on defining the right components and placing them in the right place within the System z platform.

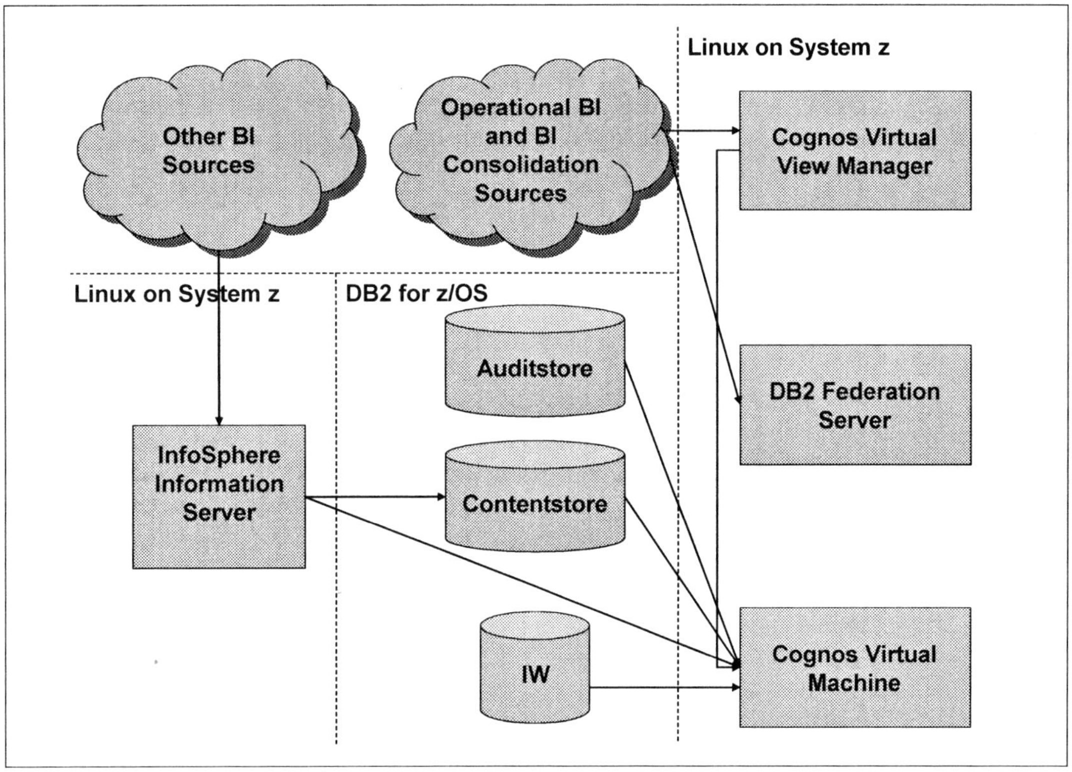

Figure 5-1 Architecture overview

In the architecture overview chart shown in Figure 5-1 there are two main areas of interest:

- On the right hand side is the Linux on System z area. It contains all the components that either are not available as z/OS native components (such as the DB2 Federation Server) or may benefit from being installed in a Linux environment.

[1] Go! Office is a client product and as such does not need special attention in terms of infrastructure planning or server sizing.

- In the middle, next to Linux on z, is the DB2 for z/OS area. The following DB2 databases can and should be hosted here:
  - Cognos Content Store[2]
  - Cognos Notification Store
  - Cognos Audit Store (Logging Database)[3]
  - Enterprise Information Warehouse (IW)

The enterprise data warehouse is the final staging area where the Business Intelligence relevant data of the company should be stored, thereby taking advantage of DB2 for z/OS synergy with System z. The largest network load is expected to happen between the data source (IW) and the report server because of the possible large amount of raw data pulled from the IW to generate the report. Some reports require huge amounts of raw data in order to be able to generate summary charts or crosstabs, which depends on the Framework Manager model. It helps if the physical location of the IW database is close to the report services.

The network traffic between report service, content store, dispatcher, and the gateway may be a single HTML page or a large number of PDF pages; this content is what the user eventually consumes.

The Cognos Go! Mobile content store currently does not run on DB2 for z/OS and requires a separate instance of DB2 for Linux, UNIX, and Windows (LUW) on Linux on System z.

The "clouds" in Figure 5-1 on page 129 represent the various types of data sources that could potentially be connected using DB2 Federation Server / Classic Federation or Virtual View Manager.

Virtual View Manager and DB2 Federation might be considered as consolidation or federation components in this architecture in case of Business Intelligence consolidation and integration of all the Business Intelligence data sources into the enterprise information warehouse. However they will likely stay as active components if the target is an operational or real-time Business Intelligence repository.

The IBM InfoSphere Information Server is one of the likely options for ETL. In this architecture it would be used to populate the information warehouse and would collect or provide metadata, which could be made available to Cognos 8 BI as business glossary or data lineage information. This integration is described in Chapter 4, "Information on Demand integration" on page 113.

Deploying these components in a separate virtual machine running Linux on System z allows us to remove them by simply removing the whole Linux instance.

Overcommitting resources such as CPU and memory allows load balancing across Linux instances when running under z/VM. On the other hand, having these components in a separate virtual Linux instance allows to adjust the virtual machine to the needs of each particular software independently from Cognos 8 BI.

[2] Go! Mobile does not support a DB2 z/OS Content Store; it uses the Cognos Content Store.

[3] Cognos Audit Store is an optional component used to store the log files in a database. The alternative is to use file system logging.

5.2.1 Cognos Java virtual machine

The Java process heap is made up by two components: the C++ (native) heap and the Java heap. Any services that have a JNI component will require the native heap. This native heap is required for Cognos authentication and content manager caching. The Java heap is required for services running in pure Java. You may increase the Java heap when scaling your application, but you must take into account that the native heap will decrease accordingly.

This maximum address space memory allocation is 2 GB for 31-bit process on Linux on System z. This translates into a Java heap size of 768 MB[4], as Java itself needs memory to work. This limit defines the number of services that can be run in one JVM. The guidelines that dictate the distribution and pairing of Cognos Services across multiple instances of application servers and profiles (JVMs) define which services need to be supported in one JVM.

A good indicator for the number of required JVMs is the number of components involved in the installation of Cognos 8 BI. These components are listed in the Cognos 8 BI installation window shown in Figure 5-2. In this case, we have shown Content Manager.

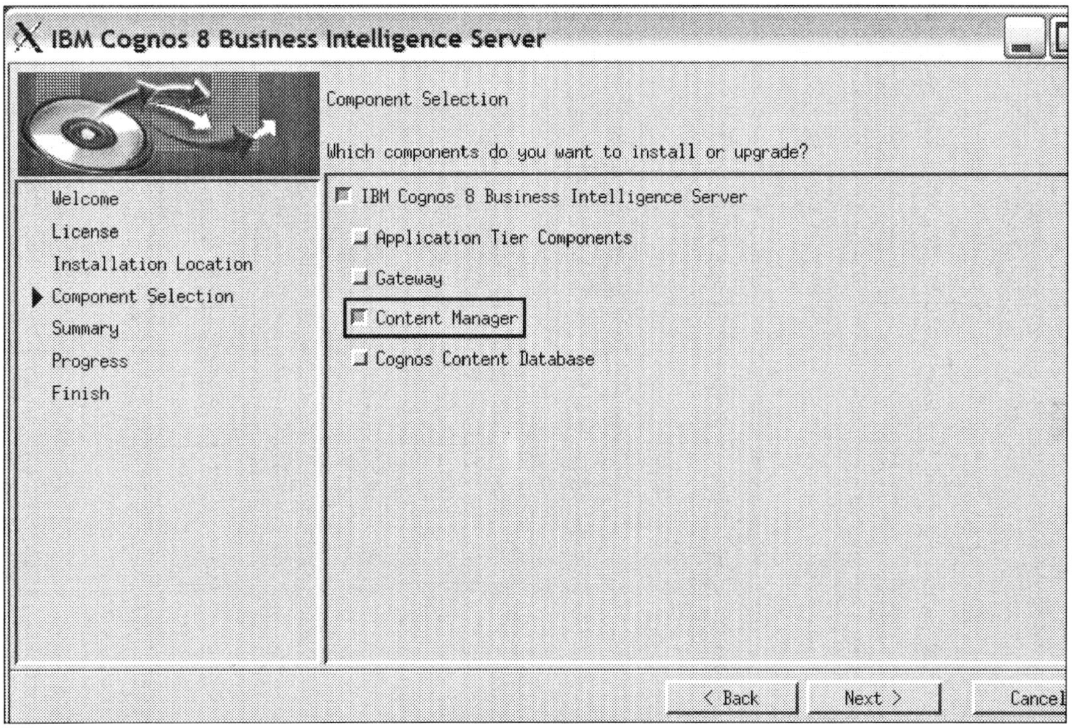

Figure 5-2 Cognos installation choice

The possible components are:

- Application Tier Components
- Gateway Manager
- Content Manager
- Content Database[5]

4 A recent WebSphere Application Server change supports a heap size up to 1.2 GB.

5 Do not install Cognos Content Database using this window. It will use Derby as the database, and this is only useful for very small systems.

It is important to note that you need to run the Cognos installation as many times as you have JVMs, but you only need to install the needed components. For the Content Manager, check **Content Manager** in the installation and clear all the other ones. For Gateway, check only the **Gateway** and **Application Tier Components**. All tiers and services must have a dispatcher to communicate with the other components.

If you create multiple JVMs for the same type of component, for example, multiple ones for report servers (Application Tier Components) then you still need to run the Cognos installation and configuration as many times as you have JVMs.

From the automation point of view, it is possible to capture the installation responses in a response file, which can then can be applied to a silent installation. The same process applies to the configuration, that is, it is possible to export a configuration and apply it silently to a Cognos instance (Gateway, Content Manager, or Content Database). The only challenge with silent configurations is the variation of port numbers, which must be unique per guest or LPAR when scaling vertically in a single server.

This translates in the 3-tier level view described in Figure 5-3. The Cognos Gateway generally provides the connection between the user and Cognos services. The Content Manager manages the metadata, and the dispatchers start all Cognos 8 services and route requests to the various services to perform the actual data retrieval, report processing, security, and systems monitoring.

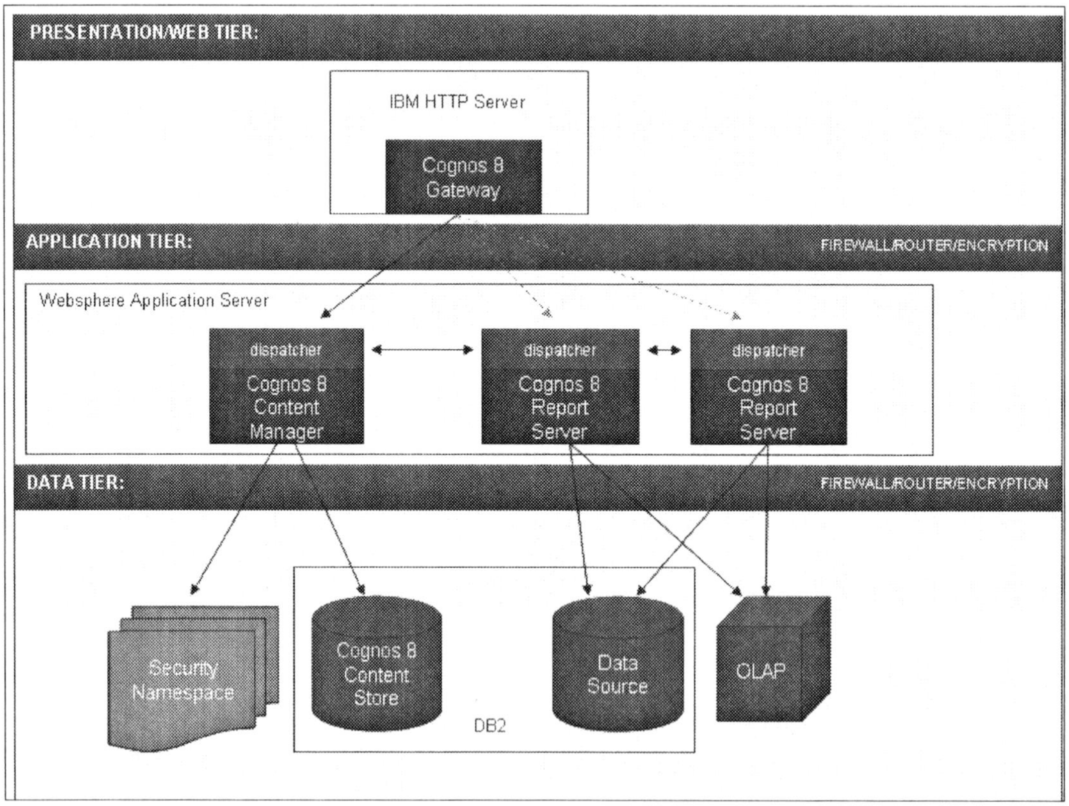

Figure 5-3 Cognos components: tier model

Gateway

The Gateway is the presentation tier component. It is the central communication point between HTTP Server and the remaining Cognos components. To avoid unnecessary cross system communication between Linux instances, it is wise to have one Gateway for each HTTP server.

Another reason to have multiple Gateways is the need for multiple authentication methods called *namespaces* in Cognos. One example is the case where you want to deliver the same Cognos instance data to your employees and business partners. In this case, you probably have an intranet authentication method for your employees (intranet ID) and an Internet authentication method for your business partners (Web Identity).

You can configure both namespaces in a single Cognos instance, but with a single Gateway architecture, any user (employee or business partner) would be asked which one of the two authentication methods is needed. This may not be desirable, especially in the case of a business partner portal.

As a namespace for authentication is a property of the Gateway configuration, multiple Gateways could be used to customize the authentication for the users.

Content Manager

The Content Manager is one of the application tier components and a key component in the Cognos infrastructure because it manages the metadata for reports and saved reports. As there can only be one Content Manager active in one Cognos instance, for maximum scalability we recommend placing this service in its own JVM.

Although there can be only one Content Manager in the Cognos instance active at a time, it is possible to have multiple Content Managers installed. The other Content Managers can be set to “stand by”, allowing hot failover in case the active Content Manager disappears, for planned or unplanned unavailability.

Dispatcher

The dispatcher is the other application tier component (as referred to by the Cognos 8 BI installation). The dispatcher manages the actual services and supports the communication to the Gateway and Content Manager. You can see the dispatcher as kind of framing interface for all services running in Cognos. There is no service without a dispatcher.

On the other hand, not every dispatcher needs to have all services installed, which allows you to reduce the load within one single JVM. If you decide to distribute services across dispatchers, make sure that at least one instance of all needed services exists somewhere on one of the dispatchers.

Report services

The report services include the batch report service, report data service, and report service.

The setting to adjust the amount of these processes in the Report Service setting is called “*Maximum number processes for report services*, and it defines how many report servers can be associated with each report service. There are two settings; one for peak time and one for off peak time. The peak time setting needs to be defined and, if you are running in a global environment, then there is no real peak time but just load differences caused by different user populations in terms of activity (such as headquarters versus branch office users).

The recommendations is generally 1.3 to 1.7 GB RAM per virtual CPU on Content Manager and Report Server instances for report servers with two BIBus processes per CPU and five threads per process (four for low affinity and one for high affinity).

For details about scalability, go to the following address:

`http://www.ibm.com/support/techdocs/atsmastr.nsf/WebIndex/WP101437`

Other BI services

Besides the report services, which creates the PDF or HTML files, there is also the presentation service, which is used for navigation of the portal and translating rendered output from the content store to the browser.

Refer to *IBM Cognos 8 Business Intelligence Architecture and Deployment Guide* for a comprehensive list of all Cognos services.

Go! Mobile services

The Go! Mobile services belong to the Cognos Go! Mobile package described in 3.2, "Cognos Go! Mobile for Linux on System z" on page 78. It is therefore not a Cognos 8 BI server core function. These services convert output of report services into consumables for mobile users using BlackBerry, Symbian, or Windows Mobile smartphones. They need to have access to the Cognos 8 content store. Although Cognos in general is a service-oriented and event driven architecture, the Go! Mobile services will definitely work best with the report services in the same JVM or dispatcher. You may want to consider using advanced routing to improve the response time for your Go! Mobile user's by providing some isolation for them from your workstation users.

Advanced routing assigns group names to dispatchers, users, and packages. With advanced routing, it is possible to route requests of special user groups (mobile user) and package groups (Framework Manager models) to special groups of dispatchers.

> **Note:** The installation of Go! Mobile requires the Cognos 8 BI Server installation directory. This does not necessarily mean the Content Manager; it could be any of the installation directories from Gateway to dispatcher. The dispatcher is the preferred location.

Index update service

Another service that interacts with the report services is the index update server of the Cognos Go! Search package described in 3.3, "Cognos Go! Search for Linux on System z" on page 84. It is run during the update cycle of the search index. It gives its content to the index data service, which takes care of storing the results. As it is able to index report contents, it needs access to report services and needs to be deployed with report services.

Although you might not be interested in indexing report content and you disable running a report in the Go! Search configuration, the configuration will still need access to the report services because it evaluates whether user searching would be able get results with this report. Some Framework Manager models may implement a row level security (row level security is implemented using security filters on query items in the framework model.) For example, a German user may only be allowed to see German data in a Cognos Package containing worldwide data.

We recommend that the relationship between report and index update services be two report services to one index update service.

If you run your environment in a geographical area with only one time zone and only a single culture in terms of weekends and public holidays, then you can simply schedule the index update during the night or the weekend. In this case, you might not need to look at distribution issues surrounding reports, Go! Mobile, and the index update service, as your whole report services could be dedicated to updating the index.

But if you are running in a global company with users around the whole world, you do not have common public holidays, weekends, or nights. In this case, you might consider dedicated capacity for report services for the index update service. Cognos would use this capacity for peak load balancing as needed in other areas.

Index search service

This service is used by the user to search for reports. This service interfaces with the index data service to obtain information. From a packaging perspective, it needs to be packaged with the index data service. If you use shared the index data service with the index update service, then you have the same dependencies as the index update service. This means that you need to package it together with report services.

This common dependency on the index data service leads to resource competition in this area. In a single time zone environment, the index update service runs at night or during weekends and the index search service runs during the business day. In a globally distributed environment both may run at the same time.

Index Data Service

The Index Data Service is the disk I/O daemon for the index search and index update service. So it needs to provide capacity for both. In a single time zone environment this means that index update service runs at night and index search service during the day. As a result the index data service needs to be adjusted to the higher of the two services in terms of load.

In a globally distributed environment without weekends and nights, the sizing of the index data service is the sum of the index update and index search services.

5.2.2 Cognos Go! Dashboard

We highly recommend that you install the Version 8.4 Fix Pack 2 or later on the IBM Cognos 8 BI server and Go! Dashboards before you install Go! Dashboards itself. With Fix Pack1 and 2, Cognos Go! Dashboard is installed on top of an existing Cognos 8 Application and resides behind the Cognos 8 gateway.

Fix Pack 2 is required if you plan to install Cognos as a WebSphere application. For more information, refer to the *IBM Cognos 8 Go! Dashboard FP1 and FP2 Companion Guide*, which can be found at the following address:

`http://www.ibm.com/developerworks/data/library/cognos/page420.html`

5.3 Scaling of the architecture

We have described the architecture in 5.2, "Architectural blueprint" on page 128.

For DB2 for z/OS based components, which are the enterprise information warehouse (IW), Cognos content store, and Cognos audit store, a great deal of best practice information about how to monitor and scale these parts already exists. For most data centers running DB2 for z/OS, this is just business as usual. We do not need to go into detail about this topic. What is worth mentioning is that a performance problem on the Cognos content and audit store will cause all kinds of problems in Cognos itself, so the DB2 for z/OS and Cognos on Linux on System z teams need to work together. The System z team is likely working independently of the other platforms, so they especially need to be informed about working together with the other teams.

The transition components DB2 Federation Server and DB2 Classic Federation and Cognos Virtual View Manager run in their Linux on z instance and can be scaled at the system level. This means that if Linux runs out of resources (CPU, memory, or disk space) you can just add what resource is needed. The same applies for Cognos Go! Dashboard if it is deployed to a different Linux on z instance. Scaling Cognos 8 BI Server and all the components recently added by the Cognos Family of products for System z is a topic that has not be developed much, so we try to explain it further in this section.

5.3.1 Initial setup of a scalable Cognos 8 BI Server instance

In 5.2.1, "Cognos Java virtual machine" on page 131, we see the components of the Cognos 8 BI Server and how they need to be packaged together.

A typical Cognos 8 BI request would be as follows;

1. The user issues a service request (such as navigating in the portal, running a report, and so on) on the HTTP server. This routes the request to the Cognos Gateway.
2. The Gateway passes the request to the Cognos dispatcher.

The dispatcher will route the request to the content manager's dispatcher, which will then confirm that the user has permission to perform this action. A passport will be issued for the session. If the request is a report run, then confirmation of an available report server is made. If the request is for navigation, then an available portal service is identified. The goal is to load balance the request. If all services are busy then the request is queued. There can only be one Content Manager on a single Cognos instance. Even though the Cognos instance can be spread across JVMs, physical computers, or even networks, the properties "talking to a single Content Manager" implicitly define the term "Cognos instance". You can have one standby content manager service per JVM, but only one active content manager service per instance.

This means that the Content Manager component is not horizontally nor vertically scalable across JVMs or application servers. In order to provide the Content Manager with maximum resources, it need to be deployed into a separate WebSphere Application Server Profile. This leads to a dedicated Java process with the full 2 GB of memory.

An HTTP server (IHS) and Cognos Gateway are in one package, as each HTTP request needs to be handled by the Cognos Gateway. If you scale the HTTP server, it is wise to have the Cognos Gateway scaled along with it.

The dispatcher contains a set of Cognos 8 BI services and depending on the overall installation, requirements may contain index services and Go! Mobile services or a combination of them.

Although within a Application Tier Installation of Cognos 8 BI Server all services are installed in the Cognos installation directory (`/opt/cognos/c8_rs1/`), they do not need to be all enabled and deployed in the application server profile. It is possible, for example, on a second or third report server, to just enable a few services (like the report services, batch report service, and report data service) to enlarge capacity on particular services. The dispatcher managing this selection of services is aware of its capabilities and registers them with the Content Manager. Cognos is smart enough to route requests to the dispatcher, which runs the services to deal with this type of request.

You create in WebSphere Application Server an individual profile for each component and deploy the Enterprise ARchive (EAR) file you created in Configuration Manager on it. Starting all the components should lead to a working environment. Be sure to manage the size of the JVMs in WebSphere Application Server; they are set up for each component individually.

Cognos provides a script called create_profile.sh, which generates a WebSphere Application Server Profile in `<installation directory>/C8SE`. This is shown in Figure 5-4.

```
svlxcod3:/opt/cognos/c8_rsv/C8SE # ./create_profile.sh c8_rsv
Where is IBM WebSphere installed to?
Input a directory, or hit enter to accept /opt/IBM/WebSphere:

Using /opt/IBM/WebSphere as IBM WebSphere location.

Generating new portdef.props file.

Input 'y' to review or edit the generated portdef.props file,
or anything else to proceed:


Executing the following command:
/opt/IBM/WebSphere/AppServer/bin/manageprofiles.sh -create -profileName c8_rsv
-profilePath /opt/IBM/WebSphere/AppServer/profiles/c8_rsv -templatePath
/opt/IBM/WebSphere/AppServer/profileTemplates/default/ -portsFile
/tmp/create_profile.sh.28487/portdef.props


manageprofiles.sh completed successfully.

To start the c8_rsv server profile, run the following command:
/opt/IBM/WebSphere/AppServer/profiles/c8_rsv/bin/startServer.sh server1

When the server has started, it can be tested via the URL:
http://svlxcod3:9255/admin
```

Figure 5-4 Sample WebSphere Application Server Profile creation script in Cognos

The only parameter is the profile name. During the installation, the procedure asks for the WebSphere installation directory and it allows you to review the `portdef.props` file. The `portdef.props` file is located in the properties folder of the WebSphere Application Server Profile. It contains the port number necessary for the Cognos Configuration as well as for the Administration Console. This Console is important for the installation of the Java part of Cognos, the WebSphere Application, where you can deploy (install) the EAR file produced by cogconfig. For more information about deploying Cognos on WebSphere in more detail, refer to *IBM Cognos 8 Business Intelligence Installation and Configuration Guide.*

5.3.2 Monitoring and scaling in Cognos for Linux on z

There are multiple levels of monitoring, which are illustrated by the layer model in Figure 5-5. The kernel is Linux on System z, the WebSphere Application Server encompasses it, and Cognos with its services encompasses both of them.

We examine the possible levels:

- Linux level
- WebSphere Application Server level
- Cognos Packages level
- Cognos Monitor level

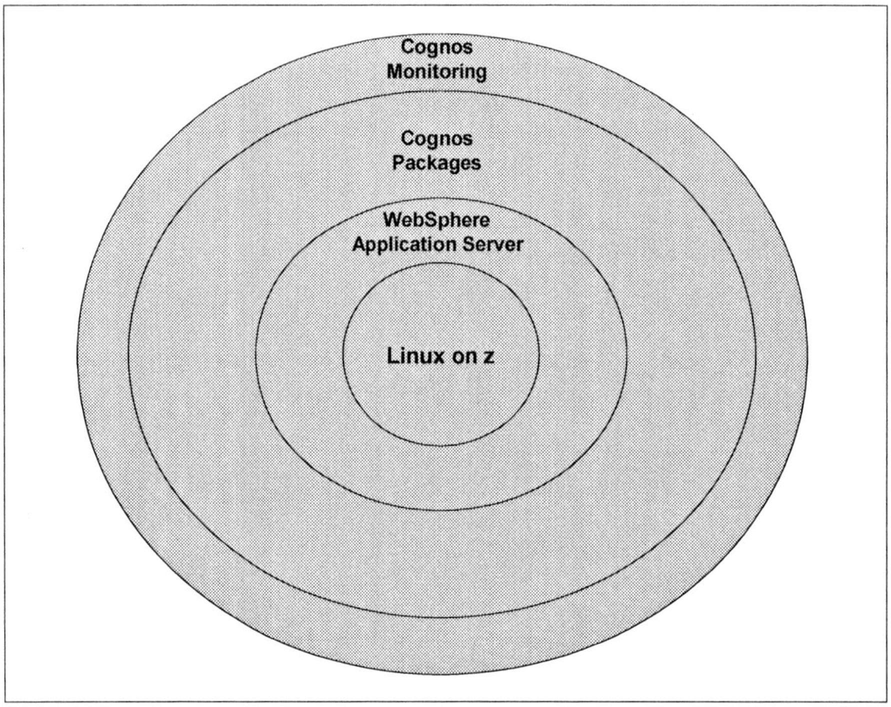

Figure 5-5 Layer model explaining of monitoring and scaling

Linux level

Obviously the size of Linux defines the space that allows for the growth of the other components. As Linux runs in a virtual environment, growing is just a matter of redefining parameters. Assuming that you have, in the beginning, a small group of users, you might start with one to two processors and 2 to 4 GB of memory. As the user community grows, you monitor memory and CPU usage and add resources.

Adding more memory requires rebooting Linux. This causes a Cognos outage. The only way to get around this situation is to create a small maintenance version of Cognos. This second Linux on z instance must have all components to run Cognos, that is, Content Manager, Gateway, and a dispatcher need to be installed. Depending on the expected workload during the outage, the environment could be in a single JVM or distributed, as with a production instance. So, when there is maintenance, you start this second instance, set the Content Manager on hot standby, and shut down you main Linux on z instance running Cognos. This will cause the standby Content Manager to become active and instantly take over the reporting.

For a smooth transition, you can have Cognos Administration shut down after the last transaction. Content Manager is in its own JVM for this reason. This technique would be only used when Content Manager needs more memory.

Presumably, you will not do maintenance during a peak load window, so this second Linux instance could be fairly small and only booted when needed.

Assuming that Linux is under good monitoring management and has a standby instance, we now look at the next layer.

WebSphere Application Server level

Both Java heap and native heap make up the Java process heap space, so specifying the Java heap size determines both heaps. Different Cognos services typically have different requirements for Java versus native heap. Cognos recommends setting the Java heap to not more than 768 MB for Content Manager or 512 MB for dispatcher. Dispatcher with report services will run better with a 512 MB heap size, as this allows Java room for I/O buffers.

You can scale this layer by adding more application server profiles (JVMs) and deploying services to it.

As mentioned in 5.3.1, "Initial setup of a scalable Cognos 8 BI Server instance" on page 136, there can only be one active Content Manager.

Regarding Gateway services, the major bottleneck in this package is actually the HTTP server. Whenever the HTTP runs out of capacity, you need to install a new HTTP server on a new Linux on z instance, add another WebSphere Application Server, and install the Cognos Gateway on it.

In order to scale the report services, you add another server profile to the WebSphere Application Server, which adds automatically a new JVM, which can be by itself scaled to 2 GB. Deploy this profile on the dispatcher, as described in 5.2.1, "Cognos Java virtual machine" on page 131 and run it. As soon as it is up and running, Cognos will balance the load across all existing dispatchers. Depending on your particular need, this dispatcher might only the report services enabled.

In order to check that a Java process is not going to run out of memory, you need to watch the size of the process memory on the system monitor. You can view the size of the virtual engine by running a query on the process ID. Use the following command:

```
PS -ef | Java
```

This lists all processes running Java on your machine. Figure 5-6 shows a sample drawn from our test system. When you run this command, pick one running one of your JVMs. In our case, the profile cognos8 is in bold.

```
root      22897      1 21 17:05 ?        00:03:37 /opt/IBM/WebSphere/AppServer/java/bin/java
-Declipse.security -Dwas.status.socket=43799 -Dosgi.install.area=/opt/IBM/WebSphere/AppServer
-Dosgi.configuration.area=/opt/IBM/WebSphere/AppServer/profiles/cognos8/configuration
-Djava.awt.headless=true -Dosgi.framework.extensions=com.ibm.cds
-Xshareclasses:name=webspherev61_%g,groupAccess,nonFatal -Xscmx50M
-Xbootclasspath/p:/opt/IBM/WebSphere/AppServer/java/jre/lib/ext/ibmorb.jar:/opt/IBM/WebSphere/AppSe
rver/java/jre/lib/ext/ibmext.jar:/opt/IBM/itcam/WebSphere/DC/toolkit/lib/bcm-bootstrap.jar:/opt/IBM
/itcam/WebSphere/DC/itcamdc/lib/ppe.probe-bootstrap.jar -classpath
/opt/IBM/WebSphere/AppServer/profiles/cognos8/properties:/opt/IBM/WebSphere/AppServer/properties:/o
pt/IBM/WebSphere/AppServer/lib/startup.jar:/opt/IBM/WebSphere/AppServer/lib/bootstrap.jar:/opt/IBM/
WebSphere/AppServer/lib/j2ee.jar:/opt/IBM/WebSphere/AppServer/lib/lmproxy.jar:/opt/IBM/WebSphere/Ap
pServer/lib/urlprotocols.jar:/opt/IBM/WebSphere/AppServer/deploytool/itp/batchboot.jar:/opt/IBM/Web
Sphere/AppServer/deploytool/itp/batch2.jar:/opt/IBM/WebSphere/AppServer/java/lib/tools.jar
-Dibm.websphere.internalClassAccessMode=allow -Xms256m -Xmx896m
-Dws.ext.dirs=/opt/IBM/WebSphere/AppServer/java/lib:/opt/IBM/WebSphere/AppServer/profiles/cognos8/c
lasses:/opt/IBM/WebSphere/AppServer/classes:/opt/IBM/WebSphere/AppServer/lib:/opt/IBM/WebSphere/App
Server/installedChannels:/opt/IBM/WebSphere/AppServer/lib/ext:/opt/IBM/WebSphere/AppServer/web/help
:/opt/IBM/WebSphere/AppServer/deploytool/itp/plugins/com.ibm.etools.ejbdeploy/runtime
-Dderby.system.home=/opt/IBM/WebSphere/AppServer/derby
-Dcom.ibm.itp.location=/opt/IBM/WebSphere/AppServer/bin -Djava.util.logging.configureByServer=true
-Duser.install.root=/opt/IBM/WebSphere/AppServer/profiles/cognos8
-Djavax.management.builder.initial=com.ibm.ws.management.PlatformMBeanServerBuilder
-Dwas.install.root=/opt/IBM/WebSphere/AppServer
-Dpython.cachedir=/opt/IBM/WebSphere/AppServer/profiles/cognos8/temp/cachedir
-Djava.util.logging.manager=com.ibm.ws.bootstrap.WsLogManager
-Dserver.root=/opt/IBM/WebSphere/AppServer/profiles/cognos8
-Dam.home=/opt/IBM/itcam/WebSphere/DC/itcamdc
-agentlib:am_ibm_15=/opt/IBM/itcam/WebSphere/DC/runtime/was61.svlxcod3Node02.server1/ -verbosegc
-Xverbosegclog:/opt/IBM/WebSphere/AppServer/profiles/cognos8/logs/server1/itcam_dc_gclog.log
-Xtrace
-Djava.security.auth.login.config=/opt/IBM/WebSphere/AppServer/profiles/cognos8/properties/wsjaas.c
onf
-Djava.security.policy=/opt/IBM/itcam/WebSphere/DC/runtime/was61.svlxcod3Node02.server1/was61.svlxc
od3Node02.server1.datacollector.policy com.ibm.wsspi.bootstrap.WSPreLauncher -nosplash -application
com.ibm.ws.bootstrap.WSLauncher com.ibm.ws.runtime.WsServer
/opt/IBM/WebSphere/AppServer/profiles/cognos8/config svlxcod3Node02Cell svlxcod3Node02 server1
```

Figure 5-6 PS -ef | grep Java: how to find the Java processes

Note the process ID (PID) right after the user starting the process (in our case, root). The process ID in our case is 22897.

If you run **cat /proc/<pid>/status**, you can see all the information about this process. This is shown in the sample output in Figure 5-7.

```
svlxcod3:~ # cat /proc/22897/status
Name:   java
State:  S (sleeping)
SleepAVG:       85%
Tgid:   22897
Pid:    22897
PPid:   1
TracerPid:      0
Uid:    0       0       0       0
Gid:    0       0       0       0
FDSize: 1024
Groups: 0
VmPeak:  1303924 kB
VmSize:  1303892 kB
VmLck:         0 kB
VmHWM:    589428 kB
VmRSS:    589428 kB
VmData:  1197248 kB
VmStk:        92 kB
VmExe:        60 kB
VmLib:     48888 kB
VmPTE:      1376 kB
Threads:        220
SigQ:   0/24576
SigPnd: 0000000000000000
ShdPnd: 0000000000000000
SigBlk: 0000000000000000
SigIgn: 0000000000301000
SigCgt: 20000001800144ff
CapInh: 0000000000000000
CapPrm: 00000000fffffeff
CapEff: 00000000fffffeff
Cpus_allowed:   00000000,000000ff
Mems_allowed:   1
task: 00000000543d6bf8, ksp: 00000000e76a7ad8
User PSW : 0705e00080000000 0000000077fb7498
User GPRS: 0000000000000000 0000000000000002 0000000000417b74 0000000000000000
           9999999800000233 000002007f891348 0000000000000000 0000000000000119
           0000000000417ba0 000000007f8913c0 0000000000000233 0000000000417b70
           0000000000417938 0000000077fbca50 00000008f7fb7482 000000007f8912b8
User ACRS: 77e62aa0 0026baf0 00000000 00000000
           00000000 00000000 00000000 00000000
           00000000 00000000 00000000 00000000
           00000000 00000000 00000000 00000000
```

Figure 5-7 Cognos Process /proc/$pid/status: check memory size

The peak memory usage is 1303924 KB, approximately 1.3 GB, which is far below 2 GB, there is no need for action in our case.

If the memory usage is getting close to 2 GB for a 32-bit OS (for example, 1.8 GB and rising), then you should deploy another instance of the report server. Do this task even if you lack physical memory for the whole Linux on z instance, because if Linux runs out of physical memory, it would use swap memory. Because all our JVMs are running Cognos, all JVMs in our environment are running a dispatcher, so Cognos will balance the load and the dispatcher will be swapped, along with the load assigned to it.

If you have a Cognos maintenance instance available, as mentioned in "Linux level" on page 138, you could boot this instance in order to either buy time or to survive a high peak load.

Running out of physical memory should be an exception. The Linux and WebSphere Application Server team should work together and the WebSphere Application Server team should have enough spare real memory available to add at least one further report server instance.

The amount of memory necessary depends on the workload, that is, how much transformation needs to be done by the report service or how many concurrent users are present. In addition to the JVM memory required, there is also a memory need for running the report server. Each of this tasks can allocate up to 2 GB if needed.

With Linux and WebSphere working well within the chosen parameters, we now discuss the Cognos Monitor level to check whether the users of the overall system are satisfied.

Cognos Packages level

The Cognos Packages are created by publishing Framework Models. These packages contain the intelligence of Cognos. If the packages contain sufficient metadata, then Cognos is able to generate SQL to move the heavy transformation work to the database itself.

In the case of Business Intelligence data consolidation or data transformation, it is often necessary to create a virtual star schema out of a data model that is not model compliant according to Business Intelligence best practices.

In such scenarios, where the heavy transformation load takes place depends on the skills of the Business Intelligence modeler using the Framework Manager. The transformation will be either in the database or in Cognos. In case Cognos needs to do the transformation, this has implications for many areas. For example, there might be more necessary data to feed into this transformation, leading to a network load between the database and the report server. As a consequence, we advise installing a report server (Cognos Application Tier Component) installed at the same campus or even the same computing center, as the data source will profit from the internal, high speed connections.

The report server is written in C++ while the report service is written in Java, so the transformation itself may lead to more allocated memory for the report server (BIBus Tsks), but should have a negligible effect on Java for a single report run. The content store database is also impacted, as Cognos generates "with" statements to implement the virtual data model in the framework model (metadata description) inside the database, from where the data is pulled. "With" statements result in the creation of temporary tables, which leads to the need of table space for these temporary tables.

Cognos Monitor level

All configurable runtime information and settings are displayed by going to the Status page of Cognos Administration inside Cognos Connection (Administrator IBM Cognos Content). The window that appears is shown in Figure 5-8.

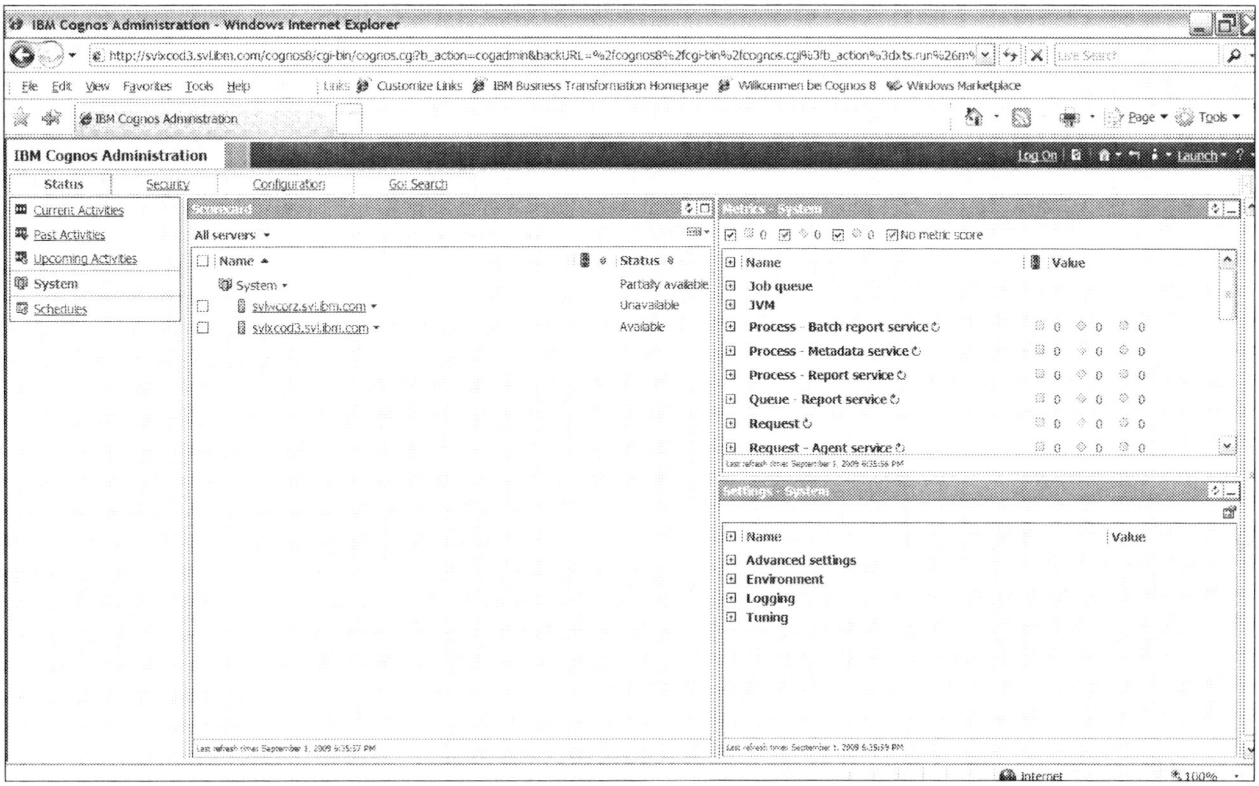

Figure 5-8 Cognos Administration status window

There are a few links on the left hand side of the pane (current activities, past activities, upcoming activities, and schedules) that allow you to monitor the user scenario on the Cognos server. There is also a link to the system dashboard of Cognos, which provides you with the Cognos view of the events.

Current, past, and upcoming activities and schedules

Current, past, and upcoming activities are dashboards that tell you what happens in terms of a scheduled activity on the system.

- *Current* activity lists the jobs that are currently due to run (pending) or are running on the system.
- *Past* activity tells you about jobs that have ran in the past hours or days. The interface divides these jobs into categories such as succeeded, failed, or canceled.
- *Upcoming* activity is a complementary view to schedules and tells you which jobs are due to run in the future (depending on your query).
- *Schedules* is the pane where you change the property of schedules, such as priority.

As these views do not include details about user activities, they are not very helpful in terms of scaling. Nevertheless, they give information about scheduled activities, which allows you to either move job activity to off peak times or re-prioritize across jobs.

Cognos System status dashboard

Clicking **System** opens a dashboard about health information of your Cognos System. A sample window is shown in Figure 5-9.

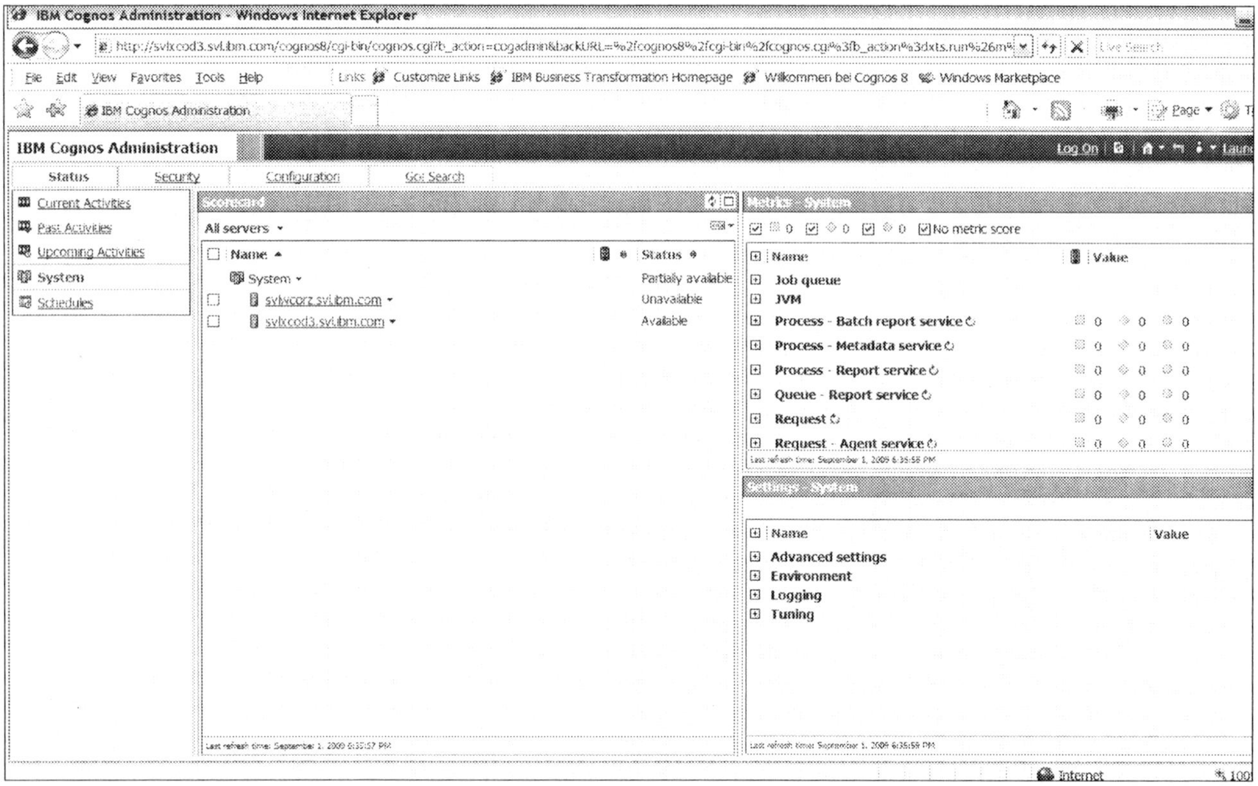

Figure 5-9 Cognos Administration: system status

The central portlet called *Scorecard* shows that two systems exist and one of them is unavailable.

On the bottom right corner are *Settings-System*. They are only visible if you click the first line in the central scorecard portlet, which is in this case "system".

If you click the little plus sign beside an item in the metrics and system settings, you can expand it and see the details. You can inspect your system by getting metrics for many different types of events: amount of processes, connections, queue lengths, and so on. For details regarding these metrics, refer to the *IBM Cognos 8 Administration and Security Guide*.

The central scorecard portlet has another interesting feature. Apart from health checks of the overall system, it also provides a drill-down feature. If you click one of the listed systems, all the portlets are updated. You see the figures just for this specific instance (system, dispatcher, and service). Underneath the system, all the dispatchers configured on that system are listed. If you then click one dispatcher, you see all the services configured for that dispatcher. This enables you to drill down and identify the system, the dispatcher, and the service causing a problem (if there is one).

Multiple figures by service for multiple level of systems and dispatchers create a massive number of metrics. To mitigate this situation, you can use the traffic lights, which are shown in Figure 5-10 and Figure 5-11. These lights are green, which indicates a “good” value, yellow, which indicates a value that is reaching a threshold, and red, which indicates that a value has exceeded a threshold. These lights will be off at an initial setup because no threshold values have been set. The threshold values you need to set depend on the usage pattern of your user population, and what is good or bad depends on the perception of your users and the scale of your system.

Not all figures can be flagged with a threshold; some are just informational. The ones to which a threshold can be assigned are the ones like “number of queue requests” and “latency”, as shown in Figure 5-10. They are indicated with a little pencil.

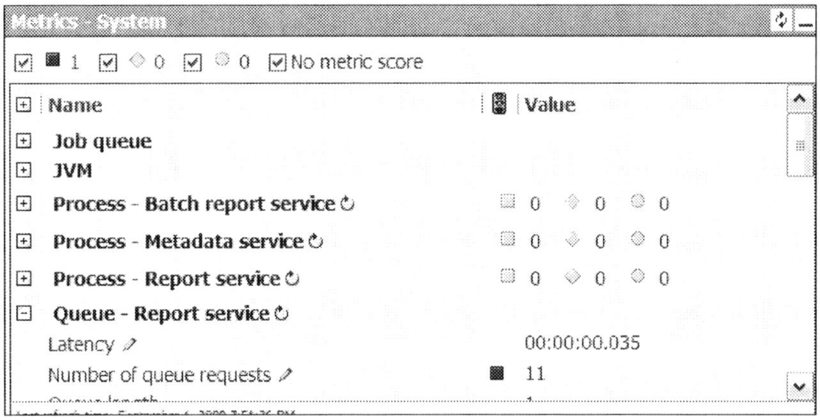

Figure 5-10 Figure with pencil

Clicking this little pencil opens a window for the threshold, where you can define the values. You define what a “good” value should be and what the upper and lower limits are in order; this allows you to set the green, yellow and red indicators.

In Figure 5-11, we demonstrate a red status by defining that small values are good and the maximum is 10. In this case, the actual value is 11, so it is flagged as red.

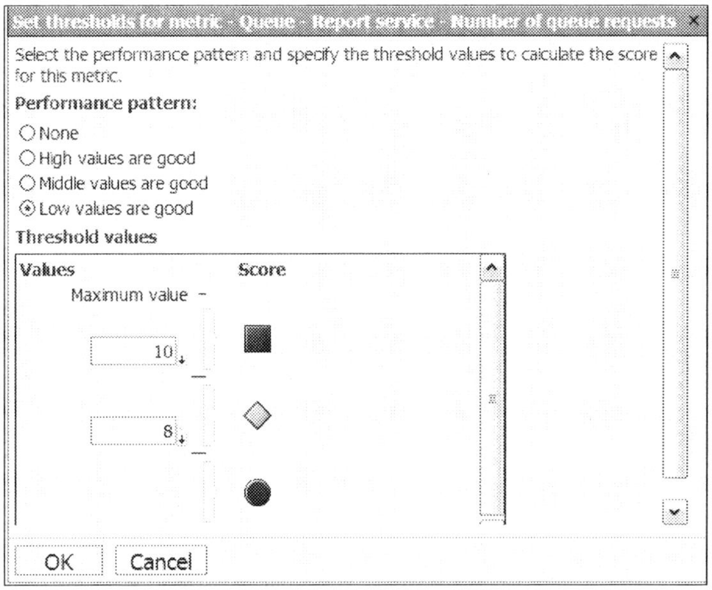

Figure 5-11 Cognos status threshold

The ability to micromanage the system comes from the origins of Cognos, where a new server added to scale the system might have a different processor speed and memory than other ones already in the system. In Linux on System z, as we scale vertically, all service components share the same logical system, may have the same JVM size, and so on.

What this means is that although you have the option to drill down to a single server, you can really manage a system at the system level. If you have added another JVM for report services (because of a resource shortage on the report services side), then you simply increase the threshold for this metric for the overall system.

However, because of interdependency, if Linux runs out of memory and one of the JVMs is set on SWAP and is no longer active, you would see, at the system level, that although your report thread level is not reached, the report request queue is growing. Drilling down the service level allows you to identify the JVM that has been swapped and make any necessary changes to it.

Scaling on the Cognos level

In "WebSphere Application Server level" on page 139, we have seen that adding new JVMs to the Cognos system provides extra capacity that is not fully utilized. The services come with standard settings, and are appropriate for an average installation of all services on one JVM.

In our case, we do not use this configuration in order to have spare resources. Each service comes with specific settings, which increases the utilization of CPU and JVM heap size. The values depend on the usage pattern. For example, reports that have a complex transformation on the Cognos server will need more memory than simple queries. If you have many small reports, you may be able to process many of them in one JVM.

To change your settings, go to Cognos Administration and select **Configuration → Dispatcher and Services** in the left pane. There you see a list of dispatchers. If you click one, it drills down to the services managed by this dispatcher, as shown in Figure 5-12.

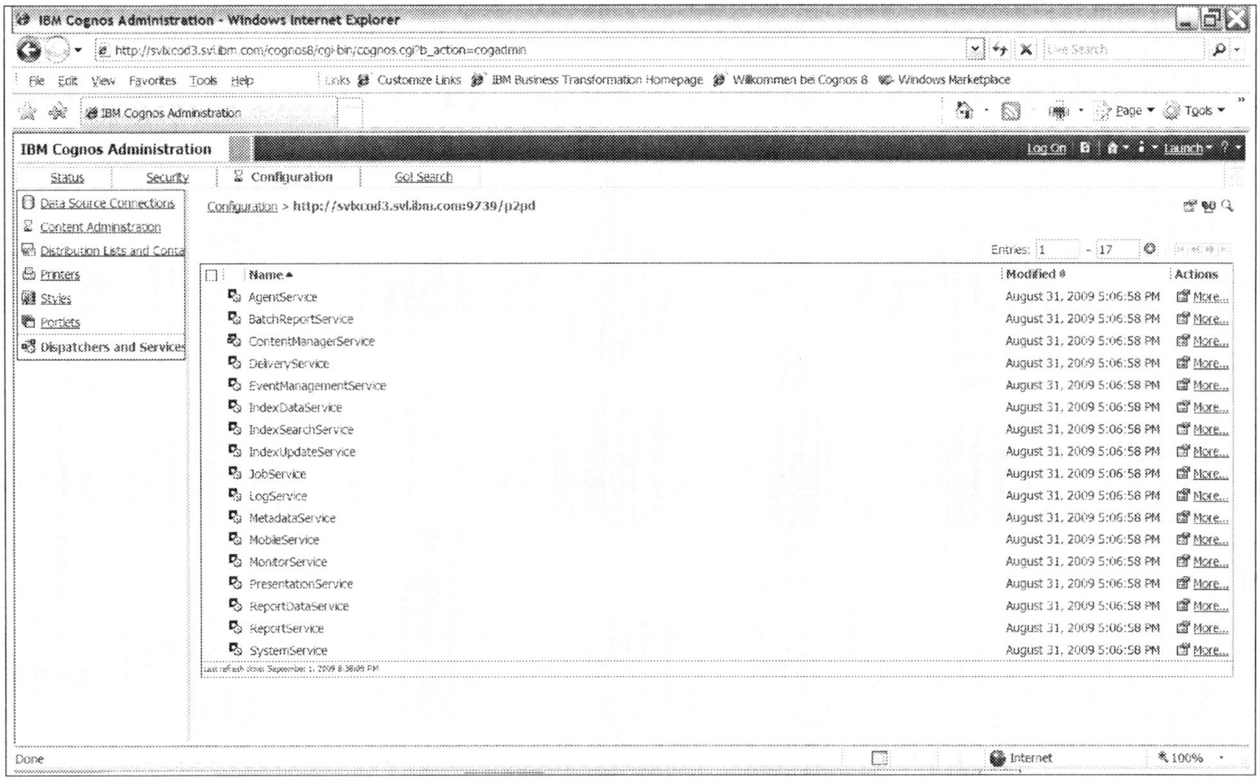

Figure 5-12 Services configuration by dispatcher

If you then click **More** in the right pane, you get the special settings for this service.

Figure 5-13 shows an example of the possible settings for a report service.

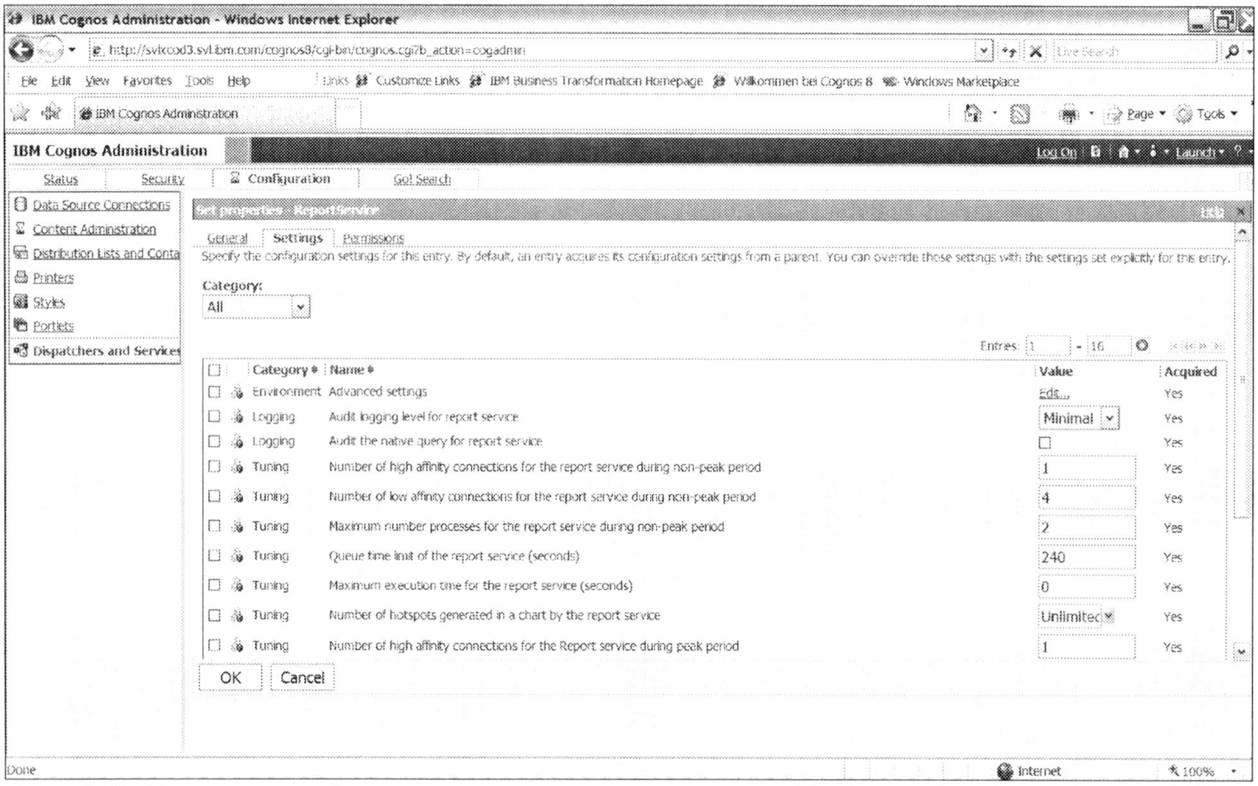

Figure 5-13 Report server settings

Report services accept low and high affinity connections to process requests from the batch report and report services. Servers also accept low and high affinity connections to process requests from the data movement service.

Low affinity requests can be handled by any report server. Typically, low affinity requests are used when a report or data movement run is initially requested and can be done by any report service.

High affinity requests are ideally handled by a specific report server. Typically, high affinity requests are for reports that were already requested and may include actions, such as going to the next page in a report. If the specific report server is not available or busy, then the report is rerun (low affinity request) on any report server and the next page (high affinity request) is directed to that server.

Affinity connections are described in the *IBM Cognos 8 Business Intelligence Architecture and Deployment Guide*.

Be aware that changing figures in these settings has an impact on the utilization of the JVM where this service is running and the overall Linux system.

These settings allow you to enlarge your system depending on the usage pattern. For a normal distribution of small and large queries run uniformly across all deployed packages on the system in a single data center, the default setup is okay.

5.3.3 Dedicated resources for packages and user groups

The chapter "Specify Advanced Dispatcher Routing" in the *IBM Cognos 8 Administration and Security Guide* describes an interesting feature of Cognos. It is possible to group users, servers, and packages (framework model) and set up rules for assigning which group of dispatchers deals with requests by certain users or for specific packages.

With this feature, a package with huge transformation could be sent to a separate set of dispatchers configured for this workload, or a special user, such as finance or a mobile user, could get dedicated dispatchers serving their requests. Depending on the importance and the overall workload of the Linux system, a dispatcher could even run on a separate Linux on System z instance with dedicated resources, such as an LPAR.

5.3.4 Globally distributed systems and special request routing

In large enterprises with branch offices globally distributed, there might be more then one information warehouse or data source used for operational BI. We discuss that topic in Chapter 2, "Scenario for deployment" on page 23. These sources can be diverse and are not necessarily in one physical location. Some might be even on a different continent.

In our introduction to "Report services" on page 133, we mentioned that the report server is probably the service with the largest workload because pulling large amounts of data from the data sources or some reports require heavy transformation to be done in Cognos. This implies heavy data traffic, which actually may increase if concurrently running different versions of this report with slightly different prompts.

One way to solve such problems is by using burst reports. Bursting is the solution when you have the same data that is going to many people and there are people specific prompts, for example, sales figures going to different departments and "bursting out" to a group of people.

Another option is to implement a Cognos dispatcher with report services in the major processing center having the desired data and route the requests requiring this data to this dispatcher. For packages requiring global data, there is no good solution; a data center supporting Cognos report services should be chosen to minimize the amount of data source related network traffic.

If no advance routing is set up in this case, Cognos will choose the next available dispatcher to serve the request. The request might fail if the dispatcher has not been implemented to access the data source.

In the case where the local data center serves only local user communities, an additional Cognos instance is probably the best choice.

5.3.5 High availability

The topic of high availability is pretty much like an insurance policy. It depends on how much you want to spend for the level of safety you require.

All Cognos components may have multiple instances through scaling, except Content Manager. As mentioned before, you could have another Content Manager on standby or even more than one on standby. Of course the standby Content Manager requires some minimal disk resources and most of the time they do actually nothing. In a z/VM virtual environment, the real CPU and memory resources associated with the standby Content Manager will be available to other virtual machines until the standby becomes active.

Having Cognos running on another Linux instance running on the same System z system offers several advantages. Having it actually up and running the whole time requires additional disks beyond the basic level, but it actually does not protect data from power failures. Again, the CPU and memory resources for Linux are virtual when running Linux under z/VM, and the associated physical resources will not be needed until the Linux instance becomes active.

To have protection in the case of local power failures, network problems, and so on, you need to have a remote data center that will not be affected by the failure.

Another issue is data access. Cognos might be up and running, but it is still unable to get to your data. A data replication solution may solve this kind of problem and also some performance problems, as all users would access the data within their geography.

Having one default global Content Manager allows the architecture to appear as a single instance while in fact Cognos services and data sources are geographically widely distributed. Standby Content Managers in all locations ensure high availability. Advanced routing may prevent processing of requests that are remote from the user location.

6

Online Analytical Processing processing comparisons

In this chapter, we describe Online Analytical Processing (OLAP) in detail by comparing the two major techniques (Cognos PowerCube and InfoSphere Cubing Services).

This chapter contains the following topics:

- OLAP introduction
- Cognos PowerCube and InfoSphere Warehouse Cubing Services
- Cubing Services overview
- Cubing Services for large cubes
- Delivering PowerCube on System z
- PowerCube security sources
- OLAP and concurrent DW maintenance

6.1 OLAP introduction

OLAP describes a special, data storage approach for query and analysis purposes, in contrast to Online Transactional Processing, which is used for transaction recording.

OLAP tools deliver a dimensional or hierarchical view of data. Many parts of a business lend themselves to being modeled or thought of as a hierarchy, such as time, geography, products, customer segmentation, and so on. Numeric values, or facts, in OLAP are called *measures*. For example, for a transaction that records a revenue of $20,000 for the selling of a white truck in Dallas, Texas in January, $20,000 is the numeric value or measure. Revenue should be the measure description, while period, location, and the product describe the key figures. Period, location, and product are different kind of descriptions and usually belong to separate dimensions. Color and other collateral information are usually defined in an OLAP environment as attributes of a main dimension.

Dimensions are often organized in single or multiple hierarchies (that is, time related information aggregates in years, quarters, months, and so on) to summarize metrics and enable data exploration by drilling down. In order to deliver analysis across many dimensions, OLAP tools usually conform to a standard query and calculation language named MultiDimensional eXpression language (MDX). Normally users do not need to be experts in query language because they are usually provided with a no-coding interface for data exploration.

Generally speaking, a multidimensional analysis helps organizations extract maximum value from their corporate data. It transforms volumes of data into information about the business, allowing users to analyze information in a business context, that is, comparisons of things, such as product or channel performance, in light of other important factors, such as regions, customers, and time. Multidimensional views enable users to quickly gain insight into business performance and trends, and improve business performance by:

- Providing visibility into large volumes of corporate data
- Presenting complex data in a business way so it is easy to understand
- Helping people stay on top of changing business conditions (market shifts, mergers, and acquisitions) and providing trending analysis
- Reducing the burden on IT by providing self-service access to corporate information
- Delivering an efficient technology that is quickly refreshed with current data

Multidimensional analysis helps you analyze a huge volume of data, from multiple perspectives. Suppose you must look at the sales data for products in several countries, for all periods of time. To help visualize data from these multiple perspectives, visualize a cube with each of the axes representing a dimension (such as country, product, and time). The implicit fourth dimension is the measures, in this case, the sales amount. The cube is comprised of a number of mini-cubes, as shown in Figure 6-1. Each mini-cube contains a measure for that specific intersection of the country, product, and time. In this case, the darker (blue) mini-cube represents the sales for the first quarter of 2008 (time dimension) for the grocery item milk (product dimension) that was sold in Germany (country dimension).

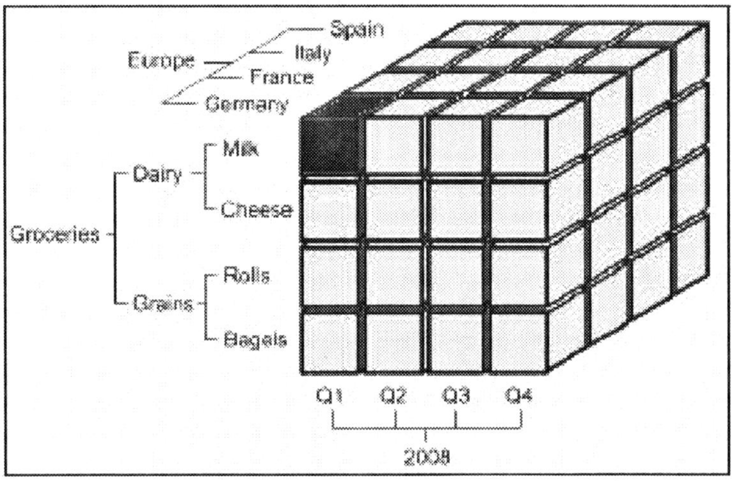

Figure 6-1 Multidimensional data represented as cube

The delivery of information within a dimensional framework that users understand means they can conduct their own analysis quickly and easily. Organizations can also extend the analysis' reach and share findings company-wide with effective reporting that helps them know sooner, understand faster, and react more quickly than the competition.

OLAP data management has been designed to address specific needs in terms of information analysis. A dimensional view makes it easier to keep the business under control, by detecting trends and behavior, such as what is the best selling product or the most valuable in terms of the profit margin. It is also valuable for comparing performance within an enterprise or against a benchmark.

OLAP technology has been evolving since the beginning, assuming different connotations, according to business requirements, hardware development, and obviously moods and trends. OLAP encompasses DOLAP (Desktop OLAP), HOLAP (Hybrid OLAP), and WOLAP (Web OLAP). Strictly looking at data storage, we can focus on a few OLAP approaches:

- Multidimensional OLAP (MOLAP),
- Relational OLAP (ROLAP)
- Hybrid OLAP (HOLAP)

MOLAP tools usually store information in a proprietary database that typically is represented as a multidimensional cube. MOLAP technology can deliver high performance data retrieval, fast data loading, and complex calculation processing. According to hardware enhancements, we have had full-storage MOLAPs that used to store pre-generated aggregation results to reduce query response time, and in-memory MOLAPs that better leverage recent improvements. Generally speaking, larger data sets, with billions of transactions and hundreds of dimensions, tend to decrease the value of a MOLAP solution. Data organized in large and flat dimensions, with thousands of members and few or none hierarchical levels, could also affect MOLAP performance.

ROLAP and dimensionally aware relational schemas apply OLAP methodologies on relational data stores, delivering slice and dice and drill functionalities, as MOLAP does, in order to limit, or avoid, data redundancy. While this option easily leverages modern hardware resources and standards and may have less limitations in terms of the number of dimensions and volumes of data, it still has a slower query response time.

The HOLAP approach is intended to combine MOLAP and ROLAP benefits by keeping MOLAP technology on smaller data sets for fast query performance and by enabling a gateway to relational data stores, with a technique that is named “drill through”, for a larger amount of data.

Using one of these approaches as a strict standard is a limit for Business Intelligence deployments in an organization; merging different solutions to be applied to specific needs may bring perceivable benefits in terms of information availability. This was the main reason that drove us in to deploy a multiple OLAP solution in consolidating Business Intelligence on System z for The Sample Outdoors Company.

6.1.1 When should I use a particular option

Defining the right choice for an intelligent Business Intelligence strategy is often a challenge. Software technology is not the only driver for a proper choice. Software just provides tools. A careful analysis of all requirements is the pillar for successful implementations. At a minimum, you need to understand what kind of features are required.

IBM System z provide a wide variety of option to consolidate Business Intelligence implementation and to deliver a high performance OLAP environment. Some considerations related to peculiar features of each solution are helpful. Table 6-1 gives good reasons to implement a PowerCube solution.

Table 6-1 Good reasons to implement a PowerCube

Business requirements	Key features
Time trend analysis and period to date aggregation	Automated time series, time dimension management, and embedded time based partitioning options
Quick comparative analysis on aggregated data	Fast delivery of dimensional models
Mobile disconnected reporting	File based OLAP generation
IT independent data manipulation	Easy deployment from Cognos 8 BI packages and reports, and friendly graphic interface
Frequent data refresh and model updates	Extremely easy and fast model maintenance and delivery

Table 6-2 addresses the key factors of an InfoSphere Cubing Services solution.

Table 6-2 Key factors for an InfoSphere Cubing Services deployment

Business requirements	Key features
Large data sets and large dimensions	High performing metadata caching
Enterprise rollout with near real time data	In memory data cache management with limited data movements
Enterprise wide standard deployment	Integrated IT management
Heterogeneous client access	Scalable, low latency OLAP
Huge data volumes involved	Top performing 64-bit environment
High performance on large inquiries	Optimization objects for automated performance improvements

6.2 Cognos PowerCube and InfoSphere Warehouse Cubing Services

The current general Cognos OLAP portfolio offers a complete MOLAP solution (easy to build and simple to deploy with PowerCubes), the in-memory, 64-bit addressing of TM1, as well as the very large database ROLAP solution of Cubing Services.

By leveraging advanced and modern standard technologies, Linux on System z enables these two main high performing multidimensional approaches:

- Dimensionally aware relational data on InfoSphere Warehouse Cubing Services: The hierarchical information is modeled in the target database environment and IBM Cognos 8 BI reads and processes this information to provide dimensional analysis capability, such as drill down and slice-and-dice.
- MOLAP approach with IBM Cognos PowerCube: As multidimensional cubes are built from any data source to accelerate decision making and information delivery across the enterprise, they incorporate business rules, calculations, and time series analysis, delivered automatically. The built-in flexibility of IBM Cognos 8 BI lets users move from summary level to transaction level detail, or from one IBM Cognos PowerCube to another or even to other different sources, so that all needed information could be just few clicks away.

In terms of alternatives, the OLAP styles fit business usage needs differently and the requirements drive the best choice:

- Who maintains the data?
- Nature of the business problem to be addressed.
- Data volume characteristics.
- Data volatility and latency characteristics.
- User population size and degree of specialization.

Each OLAP engine that has been used for The Sample Outdoors Company BI solution provides business users access to information across all Cognos 8 BI capabilities and could be shared by way of the BI front end for many other purposes.

From a user stand point, InfoSphere Warehouse Cubing Services and Cognos PowerCube have similar functionalities. PowerCubes have a valuable time dimension management, with automatically generated details, such as last period, current period, period to date aggregation, and so on. Either with Cubing Services or with PowerCube, users requests generate a standard MDX query without the user being asked to write MDX code. Users can combine the usage of Cubing Services and PowerCubes by setting up a drill through path in dashboards and reports.

IBM Cognos PowerCube

PowerCubes show relationships and trends across key business dimensions, so users see critical information in the right context. This kind of analysis provides greater business insight and supports more informed decisions. Dimensional analysis coupled with effective reporting lets people analyze trends and obtain answers to business questions by way of managed reports or dashboards.

A couple of scenarios where PowerCube can be especially useful are:

- When a limited set of information is defined to perform high performance analysis.
- To enable the fastest delivery for a BI solution (interactive dashboard, reports, or analysis).

In our scenario of BI consolidation for The Sample Outdoors Company, we produced a few departmental PowerCubes to provide controlled, consistent data sources to answer standard analysis needs. A smaller deployment grants high performance and high availability, for disconnected mobile analysis, with updates that take a few minutes and can run multiple times during a day. Those PowerCubes provide data to an internal dashboard for sales and marketing analysis across the time, products, and branches dimensions.

The strong point of the embedded OLAP engine for IBM Cognos 8 BI is that ease of building and fast loading come together. You can also add the ability to use the engine while disconnected by way of the PowerPlay client.

PowerCubes can collect a complete and meaningful set of data and keep this set "alive" and, because they are file based, they could be available even in a stand-alone environment. Furthermore, keeping the size of PowerCubes to certain limits make them suitable for multiple fast updates, even in a single day. Because they provide a highly consistent performance in large user communities, they represent the ideal solution to be accessed also by way of the Internet, with minimum disk space and memory requirements.

PowerCube data sources provide a unique look at the data when you need to perform market basket analysis or trending into the future. The automatic time series analysis allows you to easily create time bucket members, which is a very difficult task to do with relational data, and these members can be customized for more complex or forecasted trends. Time state rollups also allow implicit measures at a specific point in time (inventory); once a date's information is found, it is possible to deliver period-to-date aggregation automatically.

Transformer is the modeling and ETL tool that helps you to design and then build the PowerCube. It provides simple or advanced modeling functions depending on the modelling complexity needed. The client component of Transformer has an intuitive interface that could also be managed by advanced business users to combine corporate and non-corporate data for personal or shared use. That source data could be as simple as importing a dimension from another OLAP source or as complex as creating a report using custom SQL in Cognos 8 Report Studio for use as a data source in the cube building process, as shown in Figure 6-2 on page 157.

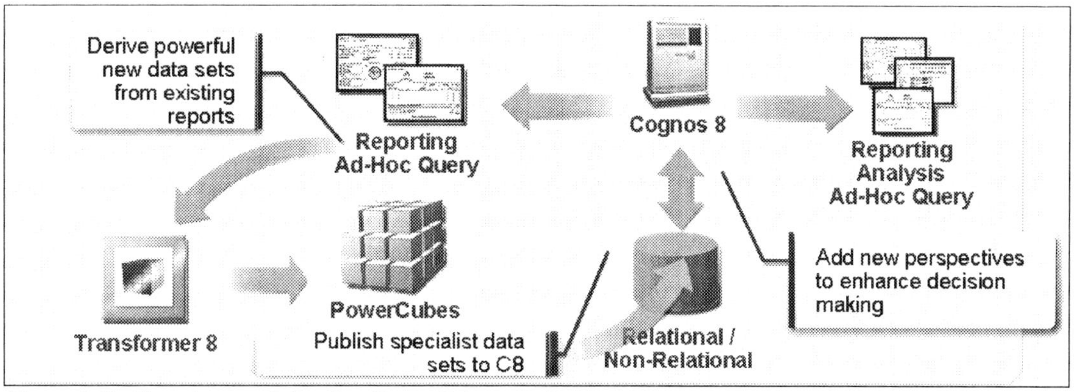

Figure 6-2 Transformer delivering PowerCubes on System z

Empowering the users reduces IT requests for unique multidimensional data sets that are used to solve business questions that span across multiple data silos. Bye dragging and dropping information, users are able to add multiple drill paths in a single dimension for alternate views of the business, or add business rules and calculations for percent growth, market share, or category counts.

Transformer also has the functionality to allow IT modelers to create business friendly multidimensional high speed data caches for users with complex and customizable data level security needs to integrate those caches with their corporate LDAP. IT departments can automate models for either structural updates or even design models from scratch. This feature reduces the need for manual manipulation of the models, thus leading to a more efficient development process that can continue without interruption.

IBM InfoSphere Warehouse Cubing Services

IBM InfoSphere Warehouse Cubing Services deploys a special environment based on ROLAP to:

- Represent relational data in a dimensional shape with embedded query optimization
- Support large multi purpose data volumes, dimensions, and user communities

Cubing Services are a key component of IBM InfoSphere Warehouse, a suite of products that combines the strength of DB2 Enterprise Edition with a data warehousing infrastructure from IBM (Figure 6-3) that works on System z with IBM Cognos 8 BI to provide OLAP access to data.

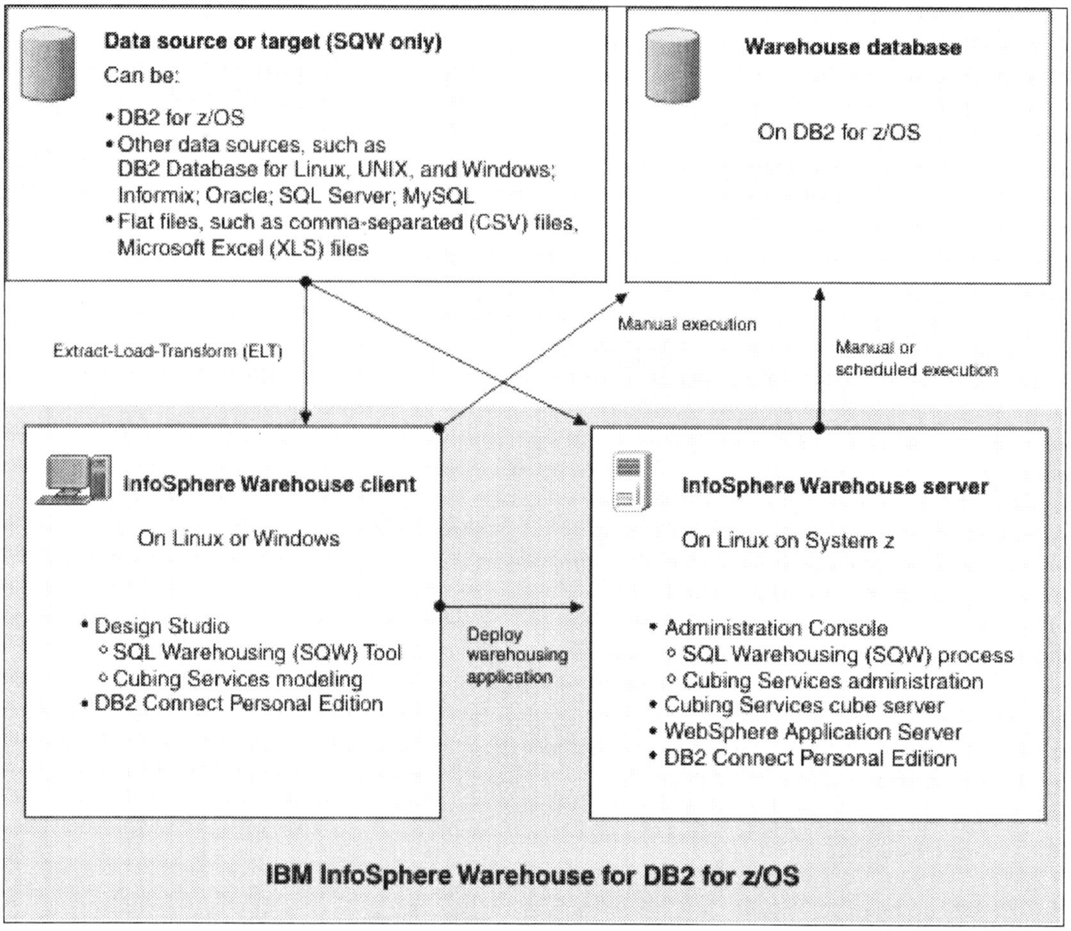

Figure 6-3 InfoSphere Warehouse architecture

Cubing Services manage data directly from InfoSphere Warehouse and include tools for multidimensional modeling to design OLAP metadata (cubes), an optimization advisor for recommending materialized query tables (MQTs) in DB2, and a cube server for providing multidimensional access to the data. Each of these components is integrated with the InfoSphere Warehouse user interfaces for design (Design Studio), administration, and maintenance (Administration Console).

The Cubing Services cube server processes multidimensional queries expressed in the MDX query language and produces multidimensional results. The cube servers fetch data from DB2 through SQL queries as needed to respond to the MDX queries. The MQTs that are recommended by the optimization advisor are exploited by the DB2 optimizer, which rewrites incoming SQL queries and routes eligible queries to the appropriate MQT for significantly faster query performance. In addition to these performance enhancements, the cube server includes multiple caching layers for further optimizing the performance of MDX queries.

The quick description of these features shows that InfoSphere Cubing Services provide OLAP capabilities for IT enterprise rollouts, where volumes and scalability are more critical than query performance. For example, in The Sample Outdoors Company environment, Cubing Services have been used to deploy multidimensional views of a large detailed data structure based on the enterprise warehouse. We collected all product related information, with a maximum level of detail, in a single dimension, and we have been able to derive facts from a fact table with millions of transactions.

Cubing Services leverages warehousing techniques and are managed by a database administrator to provide OLAP access for a large, multi-purposed data source. Since it fits better an InfoSphere Warehouse environment, it is useful for providing near real time data access.

On the System z side, Cubing Services relies on InfoSphere Warehouse and has optimized access to DB2; advanced settings for dimension management and data caching improve query performance. Cubing Services are also based on a 64-bit technology that enable a larger cache usage for huge data volumes. Furthermore, it leverages Optimization Advisor, providing more query performance improvements.

On the modeling side, a database administrator is provided with consistent, integrated design tools that provide a common environment for warehouse design. Moreover, Cubing Services applies an open standard using ODBO and XMLA APIs to increase the range of customization options.

6.3 Cubing Services overview

Many organizations have invested in data marts and data warehouses to store their relational data in a form that allows queries. This data is typically moved from the transactional systems where the data originated into another relational database that is optimized for query performance. The databases, which contain historical information, are sometimes known as *data warehouses* or *data marts*. The data marts and data warehouses are created using DB2, or other relational databases. The primary purpose of these relational databases allows users to query historical information.

Querying relational databases is easier when a dimensional model is used. Dimensional models make it easier to pose business questions related to a particular business process or business area. The structure of data, when organized in dimension hierarchies, is intuitively more familiar to users and their understanding of the relationships among data categories. Depending upon the size and complexity of the dimensional model and the business requirements, users may need the power of a dedicated OLAP server. Cubing Services enable the import of metadata from relational databases or the creation of a new set of metadata objects to dimensionally model relational or OLAP structures. InfoSphere Warehouse stores each of the metadata objects in the metadata database in DB2 for z/OS.

In this way, the data warehouse become a more useful and valuable platform for managing, deploying, and providing multidimensional data across the enterprise. Cubing Services provides easier to manage OLAP solutions more quickly and improves performance across analytical applications.

Cubing Services work by using cube metadata to design specialized summary tables (DB2 materialized query tables (MQTs)) that contain critical dimensions and levels, or slices, of the cube. The Cubing Services cube optimization process recommends creating summary tables that can improve the performance of OLAP queries. The DB2 optimizer transparently rewrites incoming queries and routes eligible queries to the appropriate summary tables for significantly faster query performance. These recommended Cubing Services summary tables can accelerate all SQL-based queries into the data warehouse, not just those queries submitted on behalf of Cubing Services.

Cubing Services core components

The Cubing Services core components provide the infrastructure to model, optimize, deploy, and execute queries against cube models, as shown in Figure 6-4.

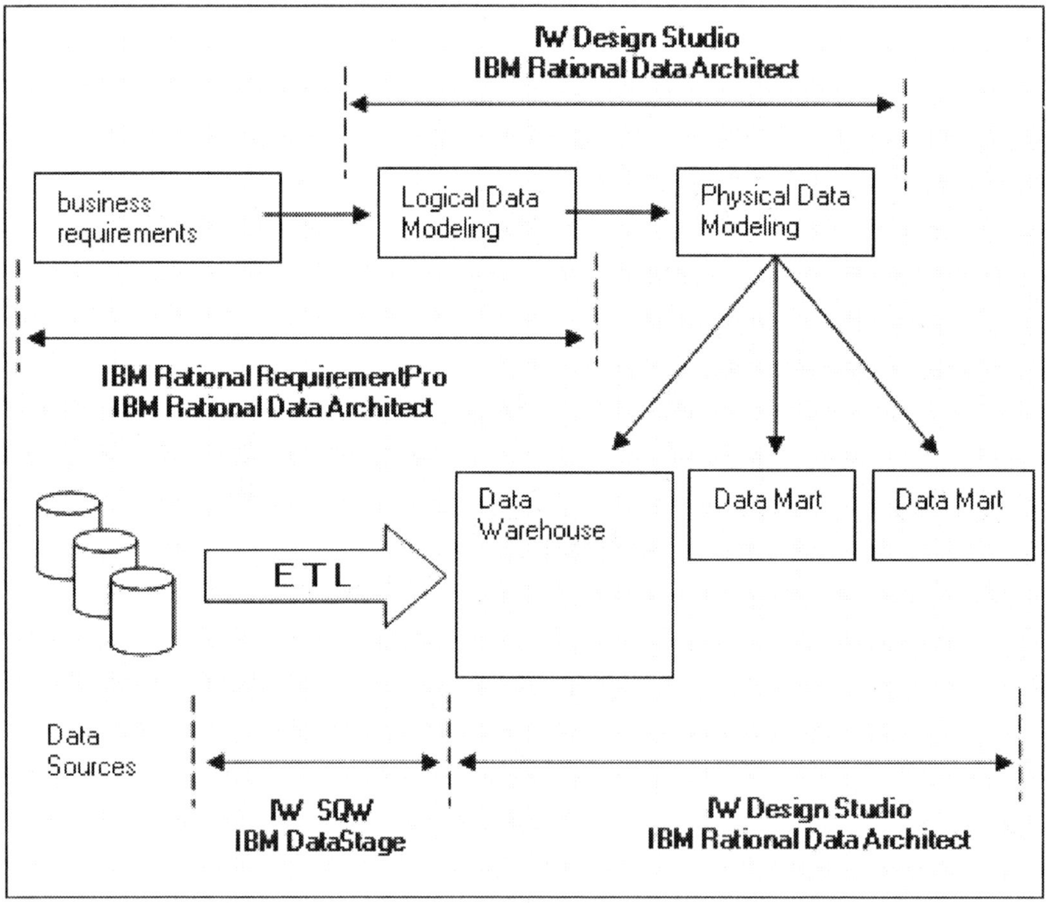

Figure 6-4 Cubing Services core components and usage

InfoSphere Warehouse Design Studio includes modeling and design tools based on and interoperable with IBM Rational Data Architect software, enabling you to design, model, and reverse engineer physical database schemas, as shown in Figure 6-5.

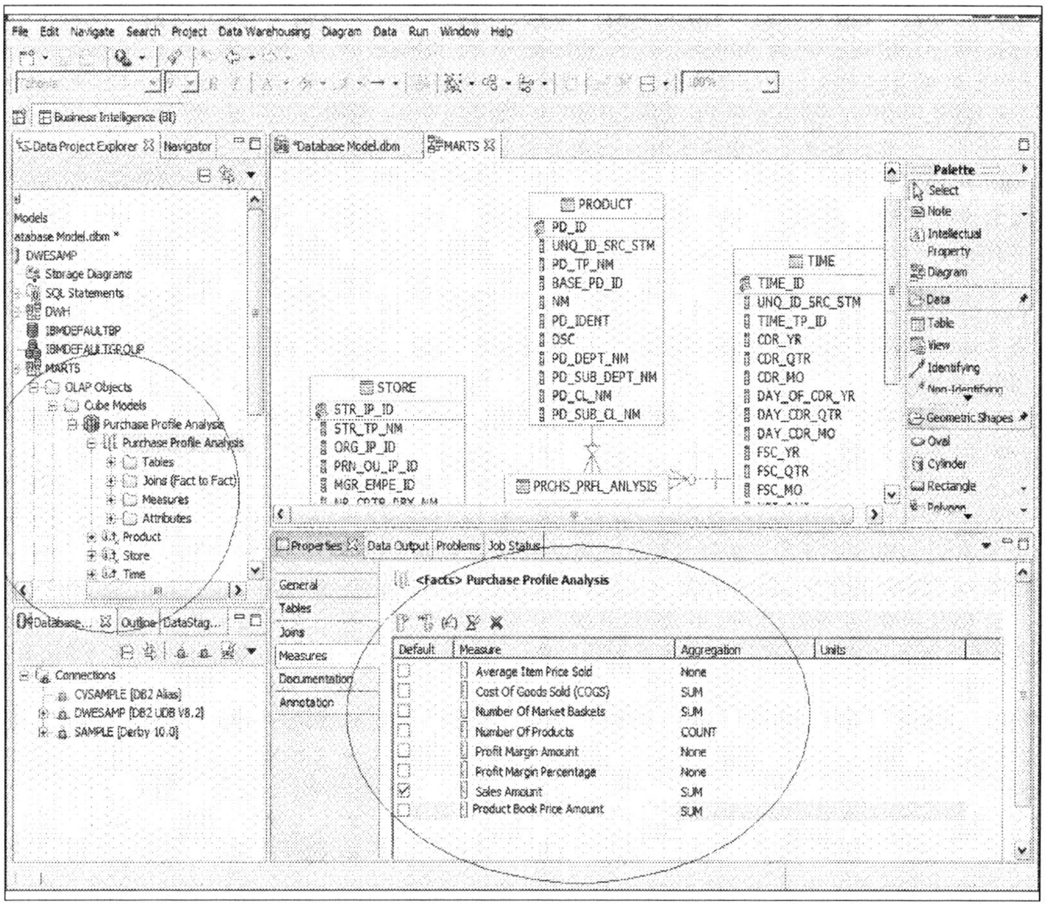

Figure 6-5 Design Studio functions

This tool provides a palette of drag and drop transformation operators that form visual data flows. These data flows are compiled into DB2-specific SQL operations that run within the warehouse database. Control flows add support for conditional processing logic, parallel processing, and special DB2 functions, such as row compression and roll-in/roll-out operations. You can use these tools to more efficiently prepare and populate data warehouse analytic structures necessary for data mining, and for multidimensional and embedded analytics.

The InfoSphere Warehouse Administration Console provides OLAP and cubing functions to manage cube servers and cubes, import metadata, and optimize OLAP queries. The Administration Console can be accessed by using a Web client that resides on any system that has connectivity to the Administration Console, as shown in Figure 6-6.

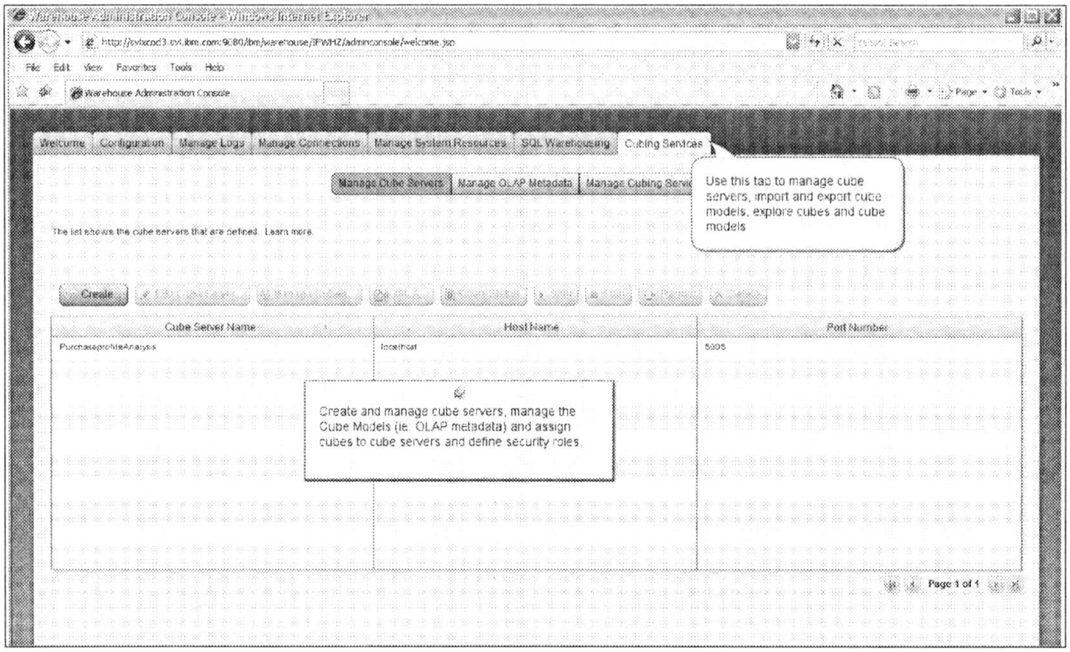

Figure 6-6 Administration Console

The Cubing Services metadata is stored in the InfoSphere Warehouse metadata database. The metadata database makes the Cubing Services metadata available for runtime access (Figure 6-7).

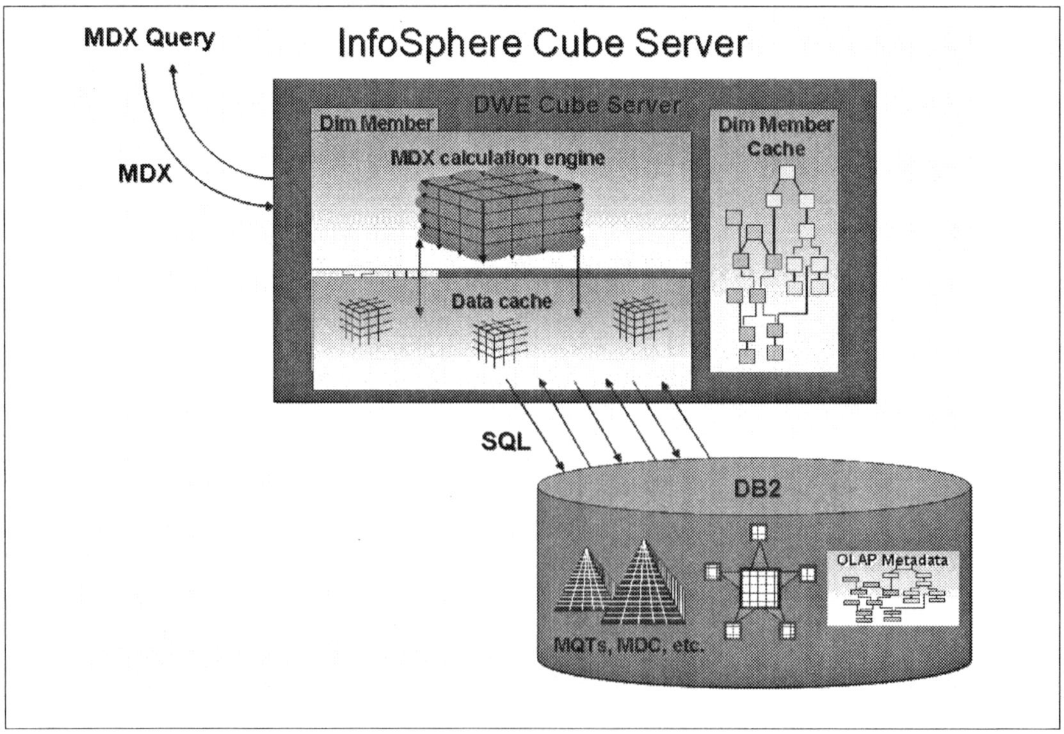

Figure 6-7 Cubing Services metadata are stored on the InfoSphere Warehouse metadata database

The Cubing Services Cube Server is a high performance, scalable cubing engine that is designed to support queries from many users against many different OLAP cubes. The Cubing Services Cube Server is designed to enable fast multidimensional access to relational data that is referenced by the OLAP cubes defined in the Cubing Services metadata database.

The Cubing Services Optimization Advisor enables you to obtain high performance for large cubes. The Advisor provides recommendations about which MQTs and indexes to build to improve SQL queries that are executed against the star schema tables.

Cube Server caching and OLAP optimization can affect performance, that is, the way a computer system behaves under a particular workload. Performance is measured in terms of system response time, throughput, and availability. Performance is also affected by:

- The resources that are available in your system
- How well those resources are used and shared

The InfoSphere Warehouse cube model represents a logical star schema or snowflake schema and groups relevant dimension objects around a central facts object, as shown in Figure 6-8. Each dimension can have multiple hierarchies. The structural information about how to join the tables that are used by the facts object and dimensions is referenced by the cube model. Also stored in the cube model is enough information to construct SQL queries and to retrieve OLAP data. Other reporting and OLAP tools that understand the cube model and that can display multiple views of a specific dimension can benefit from using the cube model.

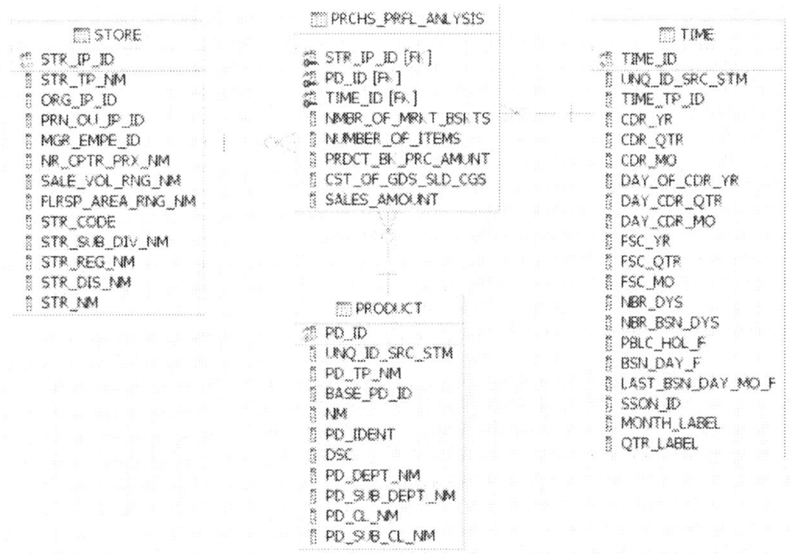

Figure 6-8 The InfoSphere Warehouse cube model represents a logical star schema

Cube models define a complex set of relationships and can be used to selectively expose relevant facts objects and dimensions to an application. Each join object that connects a dimension to the central facts object is stored with the corresponding dimension as a set. Subsets of cube model components can be used by many cubes for different analysis purposes.

A Cubing Services cube is an OLAP cube generated from an InfoSphere Warehouse model and contains a subset of the defined metadata objects. Cubes are the primary OLAP objects that are queried against a Cubing Services Cube Server using the MDX query language. The cube facts object and list of cube dimensions are subsets of those in the referenced cube model. Cubes are appropriate for tools and applications that do not use multiple hierarchies because cube dimensions allow only one cube hierarchy for each cube dimension.

Cubes can be used when optimizing a cube model to specify the regions of the cube model that are the most active and the most important. By identifying optimization slices, it is possible to define specific regions of the cube that are most often queried. The optimization slices could refer to specific cube levels, the All cube level if defined, or Any if no one cube level is significantly more important than any other cube level.

Every time data changes in the underlying database of a cube, the data within the cube might no longer be synchronized (or up-to-date) with the underlying relational data changes. A cube obtains data from queries to the underlying metadata database. When a query requests data from a cube, the Cube Server checks if the results are in its in-memory data cache. If the results are there, the results are immediately available to the application. In this case, the in-memory data cache results in fast response times. Although the results were originally retrieved from the underlying metadata database, those results were retrieved at some point in the past. If the data in the underlying data source has not changed, there is no problem. If the data in the underlying metadata database changes between the time when the cache entry occurred and the time when a query asks for the results, then the results will not match.

The Cubing Services Cube Server stores calculated results in a cache that resides in memory. These stored results are then shared among all users who access a cube model. Internally, each cube is broken down into smaller sections of results. Each of these sections is potentially stored in the cube's in-memory cache. Depending on how much memory the cube results require and how much memory is available to the cube, some entries might need to be removed from the cache. If memory needs to be freed, entries are purged from the cache. The cache is populated with queries that are made to the underlying relational database. If a query against a cube requests data that is not already stored in the cache, then that data is retrieved from the underlying database and, if necessary, old data is removed from the cache. The system performs all of these caching functions automatically.

The Optimization Advisor can help you significantly improve the performance of OLAP-style SQL queries. The optimization process includes creating, implementing, and maintaining the summary tables that are recommended by the Optimization Advisor.

A summary table is a special type of an MQT that specifically includes summary data. MQTs are a powerful way to improve response time for complex queries, especially queries that might require some of the following operations:

- Aggregated data over one or more dimensions
- Joins and aggregates of data over a group of tables

DB2 summary tables can improve query performance because they contain precomputed results from one or more tables that can be used in a query. Costly table joins and complex calculations can be computed in advance and stored in a summary table so that future queries that use these aggregations can run much faster.

The Optimization Advisor will analyze your metadata and the information that you provide to the wizard and recommend the appropriate summary tables. After running the Optimization Advisor, you will have an SQL file that can build the set of recommended summary tables. You have the option of modifying the SQL before you run it to create the summary tables.

Security control for Cubing Services is role based. Access to resources that are stored in the InfoSphere Warehouse control database, such as cubes and cube servers, can be managed by explicitly assigning user-defined roles to users, as shown in Figure 6-9.

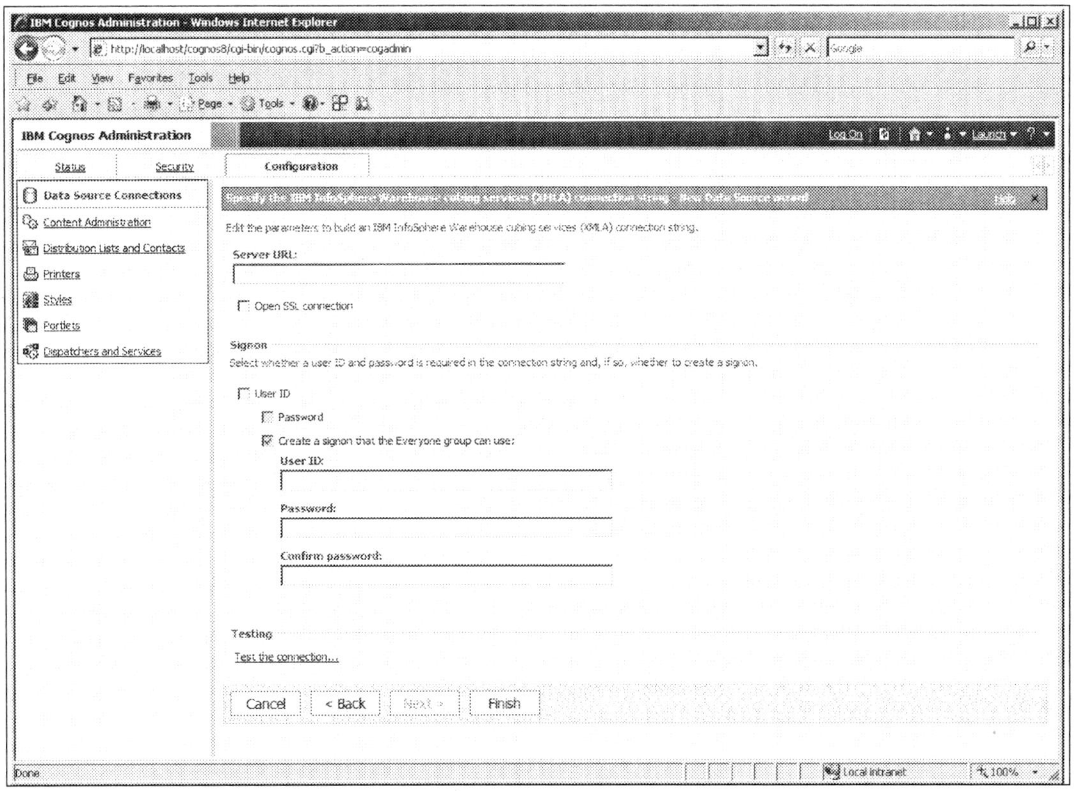

Figure 6-9 Deploying Cubing Services on IBM Cognos 8 BI: data source creation

Cubing Services users that query cubes are first authenticated by DB2. The cube server establishes user authentication by using the security configuration for DB2 on System z. Access to the cube is then authorized by the cube server security service. The cube server security service controls security at the cube level and authorizes access to cubes.

To submit a query for cubes, a user must be defined as a valid user in the DB2 instance that the cubes access. Managing roles, configuring cube security, and cube server security, are part of the Administrator privileges.

The Design Studio and Administration Console logs Cubing Services events and errors to various log files. Every message that is generated in Cubing Services is also written to one of the log files. The log files are retained until they are deleted or moved, and help to keep a history of the activity in Cubing Services. The history is useful for administrative auditing purposes and for use by IBM Software Support.

In order for the cube to be used on IBM Cognos 8 BI, it should be published in the InfoSphere Warehouse environment. Information about creating and publishing cubes using Cubing Services can be found in *Multidimensional Analytics: Delivered with InfoSphere Warehouse Cubing Services*, SG24-7679.

Because the modeling mainly take place in the InfoSphere warehouse, the effort to deliver BI packages based on Cubing Services is minimal; there are two steps that have to be accomplished in IBM Cognos 8 BI:

1. Mapping the Cubing Services data sources, as shown in Figure 6-9 on page 165.

   An IBM Cognos 8 BI data source can be created from Framework Manager or directly in Cognos Connection. Perform the following steps in Framework Manager:

   a. Create a new Framework Manager Project and follow the instruction given by the Metadata Wizard, or open an existing project, right-click **Model Namespace**, and select **Run Metadata Wizard**, as shown in Figure 6-10.

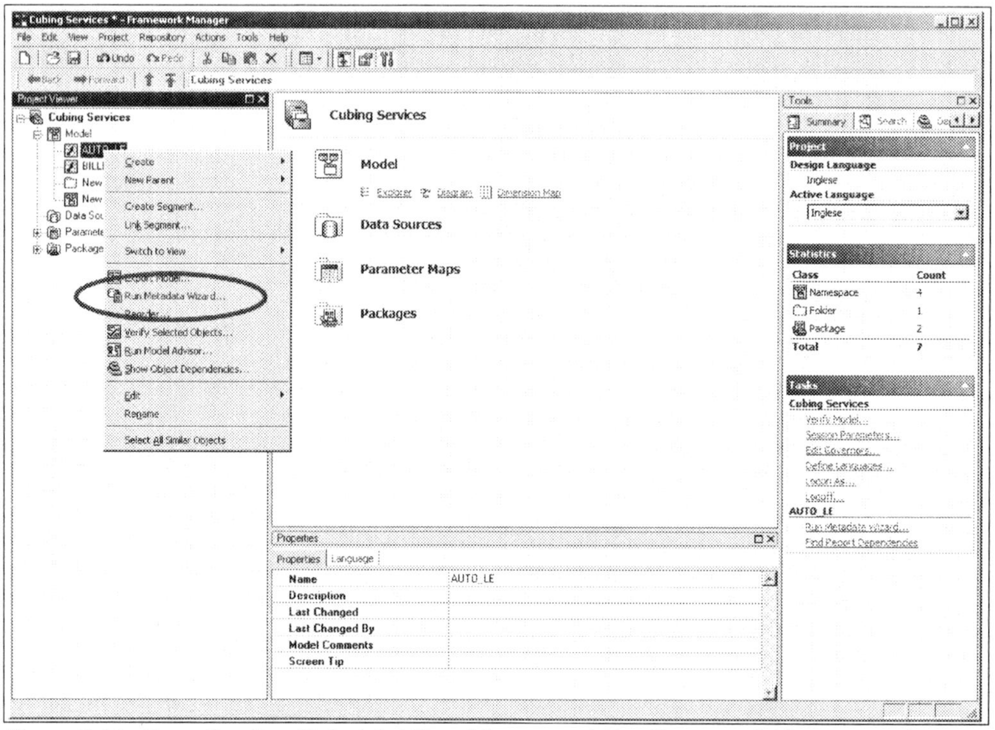

Figure 6-10 Executing Run Metadata Wizard from an existing Framework Manager project

b. Select data sources and click the **New** button, as shown in Figure 6-11.

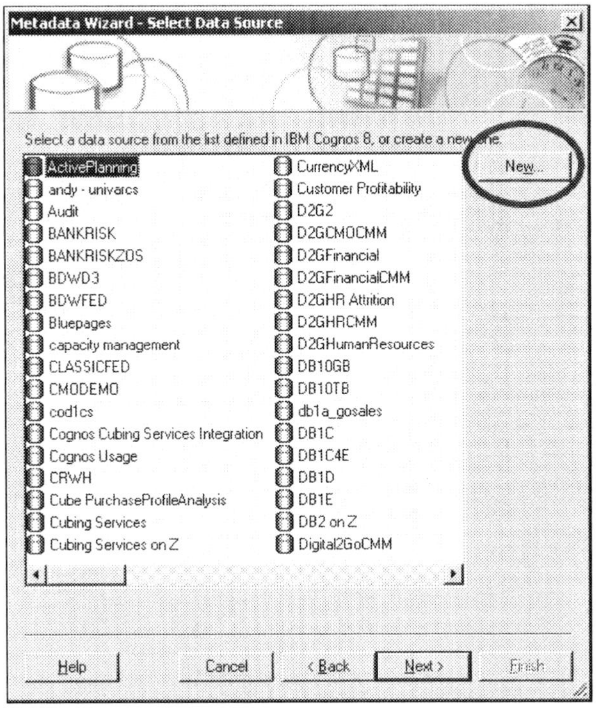

Figure 6-11 Select an existing data source or create a new one in Framework Manager

c. Provide a name for the new data source and click **Next**.

d. Select **IBM InfoSphere Warehouse cubing services (XMLA)** as the type and click **Next**.

e. Specify the server URL in which the cubes are published, as shown in Example 6-1.

Example 6-1 Publishing a cubing services data source on Cognos

```
The server URL is usually something such as servername:port/IBMXmlAnalysis.
In our sample environment we set svlxcoql.svl.ibm.com:8022/IBMXmlAnalysis
```

f. Specify, if needed, that an Open SSL connection should be used, as well as the user ID and Password, and then click **Test the connection...**.

g. Click **Test**.

h. If the test was successful, click **Close**, then **Close** again, and then **Finish**.

To create a new data source from Cognos Connection, perform the following steps:

a. Go to IBM Cognos Administration.

b. Select the **Configuration** tab.

c. Select **Data Source Connections** from the left menu and click the **New Data Source** button.

d. Give the name to the new data source and click **Next**.

e. Select **IBM InfoSphere Warehouse cubing services (XMLA)** as the type and click **Next**.

f. Specify the server URL in which the cubes are published, as shown in Example 6-1.

   g. Specify if needed, that an Open SSL connection should be used, as well as a user ID and Password, and then click **Test the connection....**
   h. Click **Test**.
   i. If the test was successful, click **Close**, then **Close** again, and then **Finish**.
2. Publishing a package that include the Cubing Services data source. Perform these steps:
   a. Open an existing Framework Manager Model or create a new one. If a new project is being created, the Metadata Wizard starts automatically; otherwise, right-click **Model Namespace** and select **Run Metadata Wizard** (Figure 6-10 on page 166).
   b. Select an existing data source or create a new one, and then click **Next**.
   c. Select the published cube of choice (Figure 6-12), click **Next**, and then **Finish**.

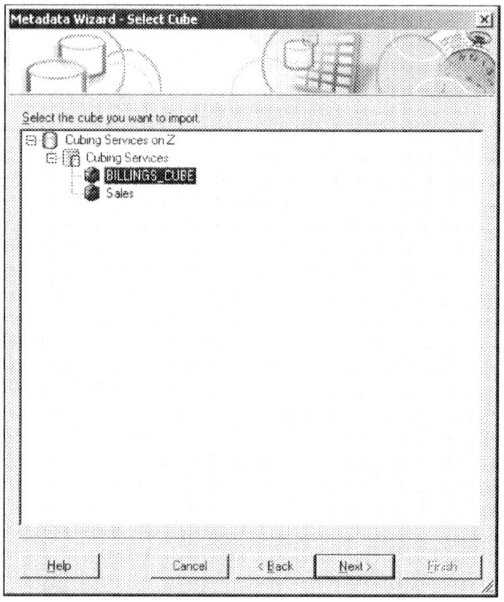

Figure 6-12 A Cubing Service published cube can be selected for publishing

d. The Publish Package Wizard will start automatically. Provide a name for the package and click **Finish**, as shown in Figure 6-13.

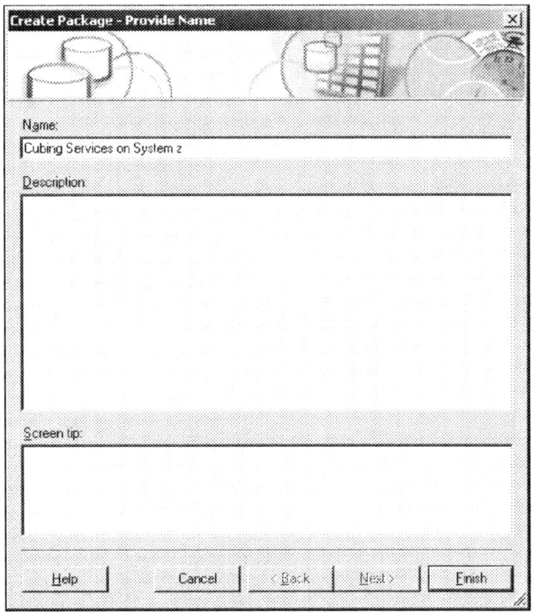

Figure 6-13 The package will be identified with a unique name

e. Framework Manager will prompt you to publish the package. Click **Yes**.

f. Choose a location for the package or accept the suggested one and then click **Next**. Model versioning is an option that will keep a number of versions of the package to avoid errors with existing reports, if the packaged was already published before, as shown in Figure 6-14.

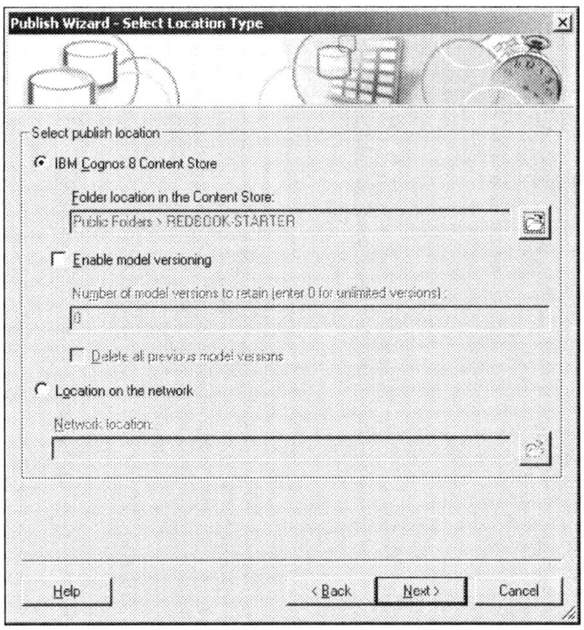

Figure 6-14 Specify what folder in which to publish the package

g. Apply security, if needed, and then click **Next**.

h. Click **Publish** and then **Finish**.

The package will now be available for analysis and reporting in Cognos Connection. When you search for the folder, it will appear as a blue folder, as shown in Figure 6-15.

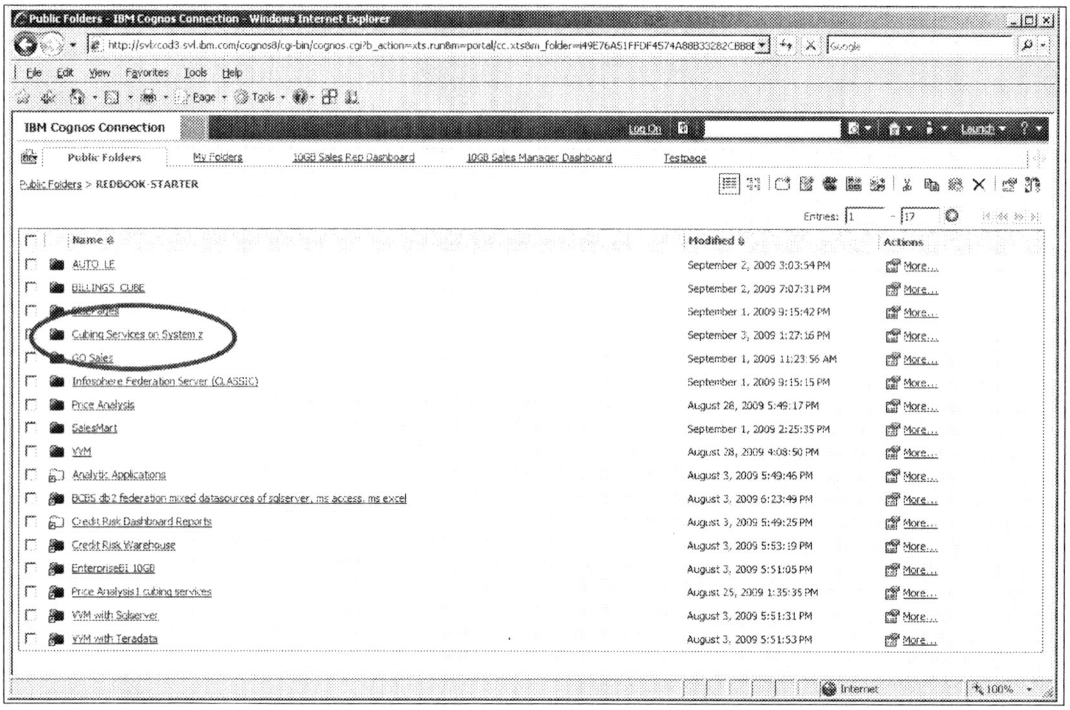

Figure 6-15 The new package based on Cubing Services is available for reporting

When you open a BI Studio, Cognos will prompt you to choose a package. The new package will appear in the list of available packages in the folder in which it has been published. It is also possible to click the package folder and then launch one of the Studios (Analysis Studio, Query Studio, or Report Studio). The new report or analysis will automatically refer to the package, as shown in Figure 6-16.

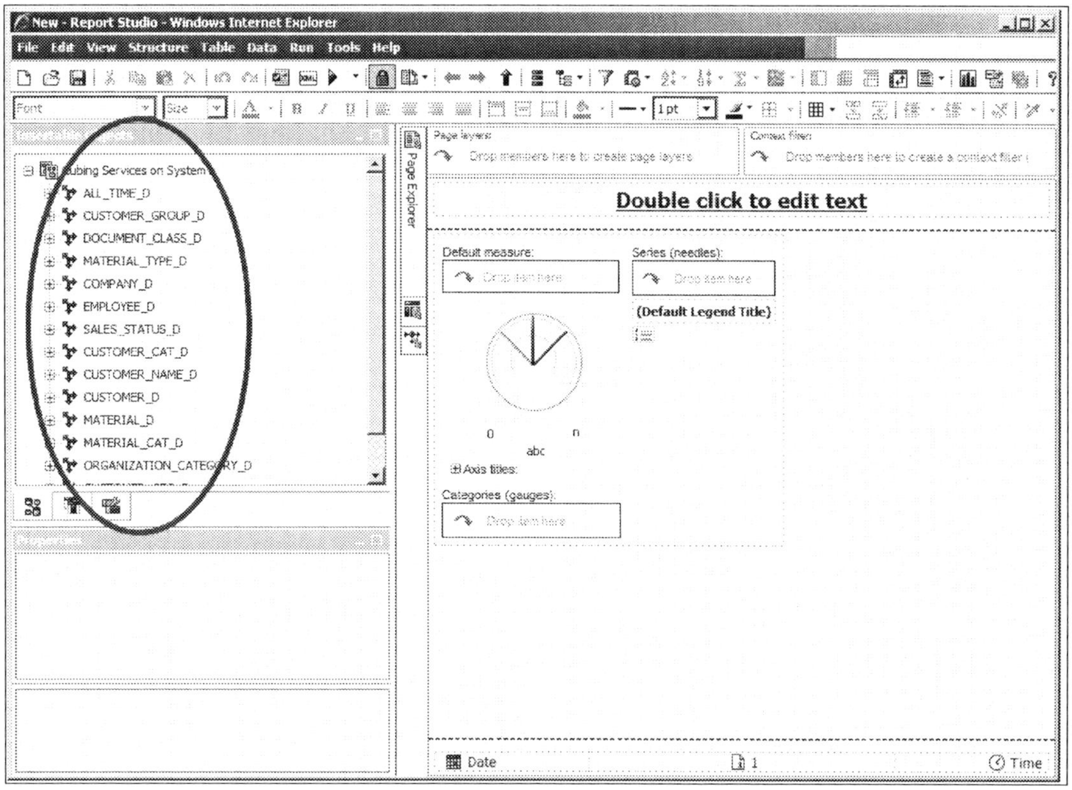

Figure 6-16 The cube structure ready to be used in Report Studio

6.4 Cubing Services for large cubes

PowerCubes can leverage its technology to deliver consistent analysis based on up to one billion rows sources. With cube partitioning techniques, it is possible to build OLAP solutions for even bigger data sets, combining incremental loads with native features that keep separate processes for data loads and query activities. When large deployments use multiple, redundant versions of the same data, using different tools, the query response time and the general benefits of even the best performing MOLAP engine are probably impacted, and become less valuable if compared with the effort needed to maintain the overall quality of the complete BI solution.

Cubing Services delivers a high performing OLAP environment that is based on large data sets that users can query easily by using Analysis Studio. If the query performance is less important than the width of the data set to be analyzed, Cubing Services can provide an OLAP approach for a large portion of a corporate warehouse.

Scalability is also be a key feature for making Cubing Services the proper deployment for large data sets that have been dimensional modeled for the Cognos 8 BI front end. For Cubing Services, scalability encompasses a number of factors: the number of cubes, the size of a cube, the number of dimensions, the number of members in a dimension, the size of the relational fact table related to a cube, the number of concurrent queries, the number of users, and so on.

The cube server runs in a single Java process, so the scalability of the cube server is fundamentally limited by the Java heap size or the process size. Because there is an upper limit on the amount of memory that is available to the cube server, a static caching policy of dimension members (which requires all members to be memory-resident) effectively limits the size or number of cubes that can be loaded at once. Under the dynamic caching policy of dimension members, not all dimension members are loaded into memory when cubes are started. The size and number of cubes that can be loaded primarily depends on the amount of disk space that is available in the file system that is used as the repository for dimension members.

Any limit on the size of a cube does not imply that the size of the underlying relational data is limited. Cubes can be defined at a level of granularity higher than the fact table, and the limiting factor is the number of members in the cube, not the size of the relational data. Provided that all the members that are defined in the cube can fit into the memory, any size of fact table can be supported (and supported better through the use of effective MQTs).

The cube server does not have an inherent limitation regarding the number of dimensions in a cube. If you are using static caching for members, all members of all dimensions must be loaded into the metadata cache when the cube is started. Thus, the cube server will support a cube that has hundreds of small dimensions, provided that all the metadata fits in memory. However, the Cubing Services optimization advisor becomes less effective as the number of dimensions increases (particularly when it exceeds 15-20 dimensions). So in those cases, the cube should be carefully designed and deployed so that SQL and MQT performance does not slow down cube access.

With a dynamic caching policy, there is no inherent limitation on the number of dimensions in a cube. The limits on the total number of members in a cube are significantly higher compared to static caching, provided that the underlying file system can store all members from all dimensions of the cube.

Dimensions, hierarchies, measures, and members of a Cubing Services cube behave just like other OLAP tools: Users can perform custom analysis or, when using a dashboard, report using a predefined navigation path.

Reports and dashboards (Figure 6-17) can refer directly to branches of dimensions, specific members, or dynamically determined sets of metadata (defined with MDX set definition formulas, such as descendants).

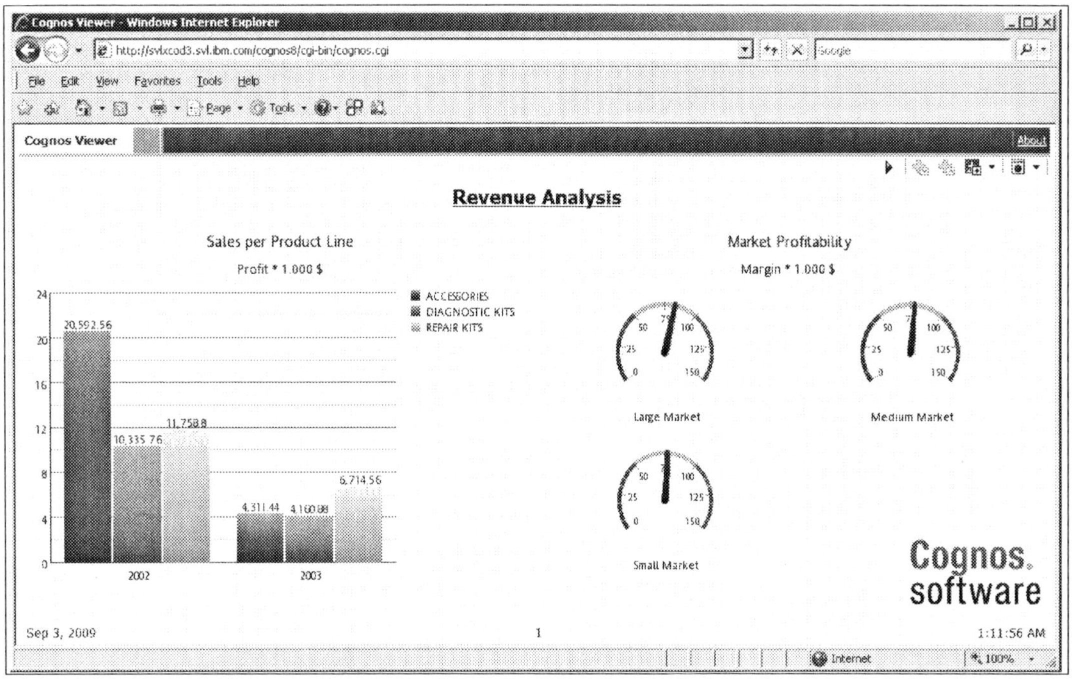

Figure 6-17 Interactive Dashboard referring to the branches and members or dynamic subsets of metadata

6.5 Delivering PowerCube on System z

When you plan to deliver BI functionalities based on PowerCubes, the following steps drive the process:

- Analyze users' OLAP reporting requirements.
- Test a prototype model.
- Identify data sources and import the facts (measures) and metadata (dimensions).
- Map metadata into dimensions, and your facts into measures.
- Verify the model and resolve any ambiguities.
- Organize the data into customized dimension views or cube groups.
- Apply security and create custom views to control access to sensitive information.
- Create and publish PowerCubes to IBM Cognos Connection.
- Manage and maintain models, cubes, and reports for optimal effectiveness.

By following these steps, we deliver some small, flexible PowerCubes to address high level BI needs across The Sample Outdoors Company. We will walk through the process of building a PowerCube to supply the sales force with flexible reports and analyses.

As mentioned in "IBM Cognos PowerCube" on page 156, PowerCubes are modeled in the PowerCube modeling tool, Transformer. Transformer has a GUI for the Windows environment, and a command-line interface for other platforms, including System z, but the modeling still needs to be done in Windows.

In order to create a new model in Transformer, you need to identify the data sources required. These data sources can be accessed in a number of ways, but for most Cognos 8 deployments, the most likely and most elegant way will be by way of an existing Cognos 8 Package, which already maps to a data source. Once in production, we advise performing updates using flat files, for performance reasons.

Daily revenue for products, country, channels, and sales force are stored in the DB2 warehouse environment that is already mapped as a data source for other BI solutions, so we refer to the package that includes this database, as shown in Figure 6-18.

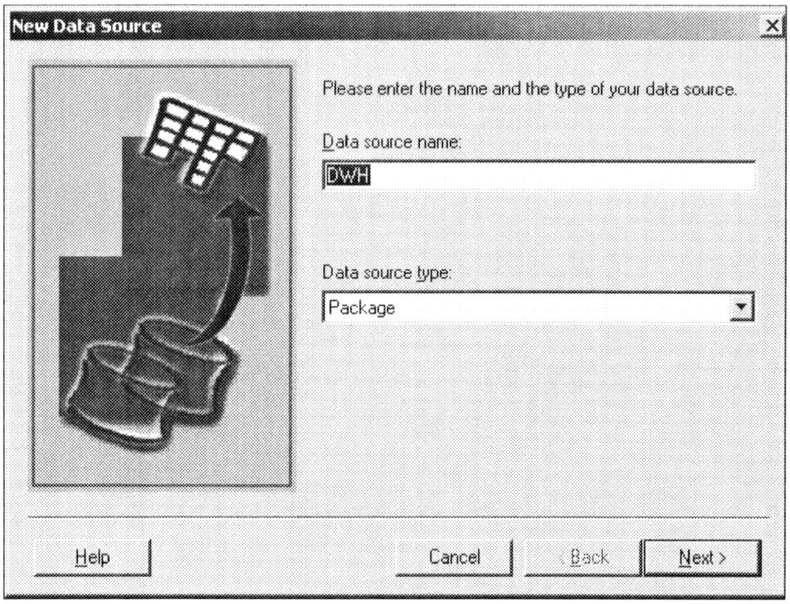

Figure 6-18 Linking an IBM Cognos 8 BI package while building a PowerCube

With IBM Cognos 8 Transformer, an OLAP modeler is able to browse the portal contents and access the areas and folders that they can usually access. When browsing the Cognos Connection portal, it is possible to select the proper package, as shown in Figure 6-19.

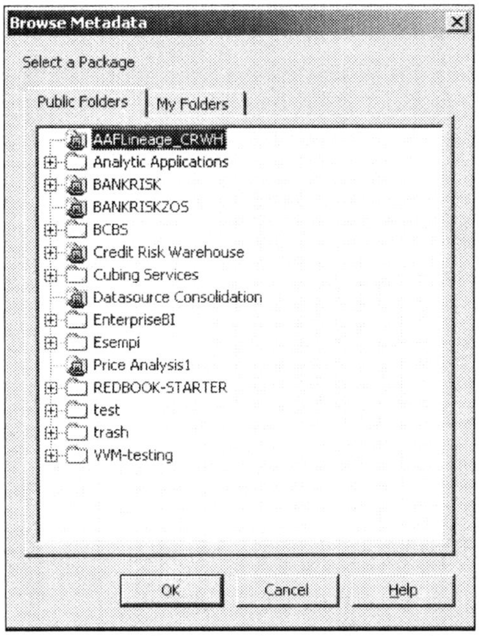

Figure 6-19 Browsing Cognos Connection to select packages as data sources for PowerCubes

Sharing sources within the BI environment allows power users with less technical skills to select and define data sources that they are used to working within the BI front end. That also means that qualified users, with few technology skills, could be involved in BI development. Entities, data structure, query items, or table views can be selected as sources for a PowerCube, as shown in Figure 6-20.

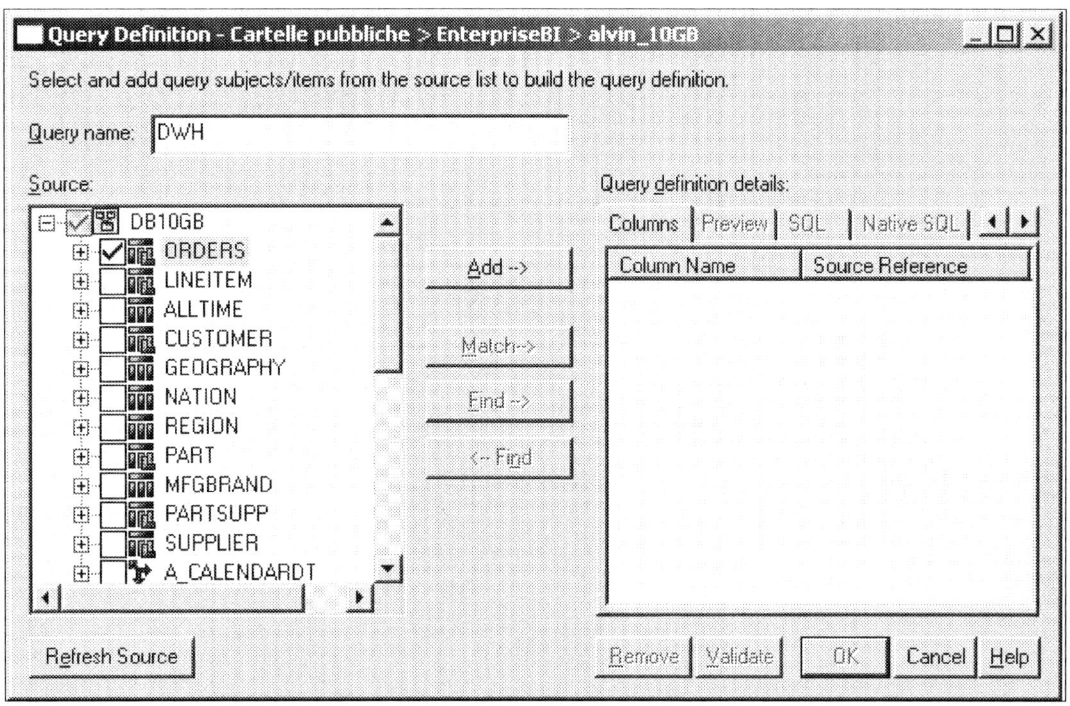

Figure 6-20 Query subject and query items are selected as sources for a PowerCube

The autodesign or manual options are used to define the structure of the PowerCube. As a best practice, instead of using a single huge query that gathers all the data needed for building the PowerCube, it is possible to define multiple smaller sources. This option provides better and faster cube building. By using the query subject from a package, Transformer leverages the way in which the model has been defined in Framework Manager.

When using multiple sources, sometimes defined relationship is available. Transformer is then able to reconcile the information by using common column or field names. Field names of sources can be modified to match. In the model for sales reporting, we manually define all the dimensions and hierarchies, as shown in Figure 6-21; every ID that is present in the fact table that has been used to link dimension information has also been used to map the source of the leaf level[1] of each hierarchy, so that Transformer will deliver a consistent set of data.

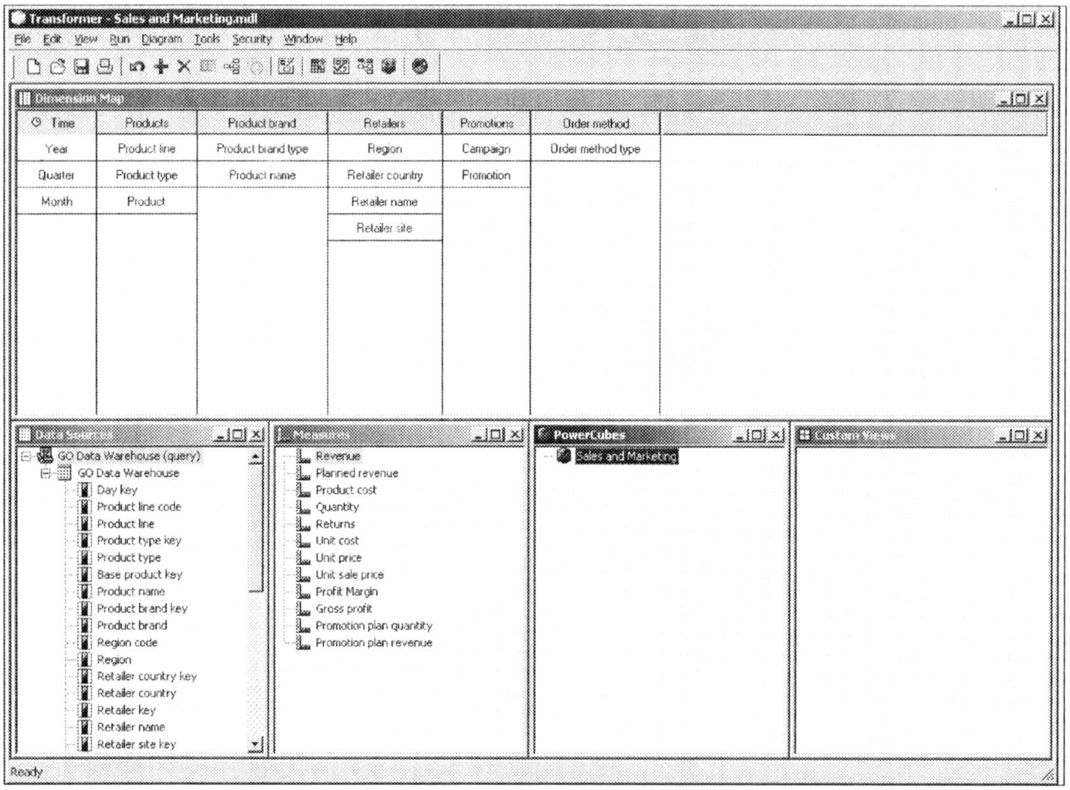

Figure 6-21 Dimension, measures, and PowerCubes defined in Transformer

[1] This is a computer search term where the hierarchical structure of the data is described as being analogous to a tree. You have a single root ot trunk, which then branches into the major or first level branches, which then themselves branch into smaller branches and so on until you reach the ends or terminal points that do not lead any further.

While defining the structure of a PowerCube, it is always possible to check how the dimensions will be delivered by creating a preview of the categories. The Categories window shows all the available categories for each dimension, as shown in Figure 6-22. It includes alternative hierarchies and allows you to define a particular behavior, such as inclusion, exclusion, or movement of branches or leaf levels.

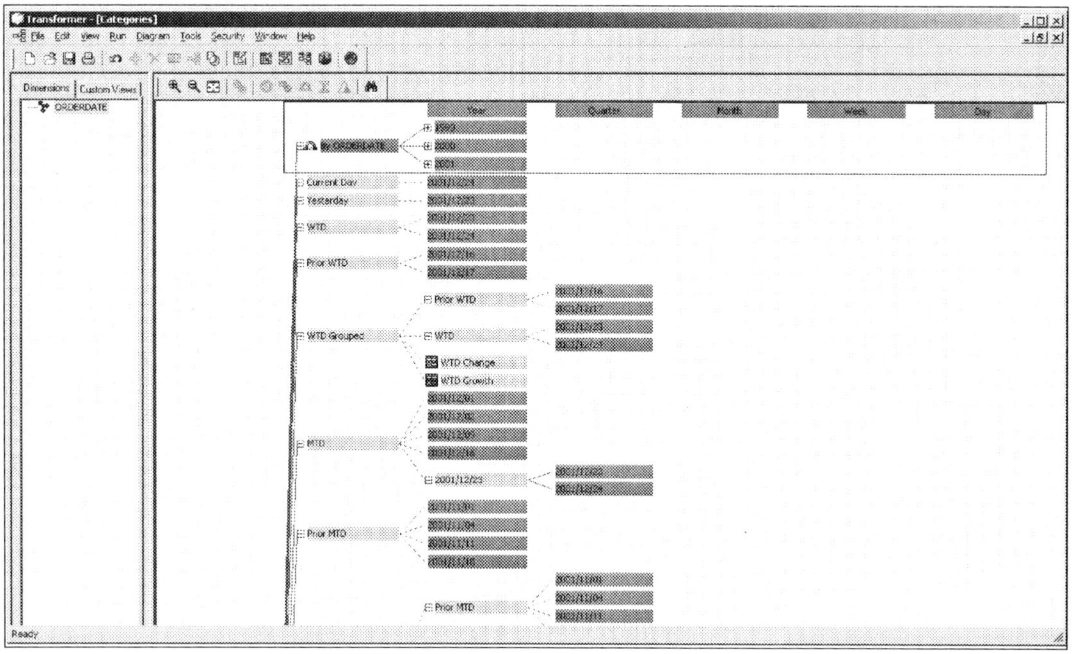

Figure 6-22 The categories window provides a preview of defined dimension and hierarchies

Not all the information needs to be available in the sources; possible requirements for derived measures or descriptions are addressed by the Transformer, which provides a powerful interface to define calculations and manipulate existing data, as shown in Figure 6-23.

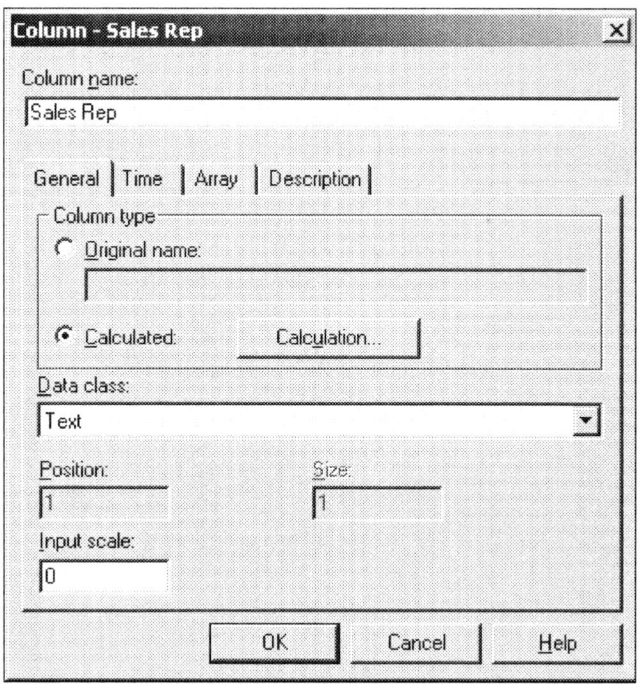

Figure 6-23 Transformer enables advanced calculation definitions, such as string manipulation

Measures and categories can be customized in order to appear in a certain format. For example, measures can be customized in terms of data format, such as currency, percentage, and so on.

The last step of the process is defining one or multiple PowerCubes that collect a dimension, measures, or a subset of them, as shown in Figure 6-24. PowerCubes can also be empowered by defining permissions based on users, groups, or profiles that come with the available authentication providers.

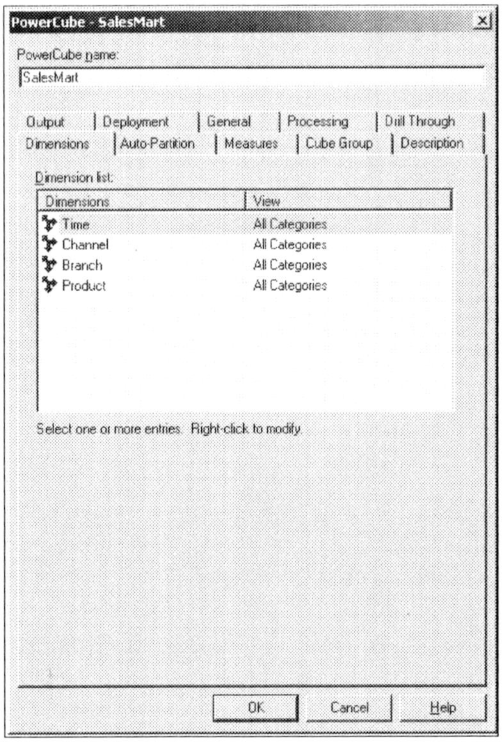

Figure 6-24 A PowerCube is defined with a set of measures and a dimension

As a best practice for IBM Cognos Transformer, we suggest testing the cube creation on Windows, using the GUI. The PowerCube could be copied on to the System z file system in order to be published (Figure 6-25) for testing.

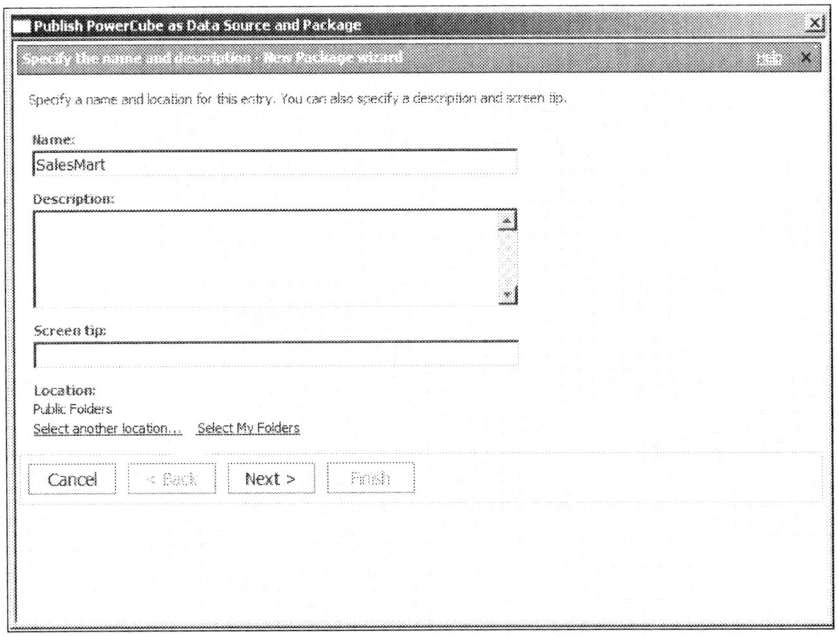

Figure 6-25 Transformer enables direct publishing of PowerCubes

Once you are comfortable with the PowerCube design, the Transformer models (the .pyj or .mdl extensions) are promoted on System z; by using IBM Cognos 8 command-line automation, they will be used to schedule cube building, updates, and deployments. This task should be done manually the first time by uploading the file into the Linux for z file system. Because Transformer provides a powerful language for model development, all the above mentioned operations can be scripted to run within System z.

Whether the PowerCubes and its model are defined on a client workstation or directly on System z, the scripting language is used to schedule and run the updates, as shown in Example 6-2.

Example 6-2 Sample command to schedule or execute a PowerCube building

```
cogtr -c -m../datasources/cubes/SalesMart.mdl

cogtr is the command line that invoke Transformer instructions
-c Generates categories and creates cubes
-m Opens the specified .mdl file or accepts Model Definition Language (MDL)
statements
```

Estimating the size of a PowerCube

The size of a PowerCube is strictly related to the level of performance. As a rule of thumb, we suggest keeping less than 2 million categories (every single element in a dimension) in a PowerCube. Due to the amount of variables that contribute to the PowerCube size that are unique to each environment, the data set and model configuration, which is an estimate of a PowerCube's size, cannot be made. The calculation of the amount of space needed to build a PowerCube can only be roughly approximated and only for existing cubes. To avoid a building process failure, we suggest having an amount of free disk space at least equal to 3.5 times the total size of the PowerCube.

Another way to estimate the amount of space required by a PowerCube building process is based on the number of categories, number of measures, and number of records in the input source. It is important to understand the size of the cube in order to discover how much disk space will be needed for the cube and working files. There are three phases during the cube build where temporary files are created (Example 6-3):

- Data Read Phase: Transformer imports the data from the transactional sources so that the amount of space required is directly based on the amount of data being referenced in the data source.
- Metadata Update Phase: Transformer goes through the files created during the Data Read Phase and copies metadata to a new file, and then the amount of space is based on the number of categories and measures in the cube. This is usually a relatively small size.
- Data Update Phase: Data from the files created during the Data Read Phase are processed and additional space is created to allow for sorting and processing of the data.

Example 6-3 Sizing estimate formula

```
((((x2 * 4) + (x3 * 4) + (x4 * 9) +8) * x5) / 1024 / 1024) *2
If this value is greater then 1907, add x6.
x2 = The total number of dimensions
x3 = The number of dimension views
x4 = The number of regular measures (not calculated measures)
x5 = The number of input records from all transactional data sources
x6 = The value of the WorkFileMaxSize setting in trnsfrmr.ini
```

6.6 PowerCube security sources

PowerCube supports simultaneous user authentication and logon using the full range of compatible IBM Cognos 8 security providers. Custom views on PowerCubes are useful to grant or deny access to sensitive Business Intelligence information. These access controls can be customized down to the query object level, not merely for the reports and cubes, but for the specific levels, categories, members, or measures within them.

Transformer supports two types of security to restrict data access across the IBM Cognos 8 reporting components: member-based security and cube-based password protection. By using member-based security, it is possible to create custom views and apply these views to specific categories (members), dimensions, or components. This filters the cube data that is shown to specific report users. Member-based security uses security objects, such as users, groups, or roles, to define user access to information, as shown in Figure 6-26.

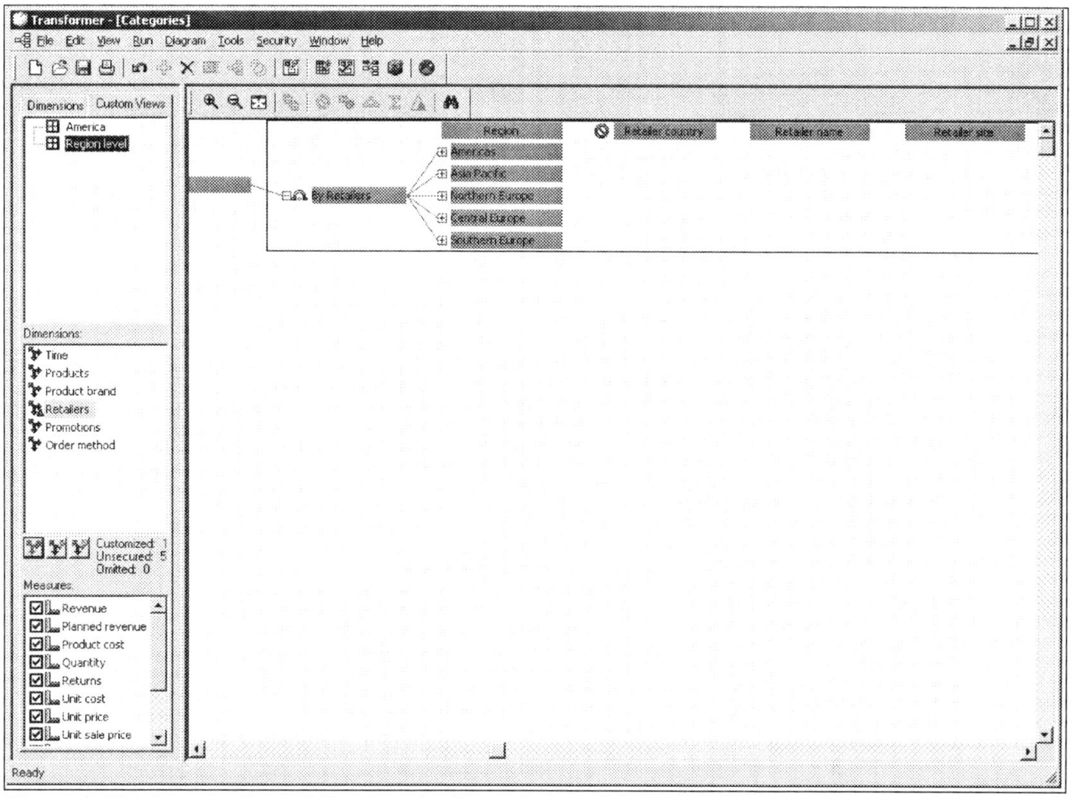

Figure 6-26 Custom views defined on the PowerCubes definition to differentiate users' access

With cube-based security, security is applied to an entire PowerCube or cube group by setting a password to restrict access to authorized users. Once the necessary levels of security to use has been determined, the process of adding security to models and cubes consists of the following tasks:

- Ensuring that the required authentication provider is configured in the IBM Cognos 8 Business Intelligence environment and that the required users, groups, and roles are available from that IBM Cognos 8 namespace by referencing the configured authentication provider
- Assigning the security objects from the security namespace configured in IBM Cognos 8 to custom views, and then combining custom views with dimension filtering to appropriately subdivide business information
- Associating access controls with PowerCubes before delivering them to your users

We should consider the business reasons for restricting access to data. For example, there might be some confidential data that only specific users are allowed to see or the configured data source may contain a large amount of information, and users need to retrieve data from only specific dimensions or levels. Also, there might be dimensions containing many categories or members, and users need to retrieve only a subset of records from that dimension.

Depending on the data source, the underlying database security may also affect user access to certain categories of information. Therefore, assigning access to a level may not guarantee that the user also has access to all the categories or members in that level.

Users, groups, and roles are IBM Cognos 8 security objects created for authentication and authorization purposes. You can add groups available in authentication providers (for example, the System z security), or you can create your own in IBM Cognos 8, as shown in Figure 6-27.

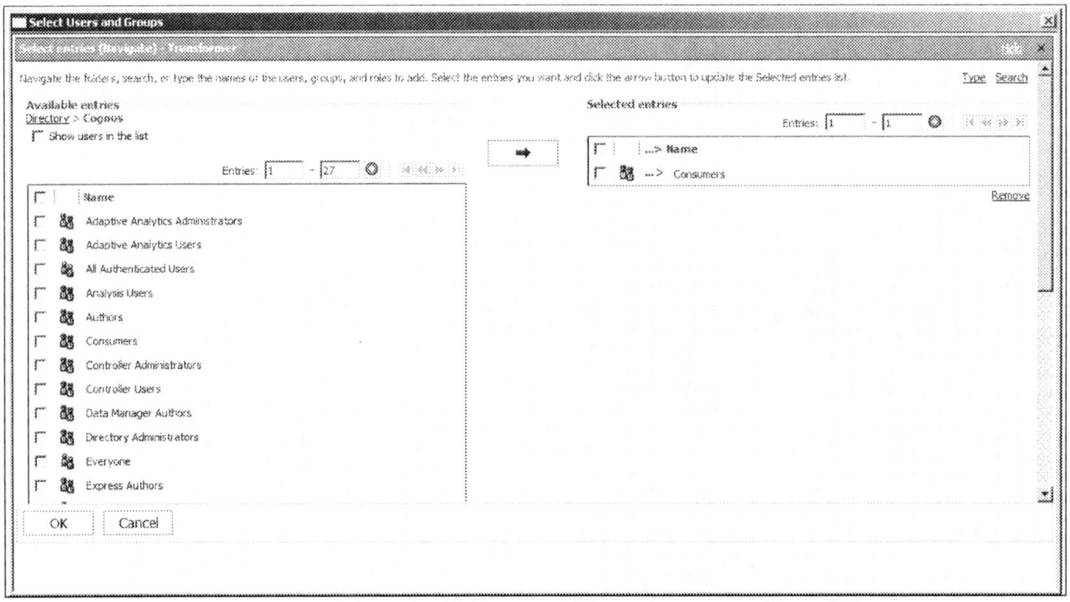

Figure 6-27 Security provider defined for IB Cognos 8 BI used to secure PowerCubes

A user entry is created and maintained in an authentication provider to uniquely identify a human or a computer account. You cannot create users in IBM Cognos 8. Information about users, such as first and last names, IDs, passwords, locales, and e-mail addresses, reside with the authentication providers.

Users can become members of groups defined in authentication providers and groups defined in IBM Cognos 8. A user can belong to one or more groups. When users are members of more than one group, their access permissions are merged; this is known as the *union of views principle.*

Groups can include individual users, as well as other groups. Group membership is part of a user's basic identity. Users log on with all the permissions associated with the groups to which they belong.

A role is a grouping that typically includes users who have similar responsibilities and privileges in your organization. Roles can include users, groups, and other roles. Individual users can belong to several groups or roles. Group and role names must be unique in a Cognos 8 BI environment.

All of above mentioned security entities are used to define security filters on PowerCubes; to secure the content of a PowerCube, the needed custom views should be dragged on to the cube definition window, as shown in Figure 6-28. A cube re-creation would be necessary to apply the security layer.

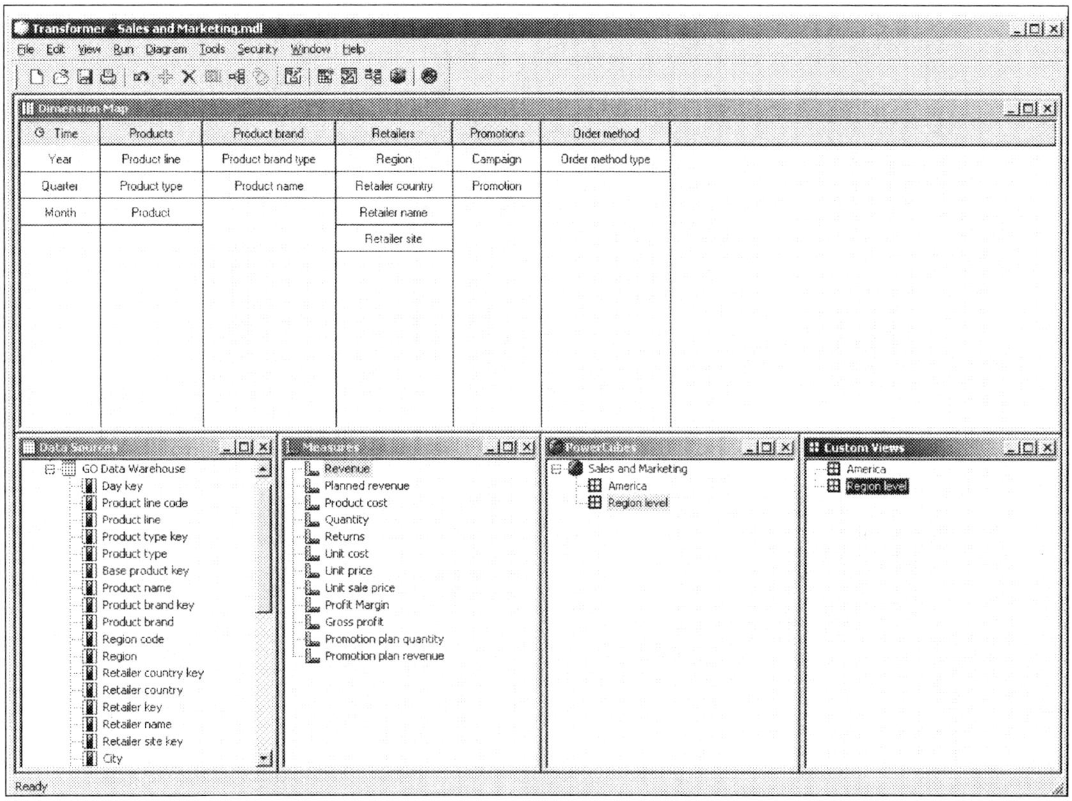

Figure 6-28 Custom views are attached to PowerCube definition

6.7 OLAP and concurrent DW maintenance

One of the key factors in delivering an effective Business Intelligence solution to the users is that these users must be enabled to access meaningful information when they need it. Financial summaries usually involve more detailed information that must be reliable and certified. Other implementations often run on aggregated views and must deliver smart capabilities in terms of comparative analysis or time trends.

As we mentioned in our discussion about MOLAP and ROLAP techniques, solutions involving massive volumes of data run better on relational databases, while analysis running on aggregates can leverage MOLAP performance.

Data source maintenance should also be considered when defining an implementation strategy; fact and structure updates on small PowerCubes require a smaller time frame. Even though InfoSphere Cubing Services delivers a high performance environment to cache data, maintenance on models and data load jobs could require more time.

IBM customers often create a corporate data warehouse to collect and organize a large volume of information. Enterprise financial reporting leverages the high level of detail available in the warehouse, so maintenance could be scheduled so that it does not impact this kind of activity. In addition, some analyses in some departments, such as Marketing or Sales, often require aggregated data availability.

For example, an international pharmaceutical company implemented a BI strategy to address those different needs by creating Sales dashboards on top of a few PowerCubes. The PowerCubes were refreshed every 12 hours to provide users with the most current information while having a minimal impact on the warehouse maintenance activities. Moreover, because the corporate data warehouse plays a strategic role in managing information assets, the company also achieved the goal of reducing the total workload generated by multiple inquiries, which had an impact on relatively small aggregated data sets.

Related publications

The publications listed in this section are considered particularly suitable for a more detailed discussion of the topics covered in this book.

IBM Redbooks

For information about ordering these publications, see "How to get Redbooks" on page 187. Note that some of the documents referenced here may be available in softcopy only.

- *50 TB Data Warehouse Benchmark on IBM System z*, SG24-7674
- *Disaster Recovery with DB2 UDB for z/OS*, SG24-6370
- *DS8000 Copy Services for IBM System z*, SG24-6787
- *Enterprise Data Warehousing with DB2 9 for z/OS*, SG24-7637
- *GDPS Family - An Introduction to Concepts and Capabilities*, SG24-6374
- *IBM System Storage DS8000: Architecture and Implementation*, SG24-6786
- *InfoSphere Warehouse: Cubing Services and Client Access Interfaces*, SG24-7582
- *Linux on IBM System z: Performance Measurement and Tuning*, SG24-6926
- *Multidimensional Analytics: Delivered with InfoSphere Warehouse Cubing Services*, SG24-7679
- *Optimizing Restore and Recovery Solutions with DB2 Recovery Expert for z/OS V2.1*, SG24-7606
- *Practical Migration to Linux on System z*, SG24-7727
- *Publishing IMS and DB2 Data using WebSphere Information Integrator: Configuration and Monitoring Guide*, SG24-7132

Other publications

These publications are also relevant as further information sources. Note that some of the documents referenced here may be available in softcopy only. Each Cognos document ships with its individual product, and also can be found at the following address:

`http://www-01.ibm.com/support/docview.wss?uid=swg27015681`

- *IBM Cognos 8 Administration and Security Guide*
- *IBM Cognos 8 Business Intelligence Architecture and Deployment Guide*
- *IBM Cognos 8 Business Intelligence IBM Cognos 8 Go! Office Installation Guide*
- *IBM Cognos 8 Business Intelligence IBM Cognos 8 Go! Office User Guide*
- *IBM Cognos 8 Business Intelligence IBM Cognos 8 Go! Search User Guide*
- *IBM Cognos 8 Business Intelligence Installation and Configuration Guide*
- *IBM Cognos 8 Framework Manager Guidelines for Modeling Metadata*
- *IBM Cognos 8 Framework Manager User Guide*
- *IBM Cognos 8 Go! Dashboard Installation and Configuration Guide*

- *IBM Cognos 8 Go! Mobile Installation and Administration Guide*
- *IBM Cognos 8 Virtual View Manager Administration Guide*
- *IBM Cognos 8 Virtual View Manager Installation and Configuration Guide*
- *IBM Cognos 8 Virtual View Manager User Guide*

Online resources

These Web sites are also relevant as further information sources:

- Business Glossary and Cognos

  `http://www.ibm.com/developerworks/data/library/techarticle/dm-0907metadataintegration/index.html`
- Cognos Software Environments

  `http://www-304.ibm.com/jct01003c/support/docview.wss?rs=3528&uid=swg27014782`
- Cognos 8 Business Intelligence for Linux on System z

  `http://www.ibm.com/software/data/cognos/cognos-8-business-intelligence/system-z`
- Cognos 8 Go! product line

  `http://www.ibm.com/software/data/cognos/products/cognos-8-go/`
- Cognos Information Center

  `http://publib.boulder.ibm.com/infocenter/c8bi/v8r4m0/index.jsp?topic=/com.ibm.swg.im.cognos.ug_cra.8.4.0.doc/ug_cra_id25289configurePortletApplicationsIBM.html`
- Cognos Proven Practices

  `http://www.ibm.com/developerworks/data/library/cognos/cognosprovenpractices.html`
- FICON channels

  `http://www.ibm.com/systems/z/hardware/connectivity/news.html`
- GDPS Family

  `http://www.ibm.com/systems/z/advantages/gdps/index.html`
- "IBM Cognos 8 BI for Linux on System z: 30,000 users in production in just four months"

  `http://www.ibm.com/software/success/cssdb.nsf/CS/SANS-7WUJEV?OpenDocument&Site=default&cty=en_us`
- IBM Cognos 8 Business Intelligence 8.4 Fix Pack 2

  `http://www.ibm.com/support/docview.wss?rs=3442&context=SS9RTN&dc=D400&uid=swg24023803&loc=en_US&cs=UTF-8&lang=en&rss=ct3442db2`
- IBM Cognos 8 Go! Dashboard FP1 and FP2 Companion Guide

  `http://www.ibm.com/developerworks/data/library/cognos/page420.html`
- IBM Cognos Analytic Applications

  `http://www.ibm.com/software/data/cognos/products/cognos-analytic-applications/`
- IBM Cognos Resource Center

  `http://www.ibm.com/software/data/support/cognos_crc.html`

- InfoSphere Warehouse - IBM product site

  http://www.ibm.com/software/data/infosphere/warehouse/
- "The strategic importance of OLAP and multidimensional analysis - A Cognos White Paper"

  http://www.cognos.com/pdfs/whitepapers/wp_strategic_importance_of_olap_and_multidimensional_analysis.pdf
- Virtual View Manager software environments

  http://www.ibm.com/support/docview.wss?rs=3442&uid=swg27014427

How to get Redbooks

You can search for, view, or download Redbooks, Redpapers, Technotes, draft publications and Additional materials, as well as order hardcopy Redbooks publications, at this Web site:

ibm.com/redbooks

Help from IBM

IBM Support and downloads

ibm.com/support

IBM Global Services

ibm.com/services

Index

S

T

U

V

W

X

Z